Drug Wars and Coffee Houses

DATE DUE

AUG 0 8 2011	
OCT 1 8 2011	
FEB 1 8	

D1203037

Drug Wars and Coffee Houses

The Political Economy of the International Drug Trade

David R. Mares
University of California, San Diego

CQ PRESS

A Division of Congressional Quarterly Inc.
Washington, D.C.

CQ Press
1255 22nd Street, NW, Suite 400
Washington, DC 20037

Phone: 202-729-1900; toll-free, 1-866-427-7737 (1-866-4CQ-PRESS)

Web: www.cqpress.com

Cover design: Pottman Design
Cover photos: AP Wide World Photos; Getty Images (flags in lower right background).

Interior photos: p. 3 Ondrej Pastirik, www.amsterdam.info (top) and AP/Wide World Photos
(bottom); p. 36 AP/Wide World Photos; p. 73 Common Sense for Drug Policy.

Printed and bound in the United States of America

09   08   07   06   05   1   2   3   4   5

Cataloging-in-Publication Data available from the Library of Congress.

Mares, David R.
    Drug wars and coffeehouses : the political economy of the international drug trade / David
R. Mares.
    p. cm.
    Includes bibliographical references and index.
    ISBN 1-56802-862-8 (pbk. : alk. paper)
  1. Drug traffic. 2. Drug control. I. Title.

    HV5801.M324 2005
    363.45—dc22

                                                                2005033643

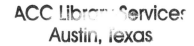
ACC Library Services
Austin, Texas

To Jane

Contents

Tables, Figures, and Boxes

Boxes

Preface

Ten years ago I was looking for a new topic around which I could organize my international political economy course. I was tired of talking about trade and finance, and my students did not really see how the knowledge necessary to understand the topic was relevant to their lives. I cast about for an issue that could be both relevant and intellectually challenging for them and for myself.

I did not know much about drugs or drug policy when I began offering my political economy of drugs course. Most students fortunately are willing to give a professor the benefit of the doubt when he announces up front that the class is an exploration for him as well. Together we searched for the missing data to answer our questions, and together we faced the frustrations of realizing that government agencies and analysts are ignoring many fundamental questions that should be investigated when making drug policy. Among these questions are the following: What is the causal relationship between drugs and crime? What are the criteria that allow a drug to be labeled "highly addictive"? Why is tobacco legal but other drugs are not? And why are the Netherlands and the United States major producers of illegal drugs?

Drug policy is, in many ways, an ideal topic for teaching students the importance of systematic and theoretical thinking. Everyone has some idea about the topic, and most have formed opinions—ostensibly based upon "facts"—about how public policy should treat these substances and those who use or provide them. I find that some of the most interesting class discussions develop when students first are presented with what is actually known (and not known) about drugs and then turn to examining the causal logic underlying specific drug policies. This exercise provides a great segue into learning about how theories help us ask the right questions, organize data, and deal with missing data. It also provides a stunning example of the real-world importance of developing testable hypotheses about cause and effect.

At the beginning of the term few students have any idea about the complexity of the drug issue internationally, nor of the broad range of policies adopted in the past and present in the United States and around the world. In addition, learning that the United States is a major producer of illegal drugs, that the nation has an extensive internal drug trafficking network, and that major financial institutions are not immune to money laundering can be an eye-opening experience for students used to a "drug consuming country–drug producing country" paradigm.

Although some students are irritated that science and medicine cannot provide clear-cut or universal policy answers, most students are stimulated by the challenge of making sense of the political economy of drug policy. They come to appreciate the political nature of public policy even on an issue that many tie to national security. I find it especially gratifying when students articulate positions distinct from my own (were I to reveal them), and appreciate it when they explain how they process information that they were previously unaware of or had interpreted differently from myself.

I have selected three analytic perspectives (social deviance, social constructivism, and rational choice) for introducing students to social science methods of studying the politics of drug policy, all based upon the dominant rhetoric and debates in the United States. Social science, with its emphasis on logical argument and empirical testing, is a particularly appropriate methodology with which to study the politics of drug policy. This book uses the context of the international drug trade to help students develop such analytical social science skills as formulating questions that can be answered logically and systematically, using theory in thinking critically about an issue, and evaluating relevant evidence to find support for any answers put forth. Students also explore the political science subfields of comparative politics (with individual countries responding differently to the same issue) and international relations (with countries influencing each other's behavior) because the drug phenomenon occurs at their intersection. At the end of each chapter students will find a list of detailed study questions designed to further these analytical goals.

Chapter One introduces readers to some of the national and international dimensions of the drug trade and the politics of creating public policy; because this is not a public policy text, however, questions about implementation and evaluation are explicitly omitted. I also provide students with an organizational framework within which to think about the links between consumption, production, distribution, and money laundering. The text makes clear that the psychoactive substance commodity system only helps them describe links; for explanation they need to work with theories of cause and effect.

Social deviance, social constructivism, and rational choice provide distinct causal variables and logics to explain why people consume, produce, or sell illicit drugs as well as launder money. Chapter Two develops students' understanding of these three theories. Each theory informs hypotheses about why the drug trade exists and how it develops, and through claims about cause and effect suggests the best possible courses of action (policy) to influence the behavior of people or countries involved. In their most abstract form, these theories compete with each other, but when done with care it is possible to combine them in distinct ways.

The remainder of the book is organized into two parts. In Part 2 Chapters Three through Six examine in turn what is known and not known about consumption, production, distribution, and money laundering. Each chapter on these topics also provides examples of policy variations across time and national borders. Students are offered real-world vignettes that illustrate how each analytic perspective explains various aspects of the drug trade. Part 2 also examines the political economy of international cooperation and conflict over contemporary drug policy. Chapter Seven identifies the advantages and disadvantages of unilateral, bilateral, and multilateral efforts, providing examples from Europe, Latin America, and the United States.

Part 3 consists of historical accounts of three national cases that are likely to generate comparative discussion and analysis. Chapter Eight follows the evolution of U.S. drug policy from its focus on crime reduction in the early 1970s, through stillborn efforts at harm reduction, to the current drug war strategy launched in the 1980s. Chapter Nine examines the evolution of Dutch drug policy away from a drug war approach in the 1960s and toward harm reduction. Chapter Ten looks at the Swedish move from harm reduction in 1965 toward prohibition in the late 1960s and the adoption of a drug war strategy starting in the late 1970s.

Acknowledgments

Many people have helped me think through the issues presented in this book. Most important among them are the hundreds of students who have explored the topic alongside me in class. Two graduate students, Travis Knowles and Joel Johnson, have served me well as research assistants, not only collecting information but also asking stimulating questions about the material. The Ronald E. McNair Post-Baccalaureate Achievement Program at the University of California, San Diego, provided a wonderful opportunity for me to work with two bright and hardworking undergraduate students, Galya Diaz and Ariana Valle, exchanging graduate school–oriented mentoring for research assistance. I must also thank the excellent Jean Trinh, my first undergraduate research assistant on this manuscript many years ago. I would also like to thank my external reviewers for their candid insights: Peter Andreas, Brown University; David Balaam, University of Puget Sound; Russell Crandall, Davidson College; Robert Falkner, London School of Economics; Michael Huelshoff, University of New Orleans; Thomas Oatley, University of North Carolina at Chapel Hill; Beryl Radin, University of Baltimore; and one anonymous reviewer. These helped me significantly as I revised the manuscript.

The CQ team has been absolutely marvelous. James Headley encouraged my interest in writing a text that would fill the large void for any instructor seeking to stimulate thinking about complex social issues rather than providing pat answers. Charisse Kiino stuck by me as I wondered whether I could distance myself from my own theoretical baggage sufficiently to do justice to other perspectives and learn something about my views along the way. Elise Frasier helped me work through organizational and presentational issues that improved the text's ability to convey information to students. Finally, Lorna Notsch provided comprehensive copyediting, and Sally Ryman shepherded me through the production process.

My wife, Jane, never wants acknowledgment, but all authors know that their life partners contribute immeasurably to the long, often difficult process of writing and rewriting. Whether offering active or silent encouragement, especially on the down days, or discussion to work through the logic of complex arguments, Jane has been an incredible intellectual partner for my entire career.

I have benefited immensely from everyone's contribution. The responsibility for all that is written here lies with me. Because one of the joys of being a professor is the opportunity to continue learning, I hope that those teachers and students who disagree with this book will write articles and books to improve upon my contribution in the effort to develop an informed and reasoning citizenry.

Chapter 1 The Drug Trade as a Global and National Phenomenon

"Well, this is a normal business here [opium poppy production in Afghanistan] and I cultivate it to support my big family. In fact I should say it is not an illicit crop but rather a blessing which saves the lives of my children, grandchildren and two widowed daughters ... my brother-in-law became addicted in Peshawar and parted from his family and nice children. But I should say that poverty is a more serious threat to millions of already vulnerable people like us. If we have a good road, electricity, water and food then we would not cultivate poppy."[1]

—*Bibi Deendaray, Kandahar*

Losing in the Paris Cannabis Cup was a disappointment for François, hurting both his pride and the price that he would be able to demand for his product. He had tended his crop faithfully, ensuring that it had the necessary conditions for a hybrid variety to thrive: constant light, steady water, and sufficient fertilizer. So it must have been the quality of the seeds from Canada. He remembered his last visit to the United States, and the marijuana that his friend was growing in a spare bedroom. It looked beautiful and produced an incredible high. This time he would specify to his supplier that he wanted seeds from the United States.[2]

—*Adapted from material in "The World Geopolitics of Drugs 1998/1999"*

The use of illegal psychoactive substances, their production, and their sale are phenomena that occur throughout the world. As the preceding vignettes suggest, sometimes a specific drug crosses national boundaries and sometimes it does not. Such examples also illustrate that production, sale, and use occur in both developing and developed countries. A look at the historical record demonstrates, in addition, that these phenomena have been around since well before modern nations began outlawing the use of psychoactive substances at the beginning of the twentieth century.

Such commonalities in usage, production, and trade contrast with the differences among the public policies that nations have adopted in the effort to regulate psychoactive substances. These policies have varied across time within the same country as well as across national boundaries at the same point in time. In many countries, including the United States, some psychoactive substances such as alcohol are legal, with restrictions on consumption only for minors (another category whose definition varies across nations). Exceptions

1

to this are countries governed by traditional Islamic law, known as Sharia, which prohibits any consumption of alcohol. Holland has become famous for its coffeehouses; the sale of marijuana and hashish has been licensed and taxed there since 1976. Britain decriminalized the possession of small quantities of marijuana in 2004, and Canada now licenses the production of marijuana for medicinal use.

The United States is a bit conflicted policy-wise. Some states permit the use of marijuana for medicinal purposes; however, the federal government not only prohibits it but also, in the name of a war on drugs, pursues suppliers even in those states that permit it. Marijuana use was actually legal in the United States until 1937; the nonprescription use of opiates and cocaine was legal until 1915. Alcohol was made illegal in 1920 only to be legalized again in 1933. And if one goes way back to 1604, England's King James I raised import duties on tobacco to curb what he considered, "A custom loathsome to the eye, hateful to the nose, harmful to the brain, dangerous to the lungs...."[3]

Over the years, countries also have attempted to influence each other's policies regarding consumption, distribution, and production of psychoactive substances, as well as the circulation of the money associated with the trade. For example, in the nineteenth century, the British exported opium from their colony in India to China to offset a trade imbalance. They in fact went to war twice with China (First Opium War 1839–1842, Second Opium War 1856–1860) to keep that market open. Eventually, after years of conflict, discussions between China and British India produced the 1907 Ten Years' Agreement, the first international agreement to diminish the opium trade.

The United States built upon this precedent to promote a prohibitionist international policy to proscribe a number of psychoactive substances. In the early part of the twentieth century, missionaries, moral entrepreneurs, and public health reformers pressured the United States government to negotiate treaties to restrict the international trade of opium and its derivatives.[4] Within the League of Nations and its successor, the United Nations (UN), more international treaties were negotiated that prohibited the domestic production and use of a variety of psychoactive substances. The most significant of these treaties are the 1961 Single Convention on Narcotic Drugs, the 1971 Convention on Psychotropic Substances, and the 1988 Convention Against Illicit Traffic in Narcotic Drugs and Psychotropic Substances.

Those treaties controlling the opium trade allowed for the distribution of a small number of licenses to select countries to produce opium for the legal international pharmaceutical market. Then in the 1980s, the United States again led the way for further regulation, this time of illegally generated money and financial assets, by the international financial system. Finally, in the wake of the terrorist attacks of September 11, 2001, the U.S. government raised the specter of profits from illegal drugs as a contributor to the financing of international terrorism.

SITUATED AMONGST OTHER CAFES AND RETAIL SHOPS IN DOWNTOWN AMSTERDAM, COFFEE-HOUSES SUCH AS THE ONE SHOWN HERE ARE PART OF THE EVERYDAY LANDSCAPE.

U.S. DRUG CZAR JOHN WALTERS MEETS WITH GEN. JORGE CASTRO, CHIEF OF THE COLOMBIAN NATIONAL POLICE, AT THE ANTI-NARCOTICS MILITARY BASE IN SANTA MARTA.

In the latter part of the century, however, the international consensus that had been steadily building since 1907 began to show signs of strain. The Dutch were the first to break away. As early as the 1970s, they dramatically broke ranks by decriminalizing marijuana. By the 1990s, the rifts had deepened, with a number of factors combining to make the study of the drug phenomenon controversial and divisive. Groups formed that argued that dealing with these psychoactive substances through prohibition created more problems than it solved. These groups offered a variety of alternatives from decriminalization to public health strategies. Their ability to gain political power varied across countries. The resulting fractures in the international consensus on criminalizing the production, trade, and use of many drugs has reopened policy questions that, while muted in the UN at present, are becoming louder within the European Union, between Canada and the United States, and elsewhere.

For example, the United States has long been known as a major drug consumer despite its vocal "Just Say No" policy positions. Now, however, its leadership of the prohibitionist position has been further undercut by the revelation of its role as a major producer of such illegal drugs as methamphetamines and as an exporter of others, including LSD and high potency marijuana. Diminished credibility of the U.S. supported prohibition prescription has given other nations greater leeway in their search for alternative solutions. The new discord on drug policy raises one more threat to international cooperation at the start of the twenty-first century.

This brief look at the illegal drug phenomenon and some of its consequences in the international arena raises such compelling questions as: Why is there so much disagreement about what policies are most appropriate to address the issue? Why do specific domestic or international drug policies change or persist? Why do rich, democratic countries produce, sell, and consume illegal psychoactive substances in the same way as poor, nondemocratic countries? And, perhaps the most important question of all: How best can an issue so awash in myths, moral inconsistencies, social prejudices, and political rhetoric be studied?

Social science, with its emphasis on logical argument and empirical testing, is a particularly appropriate methodology with which to study the politics of drug policy. This text uses the context of the international drug trade to help students develop analytical social science skills such as how to formulate questions that can be answered logically and systematically, how to recognize the importance of theory in thinking critically about an issue, and how to evaluate relevant evidence to find support for their answers. Since the drug phenomenon occurs at the intersection of comparative politics (e.g., why individual countries respond differently to the same issue) and international relations (e.g., how countries influence each other's behavior), students also gain an opportunity to explore these subfields of political science.

Because illegal drugs are such a controversial issue—people hold divergent views about their nature, the consequences of their distribution and use, and their susceptibility to regulation—this text does not refer to the *problem* of drugs, but rather to the *phenomenon*, or factual circumstances of drugs, or psychoactive substances. A conclusion about whether drugs in and of themselves constitute a "problem," and if so, what that problem might be, that is amenable to public policy regulation should come out of one's analysis of the fact that such substances exist and are consumed, rather than be the starting point for analysis.

Drug policy is the result of four factors: what is known about the effects of drugs, the nature of the market for drugs, how people think about cause and effect when thinking about drugs and human behavior or health, and the politics of the policy process. It is the interaction among these four factors that provides the foundation for explaining why national and international policies vary in their approach to specific substances as well as in how they evolve over time. This chapter focuses on the politics of the policy process—how policies are designed and get adopted—the factor I believe has the greatest single influence in this area, but one that is still insufficient to explain why governments choose the policies they do. The discussion is sufficiently abstract to be useful whether discussing democratic politicians, military dictators, or religious zealots. Such a general picture is valuable in that it allows key points in the process to be isolated. Explanations of the variation in drug policies adopted over time and across place are focused at these key points.

The remainder of the chapter is devoted to a preliminary discussion of the scientific knowledge about psychoactive substances and the nature of drug markets. Students are provided with a brief overview of what is and is not known about how psychoactive substances influence human health and behavior. A third section examines three competing descriptions of the nature of illegal drug markets: balloons, organized crime, and a systems perspective. An argument is made for the analytical utility of a psychoactive substance commodity system (PASCS) for understanding how the consumer, producer, distributor, and money launderer are intimately linked; none can be understood nor their behavior significantly altered without appreciating how they affect each other. The next chapter provides an extended analysis of the dominant perspectives held by people today about cause and effect in the drug phenomenon.

The Politics of Policy

Government policy is the result of a standard strategic political process, even on an issue like drug policy that many people believe has important, subjective moral overtones. Consequently, one needs a way to think about the policy process in general so that the key points to explain differences in policy across time and place can be identified.

The idea of a policy cycle is well accepted in the field of policy studies, although analysts differ in how they conceptualize the different phases of the cycle. Dipak Gupta, who has written extensively on the public policy process, provides a useful model that can be modified for the purposes of this discussion.[5] (See Figure 1.1.) The focus of this text is the politics of getting drugs on the policy agenda, designing a policy response, and getting a policy adopted. For our purposes, policy implementation and evaluation are placed within the study of policy analysis.

The cycle starts with agenda setting, the placement of issues on the agenda. The politics of drug policy begins here with a debate about the outlines of a national strategy to identify the problem(s) to be tackled and to articulate one or more goals to be pursued. For example, in the United States, the actual consumption of illegal drugs is identified as the key problem, and the elimination of that consumption—a drug-free America—is the goal. In contrast, in Portugal the dangers associated with illegally consumed substances are identified as the key problem, and minimizing those harms to individuals and society is the goal. This means that U.S. drug policy is likely to focus on removing a substance from the marketplace, whereas in Portugal the emphasis is on mitigating any health consequences.

Policy politics revolves around the relationship between policymakers and the groups that keep them in office, their constituents. Policymakers,

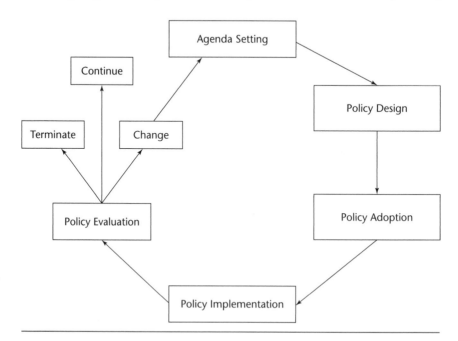

Figure 1.1 THE POLICY CYCLE

SOURCE: Adapted from Dipak Gupta, *Analyzing Public Policy*, (Washington, D.C.: CQ Press, 2001), 47.

whether in democratic or nondemocratic governments, respond to the needs of these constituents. In communist governments, the constituency might be the Central Committee of the Communist Party; in military dictatorships, it could be the commanders of the armed forces. In democracies, the constituency is found among the members of the electorate who are likely to vote and the groups whose support is vital for getting messages to and from the voters. People with the right to vote who do not exercise that privilege tend to have little influence over policy. Groups that pay for or communicate directly with likely voters are influential, but ultimately, it is their ability to affect voter decisions that matters for any policy that is not secret. Drug policy, by its very nature, cannot be secret since the goal is to provide information regarding such issues as potential legal or health costs or safer ways to use a substance so as to influence which psychoactive substances millions of people consume, produce, and distribute and how and where they do.

Obviously, drug policy isn't the only area of concern demanding attention and resources. Policymakers must devote limited time, money, and energy to each of the issues that matter to their constituents. Voters also have limited time, money, and energy; as a result, they most likely do not actively support every issue they believe important. Rather, they look for cues from their political leaders or from "experts" whom they deem knowledgeable about the issue to guide their actions. These cues help define the issue and preferred solutions; for example, drugs as a crime issue are best addressed through enhanced law enforcement policies and sentencing.[6]

Whether or not policymakers gather enough support among their constituents for a particular issue to make it onto the policy agenda depends on four variables. The first is the manner in which the issue is defined, which influences people's willingness to pay attention to it. The narrower the definition, the less likely the issue will gather support. For example, the rights of marijuana smokers don't generate mass attention, whereas concerns about the nation's natural environment generate huge rallies and considerable media focus.

An issue's social and temporal significance also draw attention. When prohibitionists label drug issues as affecting "the future of our children," they trigger concerns about long-term consequences while simultaneously raising the social significance of the issue by referring to children. Finally, the complexity of the issue matters. Simple issues are more likely to find support than are those requiring significant consideration of pros and cons. In drug policy, the claim that illegal drugs are "dangerous" is far easier for the general public to understand than is the argument that the risks associated with illegal drugs vary, are overblown, often come more from the illegality of the drugs than from anything inherent in the substances, and are not any greater than those associated with many legal drugs.

In addition to these four general factors, a sensational event may suddenly thrust an issue onto the policy agenda. Former first lady Betty Ford's revelation that she had a problem with prescription drugs and alcohol helped bring drug abuse by middle-class America into the national spotlight.

Policy Design

Once an issue has been placed on the agenda, the process of formulating a policy response begins. The manner in which the issue is put on the agenda—for example, as a crime or as public health issue—greatly influences, but does not definitively determine, the formulation of policy. Issues can be dealt with in many different ways; it is the task of the policy designers to think strategically about how to produce the outcome desired and how to gather sufficient supporters to get the policy approved.

The outcome needn't be the ultimate goal of the policy, but simply an intermediate goal that the public understands to be a marker of progress toward the ultimate goal. For example, if the goal is elimination of drug use, increased law enforcement efforts that result in larger numbers of users and traffickers in jail may satisfy the public that progress is being made. Alternatively, if the goal is mitigation of the health consequences of drug use, the public will look for such things as fewer overdose deaths or lower rates of HIV transmission. Producing the desired outcome requires a theory of behavior, or analytical perspective, that explains why people do what they do and how one might provide the appropriate incentives to channel their behavior in desired ways.

Four analytical perspectives that currently dominate debates about cause and effect on behavior are presented in the next chapter. The person or team designing the policy will probably seek advice from an outside group that has studied the issue. The choice of that outside group normally is influenced by an affinity between the analytical perspectives of the advisers and policymakers. But not always. U.S. presidents and national science associations have commissioned major studies on marijuana three times, but each time Congress and the president have ignored the findings and recommendations for a relaxation of the prohibitionist thrust of marijuana policy.[7]

The continuum of drug policy domestically and internationally has ranged from active pursuit of violators—commonly identified as a drug war strategy—to active encouragement of production and sale. The prohibition of the production and trade of a particular psychoactive substance makes international criminals and pariahs of governments and those nongovernmental actors, primarily rebels and terrorists, who openly promote these activities. In between the extremes are a variety of policy positions. These include toleration—it's illegal and the penalties may be significant, but the illegal act is ignored; decriminalization—it's illegal, but the penalties are minor; and public health—consumers are provided a variety of treatments, such as needle exchange programs to mitigate the spread of AIDS or even legal prescriptions for registered heroin addicts, for their personal health needs as well as to protect others in society.

Policy Adoption

Policymakers are driven by two factors when considering whether to adopt a particular version of a policy: self-interest and ideology. In political systems in which graft is likely to be detected and politicians can be arrested for corruption, the self-interest of policymakers that matters most is to be re-selected by the constituency, whether for the same or another policymaking position. This leads policymakers to favor policies supported by their constituents. The second factor driving policymakers is their personal belief about cause and effect in human behavior, commonly referred to as ideology. These ideologies are generally understood by the policymakers' constituents, who select the policymakers specifically because of affinities between their ideologies and the constituents' own. Given this relationship, ideologies are related to the desires of constituencies.

Policy adoption is about negotiating support from diverse groups that have an interest in an issue but can differ widely over goals and means. To understand how policy coalitions are constructed, it is first necessary to explain why people mobilize into pressure groups. Why groups have varying impact on policy also must be explored.

Let's begin with the notion that policies carry costs and benefits. All other things being equal, people prefer to receive benefits and shift costs to others. Winners are those whose benefits from a policy far exceed any costs they might pay, whereas losers pay large costs and get relatively few benefits. Organizing a response in favor of or against a policy takes time and effort and may raise problems of collective action—people can get the advantage of having the policy adopted or rejected without any cost to themselves, consequently it's not in anyone's individual interest to contribute, but with no one contributing, the policy doesn't come about. In brief, the greater the number of people who have to be organized to accomplish something, the less likely it is to happen.

Consequently, it is to be expected that people mobilize in defense of their interests if the costs or the benefits are concentrated. In the case of costs, affected groups will oppose that policy; conversely, those who would benefit from the policy generally support it. Table 1.1 indicates the hypothesized impact on the policy process of the concentrated or diffuse distribution of a policy proposal's costs and benefits. From the table, we can see that the most likely type of policy a nation will adopt distributes its costs over a wide variety of groups and concentrates its benefits on particular groups.

The distribution of the costs and benefits of a policy is not the only aspect that affects the creation of a policy coalition. Groups that confront institutional, social, or economic barriers to participation in the political process are unlikely to affect policy even if the costs of that policy are concentrated upon them. For example, in the United States young black males are significantly more likely to be arrested and spend time in jail on drug charges than are white males, even though their participation in illegal drug activity does not differ

Table 1.1 Hypothesized Impact on the Policy Process of the Concentration of Benefits and Costs

	Benefits	
Costs	*Diffuse*	*Specific*
Diffuse	Inaction	Likely Acceptance
Specific	Likely Rejection	Conflict

NOTE: As the table shows, the likely outcome of a policy issue varies depending on whether the costs and benefits are spread across the general population or concentrated on a particular group. When both costs and benefits are spread broadly, the likely outcome is inaction because there isn't sufficiently concentrated constituent support to move the issue forward. When costs are focused on a specific group and benefits are broadly distributed, the policy is likely to be rejected because the small group will be more motivated to oppose it than will the diffuse beneficiaries to actively support it. When a policy would benefit a specific group with broadly distributed costs, acceptance is likely because the group that benefits will mobilize in support, but the costs will be so moderate when spread across a large group that little effective opposition will be mounted. Finally, when both costs and benefits are concentrated, conflict will likely ensue as both beneficiaries and those who pay will be motivated to mobilize to strongly support their interests.
SOURCE: Gupta, *Analyzing Public Policy* p. 55.

significantly from that of whites (see discussion in Chapter Three). President Bill Clinton's drug czar, General Barry McCaffrey, and others condemned this unintended outcome of the overly punitive focus of U.S. drug policy.[8] Despite such opposition—since young black males, their friends, and parents tend not to vote and middle-class drug users and dealers whose parents and friends are more likely to vote tend not to go to jail—current U.S. policy still finds plenty of support among the voters.

This is the stage at which the national drug strategy, with its attendant policies, takes actual shape. The relevant interest groups bargain with policymakers, offering their theoretical rationales and public support. For example, parents might articulate family dynamic explanations, whereas medical professionals could offer clinical arguments. Policymakers, in turn, look to include enough interests to build a strong coalition behind their policies. This requires identifying who can make what deals, what they are willing to accept, and the strength of the coalition needed to get the policy accepted. If the anti-crime and pro-family voices can provide enough support to get a bill through, the public health interest groups could be ignored.

Psychoactive Substances: What Are They and How Do They Work?

The consumption of psychoactive substances, in legal or illegal form, is a common phenomenon in the United States and in most other countries. Yet the average citizen, college student, or policymaker knows little about these substances, and even then, much of what is "known" falls more into the category of urban legend than scientific fact. In the mid-1980s a frightened public believed the sensational reports of crack cocaine being so powerful and addictive that a single use could create addicts with such superhuman strength that police bullets could barely subdue them. A decade later scientific studies demonstrated that crack had no such maniacal powers. Because fact is so often fiction, analysis of policy debates requires learning more about the nature of these substances and their effects.

A psychoactive substance influences communication channels in the brain. Different types of drugs influence different channels, thereby producing distinct impacts on feelings, experiences, and behavior. These immediate effects are consistent across episodes as long as a substance is not adulterated, although the quantity used may have to increase over time because of growing tolerance. People can, therefore, choose substances to produce the feelings they desire, at least in the short term. Some long-term effects that the user may not intend are well known, including addiction, but the probabilities of developing those effects are largely unknown. Still other effects remain the subject of scientific debate.

There is disagreement concerning the exact process by which these substances influence people, but there is a strong consensus among scientists that different substances affect different neurotransmitters. For example, hallucinogens like LSD disrupt the interaction of nerve cells and the neurotransmitter serotonin, which affects "the control of behavioral, perceptual, and regulatory systems, including mood, hunger, body temperature, sexual behavior, muscle control, and sensory perception." Disassociative substances such as PCP and ketamine influence the neurotransmitter glutamate, which affects "perceptions of pain, responses to the environment, and memory." [9] Still other psychoactive substances produce artificially high levels of the neurotransmitter dopamine, which communicates pleasure to the brain. [10]

Psychoactive substances are found in some rather common food and drink whose uses are not legally regulated. Among these are chocolate and coffee. Such substances are also present in products like tobacco and alcohol whose use is regulated by a person's age or, in the case of prescription drugs, by medical license. And of course, these substances are found in the drugs that most societies began to proscribe early in the twentieth century, including cocaine and heroin, or shortly after they were developed, such as Ecstasy and methamphetamine.

Most people around the globe probably choose not to indulge in the use of those psychoactive substances that are illegal in their countries. That said, as Chapter Two demonstrates, hundreds of millions of people do try illegal drugs at some point. It is also clear that there is great diversity in the product-specific characteristics of substances—some give users a high, others make users feel down—as well as in the social and individual traits of their users. Some are rich, others poor; some have many life opportunities, others few.

"Addiction" and "dependency" are concepts that, while having no clear scientific meaning and applying to only a minority of drug consumers, permeate the views many people have of the drug phenomenon. Illegal drugs are widely believed to be particularly harmful to their users and intimately linked to violent crime because of their addictive qualities. Even the Web site of the National Institute on Drug Abuse (NIDA) usually begins a description of an illegal substance by noting that it is addictive.

The American Society of Addictive Medicine (ASAM) advocates a formal definition of addiction, which differs from physical dependence:

> The importance of maintaining this distinction has been highlighted in recent years by the emergence of the pain management movement, whose practitioners point out that in some situations (e.g., severe post-operative pain or pain associated with terminal cancer), it is clinically appropriate to give a patient medications at a dose and for a period of time sufficient to produce physical dependence. However, this alone does not lead to addiction, which always has a psychological component and is accompanied by a constellation of distinctive behaviors.[11]

There is both historical and scientific evidence that most users of psychoactive substances become neither dependent on nor addicted to those substances. Even in the case of heroin, a study by the Institute of Medicine of the National Academy of Sciences reports that only 23 percent of those who had ever used it became dependent. It may come as a surprise to many that the dependency rate for alcohol—15 percent of those who have ever used—is quite similar to cocaine's 17 percent. (See Table 1.2.)

This evidence has spurred a debate concerning the existence of addictive substances. If most users do not become addicted, then the cause of addiction cannot be the substance itself.[12] During the late nineteenth century this variation in addiction outcomes was noticed and explained in crude form by reference to "addictive personalities."[13] Modern science has discarded the notion

Table 1.2 Substance Use and Dependency Rates

Drug Category	Proportion that Have Ever Used (%)	Proportion of Users that Ever Became Dependent (%)
Tobacco	76	32
Alcohol	92	15
Marijuana (including hashish)	46	9
Anxiolytics (including sedatives and hypnotic drugs)	13	9
Cocaine	16	17
Heroin	2	23

SOURCE: Janet E. Joy, Stanley J. Watson Jr., and John A. Benson Jr., eds., *Marijuana and Medicine: Assessing the Science Base*, Institute of Medicine, National Academy of Sciences, 1999, Table 3.4, based on material from J. Anthony, Warner, L., Kessler, R. Comparative epidemiology of dependence on tobacco, alcohol, controlled substances and inhalants: Basic findings from the National Comorbidity Study. *Experimental and Clinical Psychopharmacology* 1994, 2, 244–268. http://books.nap.edu/html/marimed/notice.html.

of an addictive personality, focusing its attention on genes instead. In the case of alcohol, probably the most studied psychoactive substance, attention has been directed to familial genetic "dispositions" to alcoholism. This approach has been found to account for as much—or as little, depending on one's point of view—as 40 percent of the variation in alcoholism outcomes.[14] Yet that still leaves more than half of the variation in a drinker's alcoholism to derive from neither the substance itself nor the familial genetic links studied so far.

As students shall encounter again and again throughout this book, scientific knowledge about psychoactive substances and the links between substance and behavior are too inconclusive to provide significant guidance in policy debates. What the scientific evidence does allow at this point is that addiction and dependence are not caused by the substance itself, but rather develop from a combination of the psychoactive substance, genes, and the social context within which the consumer lives and uses the substance. Social context is not necessarily defined by economic factors. It also could be defined by how one feels about race, subcultures, or other characteristics that have social meaning.

A Commodity Systems Framework

The phenomenon of drug use is best understood by linking consumers to everyone who makes it possible for them to ingest their drug of choice. Consumers and producers are mutually dependent; neither could exist without the other. And since consumers are rarely located close enough to producers that one could simply meet the other and complete the sale, some type of transportation network must also exist. Producers and transporters, in turn, generally need access to a variety of inputs, including labor, chemicals, and in the case of illegal products, perhaps weapons and corrupt officials, to produce and transport the substance. Hence, the providers of these inputs also need to be considered. In regard to illegal products, since participants want to enjoy their profits and since spending dirty money is risky, money launderers play an exceedingly key role. Therefore, a systematic way to think about how a variety of roles are integrated to produce a product and sell it to consumers is needed.

The dominant models available for analyzing the drug trade fail to view all of these roles as part of a system whose purpose is to make a profit for its participants. The balloon model—"you punch it here, it pops out there"—is an expression of frustration that suggests that, short of "popping" the drug trade through an overwhelming use of resources, policymakers have no impact on how much air is inside the balloon or on how widespread and active the drug trade is. This view can hardly help increase understanding about why decades of effort, billons of dollars, millions of prisoners, and thousands of deaths have failed to pop or at least significantly deflate the drug balloon. Paradoxically, it also spurs people to keep trying, because they believe that if they can just get the air out of the balloon, they will destroy it.

The organized crime model provides important insights into how a major portion of the illegal drug system functions, but it doesn't provide understanding about the creation and extent of the system itself. Organized crime can develop in some parts of the system when certain characteristics are present—chiefly high value and illegality.[15] Most analyses that discuss the business of drugs mean precisely this organization of crime. But Mexican marijuana sales in the United States during the 1970s could be explained without reference to organized crime syndicates or networks, and the Medellín cartel in Colombia was certainly an organized crime unit, yet it had little direct control over coca grown in Bolivia. And the current scourge of synthetic opium use via the prescription drug OxyContin is not the result of organized crime; rather it is a decentralized process spread mainly by word of mouth and well-intentioned primary care doctors trying to stay up to date with advances in pain medication and keep happy a client base that demands such medication.[16]

Given the shortcomings of the previous two models, a systems approach is clearly needed to accommodate a more comprehensive examination. The Harvard Business School developed an agribusiness commodity system model in the 1950s that can be readily adapted to psychoactive substances, whether natural or synthetic. "An agribusiness commodity system exists for the purpose of catering to the consumer's nutritional needs, his style of living, and his society's changing value structure."[17] The categories "recreational," "psychological," or "sociological" can be substituted for "nutritional" without damaging the model, and clearly, style of living and a changing value structure are important elements in understanding how societies respond to the existence of psychoactive substances.

Essentially, a commodity system

> encompasses all the participants in the production, processing, and marketing of a single farm product, including farm suppliers, farmers, storage operators, processors, wholesalers, and retailers involved in a commodity flow from initial inputs to the final consumer. It also includes all the institutions and arrangements that affect and coordinate the successive stages of a commodity flow, such as the government, trade associations, cooperatives, ... financial partners, financial entities, transport groups...."[18]

Even in those PASCSs that are illegal, government remains an actor, since it decides on legality as well as when, where, and how to enforce laws.

The strength of the agribusiness commodity system model lies in its integrative character. From the perspective of managers of firms located in the vertical structure of agribusiness, the model provides a way of visualizing their operations within the system of which the firms form a part. The model also suggests that public policies are more effective if developed in terms of the total system and if the implications of the policies for all the segments of the system are understood. "A public policy maker cannot make a policy for one segment ... without affecting the whole structure, which will in turn affect the segment that once was viewed in isolation."[19]

Traders, producers, money launderers, and everyone else engaged in the phenomenon of supplying consumers of psychoactive substances can readily be thought of as businesspeople in competition with each other to supply a product within a legal framework that proscribes their business. This business process produces an integration of functions from production and its needs, through the distribution process, all the way to retail, where consumers send a signal back through the system by purchasing the substance.

Figures 1.2 and 1.3 diagram the general psychoactive substance commodity system for illegal and legal substances, respectively. Students should study

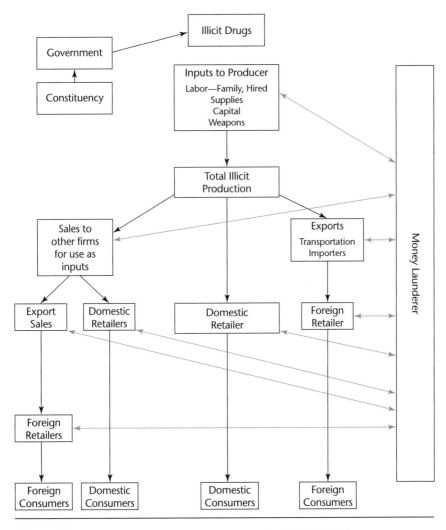

Figure 1.2 PSYCHOACTIVE SUBSTANCE COMMODITY SYSTEM: ILLICIT DRUGS

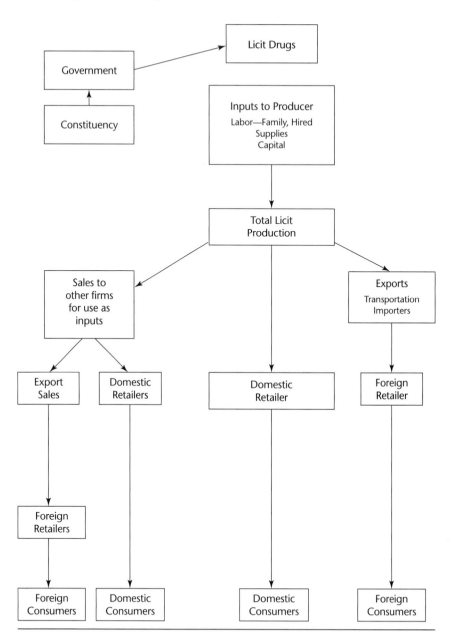

Figure 1.3 PSYCHOACTIVE SUBSTANCE COMMODITY SYSTEM: LICIT DRUGS

the systems well, noting their similarities and differences. Each phase will be explored in great detail in subsequent chapters, and the place of different participants in the system as a whole will be noted, whether that system be legal or illegal.

A systems approach suggests that before attacking a specific part of the system public policy makers should ensure that alternative means for adversaries to achieve their goals are not available or that their costs exceed the benefits of circumvention. For example, in the 1990s the United States utilized a combination of such positive incentives as crop substitution payments and such negative incentives as increased aid to militaries to pursue growers and traffickers in Peru and Bolivia. The result was dramatically reduced production in those countries. Colombian farmers in areas ignored by the United States, however, saw a new market opportunity and began producing coca. The new producers more than offset the decline in Peru and Bolivia, and the overall supply of cocaine to the United States actually increased. Now the United States is frantically pouring more than a billion dollars annually into fighting drugs in rebel-held territory in Colombia. The underappreciated consequence of all of this is that less funding is available for the positive incentives that initially discouraged production in Bolivia and Peru. Positive incentives are no longer high enough to dissuade illegal production and, as a consequence, it is again on the rise in these countries.

Similarly, the United States made great strides during the late 1980s in raising the costs of shipping drugs from Colombia directly through Caribbean waters to the southeastern United States. But because demand continued in the United States and the U.S. government had not invested sufficiently in creating an appropriate incentive structure, first in Central America and Mexico and subsequently in the Caribbean islands, Colombian shippers found ready alternative routes.

Ignoring the intimate links among all the actors in the system produces policy changes that are often met by adaptation by the targets of the policy and an outcome at odds with the intent of policymakers and their supporters. Under these circumstances it's easy to understand policymakers' frustration and retreat to the image of a balloon beyond control. Yet if the drug phenomenon is thought of as a complex and global system, policymakers and their supporters are less likely to narrowly target seemingly isolated pieces of it. Not only will frustrations be minimized, outcomes closer to those sought will be produced.

Summary

Chapter Two presents the major competing explanations for why the phenomenon of an illegal drug trade exists and why the policies to deal with it have been adopted. These explanations are theories of cause and effect: They define an issue, tell why it occurs, and suggest the best possible courses of action (policy) to influence the behavior of people or countries involved. In their most abstract form these theories compete with each other, but it is possible to combine them in distinct ways. Combinations, however, require understanding the hierarchy among the theories being used.

Chapters Three through Six examine the distinct phases in the PASCS: consumption, production, distribution, and money laundering. In each, I examine how the alternative theories explain the issue, the policy recommendations that one would expect from each theory, and the politics of making drug policy. These chapters also evaluate the existing state of knowledge about the characteristics of each phase, for example, who consumes what drugs, why, and with what consequences. Examples of policies in many countries are provided, but there is an emphasis on the U.S. experience because it offers the most comprehensive data.

In Part II, Chapter Seven examines the political economy of international cooperation and conflict over contemporary drug policy. The chapter identifies the advantages and disadvantages of unilateral, bilateral, and multilateral efforts, providing examples from the United States, Europe, and Latin America. Part III consists of three case studies, historical accounts of three nations' distinct approaches to the drug phenomenon that are apt to generate comparative discussion and analysis. Chapter Eight follows the evolution of U.S. drug policy from a focus on reducing crime in the early 1970s, through the stillborn efforts at harm reduction, to the drug war approach that began in the 1980s. In Chapter Nine, the evolution of Dutch drug policy away from a drug war in the 1960s toward harm reduction is described. Lastly, Chapter 10 turns to the Swedish experience to present a move from harm reduction in 1965 toward prohibition in the late 1960s and on to the adoption of a drug war strategy starting in the late 1970s.

STUDY QUESTIONS

1. What are the advantages and disadvantages of beginning your study of drug policy with the assumption that drugs are either "bad" or "harmless"?

2. What does highly, or powerfully, addictive mean? What would you set as the criteria for labeling something "highly addictive"? Why? Search the Web site of the Office of National Drug Control Policy, specifically the Drug Facts section (www.whitehousedrugpolicy.gov/drugfact/index .html) and count the number of substances labeled as either "highly" or "powerfully" addictive. Now find a definition of those terms on the Web site.

3. Compare the utility for analysis of describing drug markets one wants to understand and explain as 1) analogous to balloons; 2) markets controlled by organized crime; and 3) commodity systems.

Chapter 2 Analytical Perspectives for Explaining the Drug Trade

A big party is coming up this weekend. Alcohol and cigarettes will abound. Your dorm mate down the hall wants to provide the Ecstasy pills and the alcohol. He calls a friend, who calls another friend, who is waiting for a new shipment from Europe. Everyone's heard about the bust of the Hassidic young men bringing pills from, and taking cash back to, Amsterdam, but the supply is still readily available for anyone willing to pay the price.[1] And $10 to $25 is less than the price of a good concert!

—Adapted from material in Christopher A. Szechenyi's "Ecstasy bust leads to Israel organized crime, officials say"

How can the sequence of events just described be best understood? Are these criminals breaking the law, social deviants satisfying their unnatural desires, or morally weak individuals succumbing to evil? Or are they rational individuals responding to opportunities to engage in behavior that brings them some desired outcome—fun, excitement, social prestige, money—at what they perceive to be an acceptable risk?

This text compares four of the major analytical perspectives used by the public, policymakers, and social scientists to explain the drug phenomenon and policy responses. If students scan the media, listen to their neighbors, read public policy speeches, or examine academic journals, four concepts seem to dominate discussion of the drug phenomenon: deviance, beliefs, markets, and national security threats. Deviance is behavior that doesn't conform to the dominant norms, and in the approach to drugs signals a focus on abnormality as key to understanding the drug phenomenon. Beliefs are ideas that guide behavior and suggest ideological disagreements over appropriate use of psychoactive substances. Markets are places where supply and demand meet, thus emphasizing the transactional nature of drugs. Challenges to security and sovereignty are considered national security threats and highlight the international dimensions of drug use and trafficking.

Underlying each of these concepts, explicitly or implicitly, is a view of cause and effect that helps the user of that concept understand the phenomenon of the drug trade. Good social science demands that individual views regarding cause and effect—individual theories—be explicit so that their logic can be examined and their related hypotheses can be subjected to empirical tests.

Each of these concepts is linked to an analytical perspective that, as discussed in Chapter One, identifies what is important, where to look for causality, why these factors cause outcomes that are reason for concern, and how, if at all, it might be possible to vary these outcomes. In the case of the drug phenomenon, the analytical perspective that one holds identifies the particular problem of concern, such as some people use these substances or the government attempts to regulate individual use of them. It also highlights who is causing this problem, as in emotionally damaged people use drugs or politicians make policy against people's true interests. Lastly, the analytical perspective one holds demonstrates why the problem arose. For instance, emotionally damaged people use drugs to offset their pain or power-hungry politicians seek to control people's lives.

If individuals want to effect a particular outcome they must address the identified causes. For example, if analysts see psychological problems as the cause of drug use, mental health services may be offered to help users overcome their problems without these substances. Multiple policy prescriptions can follow from a single analytical perspective. For instance, both treatment for drug users or decreased availability of drugs would produce a decline in drug use. Some policy options, however, would not make sense within certain perspectives—if drug use is identified as the key problem, then legalization of such use would be an illogical response.

The task of an analytic perspective, therefore, is to make sense of the phenomenon of interest by organizing the elements of the issue in a meaningful way that allows conclusions to be reached and policy to be made that effects the desired outcome. Individuals need to follow the logic of their analytical perspective if they want to discover the answers to their questions about a particular phenomenon. For example, one analytical perspective suggests that poor people produce drugs because the selling price is high. Following this perspective, an examination of production in areas dominated by poor people should show that economic development would decrease production by providing opportunities to produce higher value crops or get a higher paying job.

Four Analytical Perspectives

Each of the four analytical perspectives most commonly used to understand the drug phenomenon provides some insight into drug trade and policy. However, each is incomplete to varying degrees in what it can explain. Readers of this text are encouraged to consider how these perspectives can be used, alone and in combination, to provide logical and empirically supported arguments for understanding the different public policies adopted to deal with the drug phenomenon across time and country.

Social Deviance

The first analytical perspective, social deviance, assumes that a common culture shares social norms and values that determine the behavior of most of the people in that society. A leading text notes that the concept

refers to behaviors or attributes manifested by specified kinds of people in specified circumstances that are judged to violate the normative expectations of a specified group. "Shared normative expectations" refers to group evaluations regarding the appropriateness or inappropriateness of certain attributes or behaviors when manifested by certain kinds of people in certain situations.

The motivation for deviant behavior generally arises because individuals or groups cannot succeed through accepted terms and thus choose to undertake activities in which they can succeed, despite the proscription of these activities by society. At times, nondeviant individuals may seek to be part of a group and wind up behaving deviantly simply because they want to fit in. This is the perception of those advocating the importance of peer pressure. Whether the motivations actually produce deviant behavior depends upon the "relative strength of the motives to commit the act and of those not to commit the act, and on the situational context and other opportunities to perform the act."[2]

There is a tendency to assume that societal norms are "natural" and inherently correct, and anyone who questions these norms is automatically suspect. This is the origin of the identification of deviant behavior as antisocial. The core argument of this perspective is that being socially deviant *causes* people to act in ways that transgress societal norms.

Analysts of the drug phenomenon who utilize this perspective believe that some individuals suffer from a flaw that leads them to violate social norms against the consumption of illegal drugs.[3] Many of these analysts assume that the national policy of a drug-free America and voters' support of legal proscription of currently illegal substances constitutes the social norm on drugs. Drinking at a college party, even by those who are underage, is acceptable because alcohol is not proscribed by society at large. Using Ecstasy, however, is by definition indicative of deviant behavior because the substance is illegal.

The nature of the flaws that allegedly cause deviance is in dispute among analysts. Some think that social and economic factors, such as poverty, child abuse, or discrimination, are key causal or contributory elements. Other analysts of this same school reject such links, emphasizing that the majority of people experiencing these social and economic factors do not engage in socially deviant behavior. For these particular analysts, genetic factors, such as low intelligence, chemical imbalances, or a familial history of addiction produce a weak character susceptible to deviance.[4] Users of illegal drugs at college parties are thus expected to have come from some type of socially or economically deprived background, to have trouble adjusting to college pressures, and to be poor students.

Although sociologists and criminologists apply the social deviance perspective to analyze the behavior of individuals, the public policy discourse and the study of international relations have been heavily influenced by the creation of an analogy between governments or nations who "misbehave" and deviant individuals. Thus, Afghanistan under the Taliban, South Africa during apartheid, or Argentina under military rule become pariah states. Colombia, with vast cocaine and heroin producing territory under guerrilla control, and post-Taliban Afghanistan with opium-friendly warlords running vast parts of the country are called failed states. The logic of these labels is that the drug use—or other undesirable behavior—occurs because a country suffers from a major flaw that makes it unable to abide by accepted norms: either it has no control over itself or its government could not survive if it stopped the unacceptable behavior.

Social deviance approaches are most useful when the relevant norms are widely accepted and only change moderately and slowly. These arguments can accommodate the fact that a society may create different laws to govern the use of distinct psychoactive substances, but such approaches have difficulty explaining such dramatic changes as the U.S. prohibition of alcohol in 1919 and its subsequent re-legalization in 1933. In addition, the widespread use of some illegal substances (for example, almost half of U.S. high school seniors have tried marijuana) renders the deviance claim a rhetorical device rather than a useful analytic approach for understanding the politics of drug policy. Consequently, the study of social deviance may not be particularly helpful for understanding and making meaningful comparisons among the politics surrounding psychoactive substances that are 1) legal, as in the case of alcohol and tobacco; 2) widely used but illegal, such as alcohol by underage drinkers or marijuana; or 3) infrequently used and illegal, like heroin.

Studies of social deviance have provided important insights when they focus on select groups of users without asserting that all users suffer from the same characteristics. Addicts are often on the margins of society, and as their contact with the mainstream decreases, they get caught in a pattern of deviance amplification.[5] This insight may go a long way toward explaining why a small group of users not only accounts for most of the illegal drug use, but also for the nondrug crime associated with such use.

To that end, this approach constitutes the theoretical basis for a crime-oriented understanding of why some individuals or groups violate the rules of behavior approved by society at large. Deviance studies have made some advances in understanding aspects of the criminal behavior of drug traffickers. As shown in more detail in Chapters Four and Five, only a minority of traffickers engages in violent behavior. Most prefer to maintain a low profile, make money, and enjoy the benefits of higher income in mainstream society.

But some drug lords, like those leading the Medellín (Colombia) and Tijuana (Mexico) cartels, pursue fame through violence, even at the cost of risking the billions of dollars they have already made. As a number of biographies illustrate, many of these violent drug lords were petty criminals who saw violence (which one can argue constitutes deviant behavior in most societies) as a way of exerting a degree of control over their environment and as a means of distinguishing themselves.[6]

However, because a focus on social deviance assumes that the substance under consideration is illegal, it doesn't help explain why there are variations in the legal status of psychoactive substances across place and time. In addition, while it is true that there can be socially disruptive and illegal behavior (beyond mere consumption) associated with these substances, this is not usually the case, and individuals who are not under the influence of psychoactive substances engage in many of the same behaviors. The challenge for social deviance analysts then is to develop measures to indicate when a norm becomes a social norm, what threshold is necessary to suggest that a social norm has become weak enough to render the label "deviance" obsolete, and the determinants and processes of norm change as mentioned earlier.

Rational Choice

A second analytical perspective, rational choice,[7] builds an argument that explains human behavior by emphasizing the rationality of choices made by individuals. A number of key concepts define a rational choice approach to analyzing the behavior of humans and of the communities they create.[8] First, actors are assumed to be instrumentally rational and egoist. This simply means that individuals, groups, or states (actors) want what they themselves define as best (egoist) and act in a manner designed to achieve it (rational). Being instrumentally rational does not imply that actors know all the relevant information. Rather it means that, given the information they have, they choose to do what appears will help achieve their goals. Choice thus plays a key role in a rational choice approach.

The existence of choice implies options—in models of strategic interaction these are called strategies—and a ranking of those options by the actor. Choices are perceived by actors to produce different outcomes, and they make choices based on how those outcomes correspond to what they desire. Actors also are assumed to have preferences concerning the rankings among outcomes; that is, they prefer the outcomes, not the options themselves. Taking psychoactive substances is therefore a strategy to achieve an outcome, such as dancing all night, getting instant gratification, or relaxing, that is preferred to the other expected outcomes, like getting too tired or drunk to dance or watching TV alone, if one does not take the drug.

A rational choice approach assumes that actors usually engage each other in situations characterized by strategic interaction: the outcome of their interaction is the combined result of what each wants and does. This means that neither actor might have chosen the outcome achieved. Instead, the outcome came about because of choices each actor made while anticipating what the other might choose. For example, a student at the party might consume a tainted drug rather than untainted Ecstasy and become critically ill instead of dancing into the night, an outcome that was not the intent of either the student or the policymakers who made Ecstasy illegal.

In addition to the individuals involved, a rational choice approach takes into account the institutional context within which an action occurs. Institutions are rules that guide behavior. They can be explicit as in the case of laws or implicit as in cultural, social, or group norms, and they can be embodied in formal organizations or simply constitute the social context within which actors interact. These rules provide incentives, both positive and negative, for certain types of behavior. Rational egoistic actors consider these costs and benefits when evaluating outcomes and choosing their actions. Rational choice analysts do not assume that everyone who violates these rules is deviant; such violations might simply signal the weakness of the rules themselves.

This element of choice holds whether actors behave in accordance with the law or act outside of it. It is also true for addicts, in the sense that the first use of a substance was a choice influenced by a variety of positive and negative incentives. It is important to realize that since the dependency rate for illegal substances is well below 25 percent for most substances, the first decision by addicts to use drugs can be made, with some rational justification, in the belief that they will not become addicted. In addition, some addicts are able to respond to decreased availability or greater risk by cutting back on consumption, even abstaining for months at a time, until the supply situation becomes more favorable.[9]

As shown, the centerpiece of the rational choice approach is the focus on this act of choice: why consumers consume, producers produce, traffickers traffic, and money launderers launder. These analysts focus on understanding the choices individuals confront and the incentives for choosing to consume, produce, traffic, and launder. The rational choice approach also allows movement beyond the sterile chicken-or-egg debate about whether drug consumption is demand- or supply-induced, by demonstrating how supply and demand are intimately related.

Such an approach can also help expand understanding of how countries respond to the existence of psychoactive substances. By recognizing that the distribution of benefits and costs of different policy options across different actors influences preferences and behavior, clarity of comprehension can be gained of the different ways in which the same society treats distinct psychoactive substances, for instance, alcohol and marijuana in the United States. Greater understanding can also be acquired regarding how countries vary in their approach to the same psychoactive substance; for example, the United States prohibits marijuana even as the Netherlands decriminalizes it. Policymakers respond strategically to the preferences of the people institutionally empowered to select them. As a result, public policy has to be understood in terms of political influence and the distribution of costs and benefits of alternative policies.

Like the other analytic perspectives, rational choice approaches have weaknesses. Preferences are assumed or derived after the fact by reasoning backward. For example, analysts might say, "Given this strategic context and this outcome, the actors must have valued these choices above these other options." This problem with preference formation occurs because the rational choice approach provides no way of understanding how rational individuals determine their value structures. As a shortcut, individuals are assumed to want more rather than less and what they want is often assumed to be material in nature. But even if students wanted to dance more at the dorm party, their value structures might lead them to reject both alcohol and Ecstasy despite the impact on their ability to dance and the minimal chance of getting arrested. The rational choice approach does not help increase our understanding of how students came to have their value structures.

Constructivism

The constructivist approach insists that individual behavior is fundamentally influenced by socially constructed norms. Consequently, behavior related to drugs, including policy choices, depends upon the way in which relevant actors conceptualize the phenomenon of psychoactive substances and policy options. Constructivists begin their analyses from the point of view that "ideas, which can only exist in individuals' heads, are ... socially causative."[10] By this they mean that facts derive their meaning from the viewer's preconceived notions rather than from inherent factors. For example, in the drug trade, consumption, production, and trade of psychoactive substances, as well as the laundering of money generated by these activities, are indisputable facts. In that sense, each constitutes a "phenomenon."

Constructivists note that understanding of the meaning of these facts varies by substance, time, place, and even by the social characterization (class, ethnicity, national origin, gender, age, or race) of those involved. Americans tend to see the person who brought booze to the dorm party as simply a partier, whereas they are likely to find more negative words—irresponsible, pusher—to describe the person who brought the Ecstasy. This despite the fact that both individuals broke the law, that both substances are dangerous to users, and that alcohol is often associated with violent behavior by the user when Ecstasy is not. Constructivists, therefore, argue that there is no inherent reason why drug use should be considered deviant or illegal. Rather, such social and legal norms, and any subsequent categorization of behavior as deviant, are generated by particular groups in particular societies at particular times.

Although constructivists focus on norms, they differ from social deviance analysts because they believe that norms are constantly being challenged and altered. Consequently, deviance is not an explanatory category. It is a descriptor with negative connotations that reflects the views of those using it rather than a powerful causal argument or an objective concept that promotes the understanding of a phenomenon. Understanding why alcohol is legal and Ecstasy illegal requires more examination of those presenting the arguments than study of the substances themselves.

Users consume, producers produce, and traffickers sell because they perceive their actions to be acceptable, not because they conceive of themselves as failures. "Toking up" a marijuana joint at a social gathering is seen as akin to sipping wine at a reception. To constructivists there are no bad norms from the perspective of those who promote them.[11] One instead needs to understand the competition among norms to explain behavior. That competition revolves around norm entrepreneurs and institutions.

Ideas are constantly available, so constructivists look to norm entrepreneurs to explain which ideas become group norms. The entrepreneur believes in the idea and therefore provides information about it and its benefits and develops a coalition to support it. As this coalition gains adherents the idea becomes accepted and, if successful, institutionalized into group norms. These norms become internalized; group members begin guiding their behavior by them subconsciously.

In fact, ideas can become so influential that they matter more than hard evidence. The gateway theory about marijuana leading to hard drug use—despite a plethora of evidence to the contrary and the growing evidence that alcohol and tobacco use predate marijuana use—sounds logical. It also gives parents reason to worry about marijuana, even as they downplay the relevance of alcohol or tobacco.[12]

The constructivist perspective forces individuals to deal with the fact that drug policy is partly the result of subjective perceptions about different substances and about consumers and nonconsumers, as well as the entire range of people involved in the drug phenomenon. But this perspective also has its own fundamental weaknesses; methodologies have not yet been developed with sufficient social scientific rigor to determine the origins of ideas in individuals or to test for the existence and power of specific ideas in explaining their dominance over empirical evidence, individual behavior, and policy preferences. Constructivist analysts need to develop arguments about when these idea entrepreneurs will arise, the direction of their policy prescriptions, and the chances for their success in building a coalition sufficiently powerful to influence policy.

Realism

The final analytic approach, realism, focuses on explaining how domestic public policy relates to a global market as well how a government behaves internationally. Realists focus on threats to a nation, and these threats are not limited to conquest by military means. But simply claiming that national security is at risk does not automatically make someone a realist. The use of a realist analytical perspective requires following the logic of realist theory.

Realism assumes that international politics occurs in a condition of anarchy—a context in which no set of rules is binding on all states—and that each state seeks to preserve its own sovereignty, which is understood as the ability to respond to international opportunities and challenges as it believes best fits its interests. In this context, subordination, subjugation, or elimination of states is a constant possibility. States therefore compete with and mistrust each other on matters that could affect their ability to survive, thrive, and make policy decisions that respond to their own best interests. As a result, power in its military, diplomatic, and economic forms is the chief currency in international politics; cooperation on important matters is limited to immediate self-interest and, consequently, will be brief and unlikely to be fully adhered to by any nation.[13]

Realists begin by asking whether any component of the psychoactive substance commodity system (consumption, production, distribution, or money laundering) weakens the nation in international competition. Such weakness might come from a diverse combination of domestic and international sources. For example, if heroin addiction could potentially become widespread, the economic costs attributable to use per se (health care costs, absence from work) could divert an important percentage of money from the economy or the defense budget and might also subvert an antiterrorist government in Afghanistan. Realists could then conclude that heroin use in the United States (although Americans get most of their heroin from Colombia) and Europe poses a potential national security threat to these regions.

All of this means that realists do not automatically support a drug war policy. A realist needs to know the actual costs of drug use and the opportunity costs of diverting funds to combat that use. If drug use is not a threat to a nation's ability to compete internationally or the diversion of resources to combat the threat is affordable, a realist perspective would suggest not getting involved in the policy debate, or if one did, such a perspective could not help one decide what should be done.

It might, however, be especially useful in understanding why the U.S. position on drug use dominates international policy. Because the market for drugs is international in scope, power differentials among states determine which policy options governments adopt. Stronger states are expected to be more unilateral in their foreign policy on drugs, whereas weaker states follow the lead of the most powerful states. Following the lead means that the powerful states force weaker states to pay higher relative costs. Hence, the U.S. government severely conditions its aid to Colombia on that country's willingness to spray herbicides over coca, poppy, and marijuana fields, a practice that would violate federal Environmental Protection Agency (EPA) laws in the United States.[14] Realists also expect that antidrug efforts are unlikely to be top

> ### Box 2.1 Realism, Foreign Governments, Drugs, and U.S. National Security
>
> The George W. Bush administration is vocal in its criticism of the North Korean government's participation in the drug trade, declaring that such behavior indicates the rogue nature of that government. Meanwhile, the post-Taliban government in Afghanistan is accused by many observers of not pursuing poppy eradication and drug traffickers because members of the government participate in those activities, as well as because the Karzai government needs the support of the warlords involved in the drug trade. The consequence is that, after the Taliban's near elimination of the crop, production is flourishing in Afghanistan once again. Unlike its condemnation of similar behavior by the North Koreans, however, the current Bush administration does not criticize the actions (or rather, inaction) of the Karzai government. A realist would explain this difference in treatment by emphasizing the priority of the war on terror over the war on drugs and the fact that the Karzai government is an ally of the United States, whereas the present North Korean government has already established itself as a threat because of its decision to reinstitute its nuclear weapons program early in the twenty-first century.

priorities for most governments; consequently, policy on drug issues will be subordinated to security or economic concerns.

A major weakness of realism in explaining drug politics is that it has no theory in regard to domestic politics. Causal arguments about the domestic politics of drugs can't simply be extrapolated from the international relations argument that governments act as if they were rational, unitary actors or that institutions have little influence over actual behavior. After all, realists argue that the chief difference between domestic and international relations is that the domestic political order is hierarchical, not anarchic.[15] Consequently, institutions that support that hierarchy have an effect on who decides policy and on the distribution of costs and benefits of different actions and, therefore, on the perception of threat by the policymakers.

Combining Perspectives on Drug Policy

Readers may protest that multiple views about the phenomenon have been presented here as opposed to just one. True, but inevitably, one conceptualization dominates each individual's perceptions. The existence of other issues may be recognized, but they will be interpreted within the context set by a fundamental conceptualization of what drugs represent to the individual and who is involved in the psychoactive substance commodity system (PASCS). In the following examples, one perspective dominates, but other perspectives contribute to the explanation of why public policy needs to address the drug phenomenon.

- Participants in the illicit PASCS are, by definition, social deviants. They need to be restrained by high costs for their deviant behavior and they represent a national security threat if their values are allowed to attract others through a war of ideas or peer pressure. These deviants may need personal health treatment, but that should be administered either in prison or under court supervision.
- Individuals make choices. Some of these individuals, but not a majority, may be deviant; others are simply seeking to increase their pleasure at what they perceive to be acceptable costs. Pleasure is individually defined; a national security threat depends upon the resources—economic and human, such as lives ruined by the use of drugs—spent on consumption. Personal health treatment and information can decrease those costs to a nation without infringing upon civil rights.

In the search for an understanding of the politics of drug policy, it is useful to distinguish among five distinct national drug strategies that nations might pursue: demand reduction, supply reduction, crime reduction, harm reduction, and civil rights protection. Although most national strategies may discuss reducing demand and supply for illicit drugs, associated crime, and harm to the consumer and society as well as protection of civil liberties, they can differ in the relative priority given to each. Some nations may insist that publicly financed harm reduction be provided to users only after they have entered the criminal justice system; others would keep law enforcement out of the picture entirely in order to attract illicit drug users to rehabilitation centers, needle exchanges, or safe injection rooms. In this latter example, harm reduction policies are an alternative to deterrent and punitive policies because policymakers believe that reducing harm takes precedence over deterring use or reducing crime.

Determining which national strategy a country has adopted requires analyzing budget allocation and policy implementation at the point of contact with someone in the PASCS. But students must beware: government budgets are quirky and opaque by design.[16] Money allocated for one policy might be diverted into another as agencies are assigned new tasks; old functions might be taken out of the drug control agencies altogether but still carried out by new agencies whose budgets do not show up on the national drug tally sheet.

Demand Reduction

A national strategy that gives priority to reducing demand does not deny that producers, distributors, and money launderers exist. Policymakers may even dedicate some resources to pursuing people and disrupting supplies in these phases of the PASCS. But the logic of this national strategy is that the key driving force in the entire phenomenon is the demand for illegal drugs. As demand falls the incidence of all the other issues related to drugs is expected to decline in turn. For example, the decrease in demand should produce falling prices, falling prices mean that profits for producing and selling these substances decline, and declining profits translate into people turning to other pursuits to generate an income. The ultimate expression of such a demand reduction strategy would be a population in which "just say no" actually happens; for example, in fundamentalist Muslim countries people willingly choose or are socially pressured to not drink or smoke.

Supply Reduction

The attraction of a supply reduction strategy lies in both economics and politics. As supplies decrease, price increases and demand falls. If supplies keep drying up, demand will keep falling. As already indicated, even heroin addicts decrease their use in response to price increases. In addition, such policies focus on people who seem to be particularly disreputable—pushers, terrorist organizations, greedy bankers—and not on the victims of their perfidy or bad genes. Since production, distribution, and money laundering are all important for supply, policies to reduce supply can focus on any or all of these phases of the PASCS. The U.S. focuses on interdiction of cocaine imports and elimination of the coca crop are supply reduction strategies to deal with cocaine consumption.

Crime Reduction

This national strategy focuses on crimes other than those committed by getting the illegal substance to consumers or by consumption. Examples are property crime—burglary, shoplifting—committed by users to generate money with which to purchase the illegal drugs, or violent crime by users for the same purposes or by distributors and money launderers to enforce their claims for a larger piece of the illegal pie. Property and violent crime committed by people as a result of drug use, such as driving while high, or battery and assault while in a drug-induced paranoia, also fall into this category. Richard Nixon's support for methadone and other treatment programs for heroin addicts was stimulated by concern for crime reduction.

Harm Reduction

The basic idea behind harm reduction strategies is to reduce the potential negative effects to users and society that result from use of illegal substances. These harms are usually health related and can include death by taking an overdose, mixing substances, or consuming adulterated substances, or the spread of HIV to the sexual partners of intravenous drug users. Because these substances are illegal, their purity, dosage, and interactive dangers with other drugs are unknown to most individuals.

To the degree that a potential user is deterred by the threats inherent in consuming illegal drugs, harm reduction may increase use even as it reduces the associated health risks. For the comparative analysis of national strategies, it is important to distinguish between use and harm. Some analysts see use of illegal psychoactive substances as harmful in and of itself, but the decriminalization of these same substances in some countries suggests that those harms are acceptable to those societies. Portugal's recent decriminalization of the consumption of all psychoactive substances, including the possibility of mandatory treatment if an individual's consumption becomes problematic, is an example of such a situation.

Civil Rights

A national strategy that puts the safeguarding of citizens' civil rights as the number one priority focuses on the right to privacy, a respect for property, and a person's right to individual liberty. The fundamental principle guiding this strategy is that it is more important to limit government's power and its intrusion into the private lives of citizens than it is to stop or significantly decrease the demand for, and supply of, psychoactive substances. Some, but not all, advocates of the primacy of civil rights also believe that it is an individual's inherent right to decide whether or not to use any psychoactive substance as long as that individual takes responsibility for the economic, social, medical, and criminal consequences of that use. This focus on the safeguarding of civil rights is the way most contemporary Western societies treat alcohol and nicotine consumption, except in those countries that regulate secondhand smoke; such regulation is a harm reduction strategy.

Explaining National Strategies

Analysis of why a particular national strategy is chosen cannot proceed by simply reasoning backward from strategy to analytic perspective. It's true that some perspectives cannot logically favor some strategies; for example, a social deviance analyst would be hard pressed to organize a policy around the notion of harm reduction. But in other cases the relationship between analytic perspective and strategy is not as clear-cut. A strategy heavily based upon demand reduction does not necessarily imply that the coalition backing the plan is led by policymakers and constituents who view the drug phenomenon through the lens of social deviance.

Proponents of other analytic perspectives could also favor demand reduction policies but for different reasons. Table 2.1 illustrates the complexity of linking policy to analytic perspective, and thus shows the need to investigate the actual case to see which perspective, or combination of perspectives, actually does the

Table 2.1 Analytic Perspective Hypotheses Regarding Adoption of National Drug Strategy

Strategy	Analytic Perspective			
	Social Deviance	Constructivism	Rational Choice	Realist
Demand Reduction	Consumers are deviant and must be stopped.	Consumers are vulnerable and must be helped.	Consumers need information regarding harms to themselves from a drug or the law.	Why consumers consume is irrelevant; what matters is that consumption is threatening nation's ability to compete internationally. Production-related issues threaten government or that of an important ally.
Supply Reduction	Consumers are deviant but can be helped; those who supply the drug are "merchants of death" and must be stopped.	Consumers are victims; pursue those responsible for spreading the problem.	Users are rational consumers; increase cost of supply and use will decline.	
Crime Reduction	Crime intimately connected to desire to use and supply drugs.	Fear drives constituents, whether crime rate is high or not.	Crime rate perceived high by constituents and as connected to drugs.	Drug-related crime threatens government or that of an important ally.
Harm Reduction	Unlikely that a social deviance analyst would support this strategy.	Consumers perceived as victims; psychoactive substances perceived as largely within acceptable bounds, if their worst aspects are mitigated.	Costs of prohibition are high, and there is a weak link between drugs and crime; some people will always use and society needs to protect itself against spread of harm by users.	Harm to drug users creates significant opportunity costs that threaten ability to defend nation.
Civil Rights Protection	Constituency fears an increase in the police power of the state more than the harm caused by drug use because power corrupts politicians and law enforcement.	"Our bodies, ourselves;" right of individual to decide gains support as knowledge of the exaggeration of the harm directly related to it spreads.	Constituency feels secure from crime and deviance but has concerns over the budget for reduction strategies and has concerns over giving the government more ability to control personal choices.	Unlikely that a realist analyst who perceives drugs as a national security threat would support this strategy because the nation matters more than the individual.

Table 2.2 Analytic Perspective Explanations for International Policy Process

International Policy Process	Analytic Perspectives			
	Social Deviance	Constructivism	Rational Choice	Realism
Unilateralism	Governments of potential partners are corrupt and weak, so nation must go it alone	Primacy of a national security viewpoint makes leaders unwilling to work together.	The benefits achievable by acting alone outweigh the costs associated with cooperation.	Great power imposing its will on small powers.
Bilateral Cooperation	Only two governments are strong and honest enough to work together to control the drug trade.	Only two governments are driven by similar ideas regarding the PASCS.	Two governments are exploring the possibility of creating an international institution because both are unhappy with the payoffs of acting unilaterally.	Two great powers find it in their short-term interest to work together and keep others out of the agreement in order to have greater control over the distribution of the benefits produced.
Multilateral Cooperation	Many governments are strong and honest.	There is recognition by countries that the psychoactive substance commodity system is global and that effective policies must therefore also be global.	An international institution has been created to deal with the drug issue.	Policy produced is mainly rhetorical or one or more of the great powers are providing the collective good of a drug policy; other countries are free riding.

best job of explaining why and how the policy was adopted. In short, systematic and logical thinking is necessary but is not a substitute for empirical evaluation.

In addition, Table 2.1 relates how the analytic perspective justifies its support for a particular national strategy. Empirical analysis means investigating the process of coalition building to ascertain whether important partners in the policy coalition articulated these rationales. Each analytical perspective produces distinct hypotheses to explain the selection of a national strategy to deal with the phenomenon of psychoactive substances.

The distinct analytical perspectives can also help one understand the process through which international policy is made, and therefore how a specific country's national strategy influences another's. International policy can be the result of three processes: unilateralism, or one nation imposing its preferred policy on the rest; bilateralism, or two countries negotiating and agreeing upon a common policy; and multilateral cooperation, or multiple countries negotiating and agreeing upon a common policy. Table 2.2 summarizes the logic by which each perspective would explain why a particular international process was chosen for discussing the drug trade.

Summary

Analytic perspectives help make sense of complex phenomena and guide the search for causal relationships. Especially when addressing controversial topics, it is important to follow the logic of causality advocated by a particular analytic perspective as well as gather the empirical evidence to support a particular argument for why a nation adopted a particular national drug strategy.

The following chapters more closely discuss the evidence for why people become involved in the distinct phases of the PASCS and the consequences of this involvement. The causal logic of the different analytic perspectives and the data will help evaluate which arguments best explain the politics of drug policy.

STUDY QUESTIONS

1. Why can't the facts in regard to drug use, crime, and addiction determine how the "drug problem" is defined?
2. What is the purpose of an analytic perspective?
3. Which of the four analytic perspectives do you think you will give primacy in your analysis of the drug phenomenon? Why?

Chapter 3 Conceptualizing Consumption: Drug Use and Drug Users

On December 21, 1970, Elvis Presley arrived at the White House bearing an unexpected offer for President Richard Nixon: his assistance in the war on drugs. Caught by surprise but more than happy for the assistance of such a celebrity, the president posed for a picture with the rock star. He also arranged to provide him with an honorary badge to designate Presley as a special narcotics agent. Less than seven years after this meeting, Elvis died suddenly at the age of forty-two. The autopsy report (kept sealed until 1990) revealed that he had fourteen different drugs in his body at the time of death and a history of drug abuse.[1]

—Compiled from "When Nixon Met Elvis," National Archives and
John Cassidy's "Presley's death on prescription finally revealed,"
Sunday Times (London)

It is appropriate to begin the empirical section of this book with an examination of who uses what. Whether individuals think that there is a drug problem or not often depends upon who they believe consumes what drugs and what the effects of these drugs are for the users and for society. How consumption and the consumer are conceptualized, in addition to affecting analysis, fundamentally influences the policies adopted regarding supply and demand. As this chapter demonstrates, even this simple starting point—who uses what—thrusts one deep into philosophical, moral, social, and political debate. Some of this debate is the result of the absence of data, but most of it is created by advocates of particular analytic perspectives, who emphasize different "facts" about drug use and its consequences to make their point.

Social reality is so complex that facts can be difficult to separate from context and perspective. When individuals try to construct a comprehensive picture, they confront three different types of facts: those that are indisputable, such as marijuana can get you high; those that are debatable, such as cocaine is highly addictive; and those that are missing, including the addiction rates for different psychoactive drugs. Given that some facts are debatable or missing, there is a choice of how to proceed. The focus can be placed on the facts that support a particular view, or the ambiguity and absence of data can be exposed and suggestions made as to why the missing data is expected to support a particular view, or as comprehensive a picture of the phenomenon as possible can be developed and then tested to see if a particular view stands up.

35

ELVIS PRESLEY MEETS WITH PRESIDENT RICHARD NIXON ON DECEMBER 21, 1970 TO OFFER HIS AS-
SISTANCE IN THE WAR ON DRUGS.
SOURCE: AP/Wide World Photos.

Whereas the first tack turns serious discussion into a debating match but doesn't help increase understanding of either the illicit drug phenomenon or provide a good basis for thinking about public policy options, the second and third choices require the type of analytical thinking that is the strength of social science analysis and can lead to more effective public policy.

Although this chapter generally focuses on drug use in the United States, it is an international phenomenon. One of the distinguishing factors about the U.S. experience is the data available about drug use. No other country has such systematic and comprehensive material tracked over time. Some nations don't survey this issue, and those that do differ in the years surveyed, measurement methods used, and population samples from which they draw for their analyses. Comparisons about drug use internationally and in many cases within the same country over time must, therefore, be suggestive rather than precise or conclusive.

Thinking about the Data and the Questions We Want to Answer

Any analysis of a phenomenon requires that analysts make distinctions about what they are studying. The first distinction many people make when discussing drugs is between those that are legal and those that are illegal. Yet analysis cannot proceed fruitfully by taking this distinction as a given. As seen in Chapter One, some substances have been legal at some point in time, some have been illegal and then have been legalized, and some countries have decriminalized the use of all drugs.

These differences in legal regime need to be explained rather than simply ignored. They can help illuminate how ideas, morality, science, economics, and politics interact in public policy. While many issues that concern people about drugs are related to the legal regime under which they are consumed, not all are. For example, the issue of addiction crosses the boundaries between legal and illegal. A prime example of this is alcohol, a psychoactive substance that is legal in the United States but which has the potential to have serious addictive effects on consumers.

Addressing questions about drug use and users requires that one understand how best to use available data. However the data are organized, the important thing to remember is that it cannot be used to make arguments about precise numbers or specific individuals, but only to draw a general picture of the phenomenon and to track trends over time. So before I begin an examination of who uses, I'll say a few words about my decision to include which drugs over which specific time period and who is represented in the surveys about consumption.

The identification and definition of the substances that come to mind when people think about the "drug issue" tend not to capture the complexity of the phenomenon. Analysts disagree on which drugs to study; consequently, they focus on different ones, often for convenience or because they have preconceived notions of which drugs and which users represent problems. A quick scan of the media and materials on the drug issue suggests that in the United States the focus has been largely on an unholy trinity of marijuana, cocaine, and heroin. Yet the drug phenomenon has always been much greater than these three, as the U.S. experiment with alcohol prohibition from 1919–1933 and the current debates over tobacco illustrate. Fortunately, public policy makers in the United States are now seeking a more comprehensive picture of the use of psychoactive substances in society. Since 1979 the major national surveys sponsored by the National Institute on Drug Abuse (NIDA) have included questions concerning tobacco use; anabolic steroids were added to the surveys in 1989, and still others have been added in the subsequent years.

At the global level the biases are even greater. In 1998 the UN General Assembly tasked the UN Office on Drugs and Crime (UNODC) with publishing "comprehensive and balanced information about the world drug problem." The 2004 report was less than comprehensive. For example, it did not include the use of such inhalants as glue and paint, nor was the use of prescription drugs without a prescription addressed. Alcohol and tobacco use also were not studied.

Another major factor that surfaces in the discussion about drug policy is the time periods that analysts use in their arguments. The U.S. government has collected systematic data only since 1971 for household residents over the age of twelve—using the National Household Survey on Drug Abuse (NHSDA)—and only since 1975 for high school seniors—through such programs as the "Monitoring The Future" (MTF) survey. Since drug use varies over time, analysts can argue about trends by defining their time periods differently. For example, drug use in the United States went up in the late 1970s, fell dramatically in the mid-1980s, leveled off in the early 1990s, and gradually increased by 2001, albeit to levels still far below the peak reached in the 1970s. Advocates of the drug war approach to curtailing drug use tend to begin their analyses in the 1980s, arguing that use went down when the U.S. government got tough on drugs and leveled off because people began questioning the appropriateness of punitive measures. Opponents of drug war policies date getting tough on drugs to President Richard Nixon's declaration of drugs as "public enemy number one" in 1971 and use the up and down trends over the next thirty years to dispute the usefulness of the get tough approach.

The choice of a specific time period for analysis is inherently neither correct nor incorrect—relevance depends upon the question being asked. What is important for analysis is to justify why a particular time period makes sense. This means clearly articulating the reasons why the analysis is best couched in those terms and then examining the logic behind such justifications. For most questions one would want to analyze the longest time period for which data are available in order to see if fluctuations in use over time or under specific policies better account for changing patterns in use. But if one wanted to track use of a specific drug, it might be more useful to compare its use to the use of other drugs in a specific time period. For example, a question about the popularity of Ecstasy should consider the use of other drugs during a period when Ecstasy has been used, but not before.

An additional factor to consider when conducting an analysis is who is being tracked. Early surveys in the NHSDA sample overlooked the homeless and those living in such institutions as prisons, mental institutions, and rehabilitation hospitals. However, in 1991 the NHSDA was redesigned to include populations in mental and rehab institutions, whose drug use is likely to be higher than that of the general population.[2] Also in 1991, NIDA began providing national estimates of drug-related emergency room admissions through the Drug Abuse Warning Network (DAWN) and eighth and tenth graders were added to the MTF survey. Since 1980 the Department of Defense has periodically conducted surveys of drug use among U.S. active duty personnel around the world, and the Justice Department began commissioning studies of drug use among federal and state prison populations in 1986.

Although the United States has collected systematic survey data about drug use since 1971, European countries have only recently begun to be more systematic in gathering and organizing information about their drug phenomena. The largest comparative survey, the European School Survey Project on Alcohol and Other Drugs (ESPAD), is modeled after the MTF in the United States and now covers thirty-five countries. Taken in 1995, 1999, and 2003, the surveys only canvassed sixteen-year-olds, however, rather than eighth, tenth, and twelfth graders as in the United States, and many countries sampled only regions or major cities. These surveys also did not include dropouts, and they were not evaluated for statistical significance.[3] Consequently, they are best used to appreciate the situation within Europe rather than for comparisons with the United States. The European nations also do not have anything comparable to the NHSDA for their general populations at this time.

In the Western Hemisphere, the Inter-American Drug Abuse Control Commission (CICAD), formed by the Organization of American States (OAS), began surveying students in 2003, but only in seven of thirty-five member countries.[4] School children aged thirteen, fifteen, and seventeen were surveyed, but given the dropout rates in developing countries, the limitation of the survey to children in school means the resulting data are less comprehensive—and subsequently, less informative—than they could be. And, as in Europe, surveys of the total population or those in jail have yet to be undertaken among the nations of the OAS.

The Illegal Use of Psychoactive Substances

Drugs have been such a major part of socialization via the media, politicians, police, spiritual and lay counselors, parents, and peers that pretty much everyone has a notion of who consumes drugs and why. It is unreasonable to expect readers to wipe the slate clean on this issue, but it is an issue best studied with an open mind.

As previously mentioned, the unholy trinity of marijuana, cocaine, and heroin dominates debate in the United States. Yet a huge range of psychoactive substances is consumed illegally in the United States. Some of these are from domestic sources such as marijuana farms and greenhouses, meth [amphetamine] and LSD labs, kitchen-stove produced meth and GHB (Gamma Hydroxybutyrate, also known by multiple street names and as a "date-rape" drug), or prescription drugs diverted from the legal market. Others are

Box 3.1 **Write down your answers to the following questions and use them to contribute to class discussion.**

What does the "average" user of illegal drugs look like in terms of age, race/ethnicity, gender, and employment? Does this vary significantly by drug used?

Which drugs are most widely used illegally?

What is the correlation between illegal use of drugs and crime, distinguishing the latter in terms of property crime and violent crime?

imported—Ecstasy from Europe; high-potency marijuana from Canada; and marijuana, cocaine, and heroin from a number of developing countries. Some drugs replace others as fashion shifts, fear or curiosity ebbs and flows, or supply becomes problematic. Some are used in combination with other psychoactive substances, legal or illegal; in such combinations, alcohol use far outstrips the use of a second illegal substance.[5]

Tables 3.1 and 3.2 present the psychoactive drugs most commonly consumed by twelve- to twenty-year-olds in the United States in 2000. (The NIDA eliminated college students as a subgroup in the most recent volume.) The tables make clear that by the tenth grade, alcohol and tobacco are the leading psychoactive substances used illegally by youth, followed by marijuana. No other substance rivals these three in terms of use. After marijuana, the illegal drugs most used by high schoolers and college students are amphetamines without a prescription, followed by Ecstasy and tranquilizers without a prescription. For high school seniors specifically, amphetamines again head the list, followed by Ecstasy, with hallucinogens tied with the illegal use of legal tranquilizers for third. Inhalants place fifth. For tenth graders, the top five substances are amphetamines, inhalants, Ecstasy, tranquilizers, and hallucinogens.

In short, across all of these age groups in the United States the use of illegal drugs or the illegal use of legal drugs is a phenomenon that cannot be characterized, understood, or analyzed by focusing on marijuana, cocaine, and heroin.

Analysts in charge of tracking drug use for the U.S. government are often surprised by the appearance and rapid expansion of new drugs or old drugs used in new ways and are late to respond. For example, Ecstasy (MDMA) had been used for psychotherapeutic purposes in the 1970s but its utility was judged minimal and it was banned in the United States in 1988. Use of the banned drug then escalated dramatically in the 1990s,[6] but it was not until 2001 that surveys caught up with reality and began to ask about current and recent use.

At the turn of the millennium, illegal use of the synthetic opiate Oxycontin, meant for relief of back pain and legal with a prescription, caught the government off guard. The 2001 NHSDA did not investigate past month or past year use, but only lifetime use, probably because in 1999 and 2000 only 221,000 and 399,000 people, respectively, were estimated to have ever used it. But the 2001 survey revealed an increase of almost 250 percent for lifetime use, a clear indication that past year and past month use must have risen dramatically.[7] Yet two years later, the 2003 MFT survey of high school students still did not ask about current Oxycontin use.

Among European countries, the characteristics of illegal use of psychoactive substances vary, but cocaine and heroin are not even on the ESPAD list for sixteen-year-olds. (This absence is most likely because these two drugs are expensive and generally consumed by people once they have greater sources of income than those of the average sixteen-year-old. Given the European focus on harm reduction, these governments may want to know only about the most consumed drugs, whereas the U.S. government, with its drug-free

Table 3.1 Psychoactive Substance Use
Last 30 days, by Age Group and Substance (national percentages for 2000)

	Any Illicit[a]	Marijuana/Hashish	Heroin	Cocaine	Crack
Age Group					
8th Grade	11.9	9.1	0.5	1.2	0.8
10th Grade	22.5	19.7	0.5	1.8	0.9
12th Grade	24.9	21.6	0.7	2.1	1
College Students	21.5	20	0.2	1.4	0.3
Young Adults (19–28)	18.1	16.1	0.1	1.7	0.4

	Amphetamines[b]	Methamphetamine[c]	Hallucinogens[d]	MDMA (Ecstasy)
Age Group				
8th Grade	3.4	0.8	1.2	1.4
10th Grade	5.4	2	2.3	2.6
12th Grade	5	1.9	2.6	3.6
College Students	2.9	0.2	1.4	2.5
Young Adults (19–28)	2.3	0.7	1.2	1.9

	Tranquilizers[b]	Barbiturates[b]	Inhalants[d]	Been Drunk	Cigarettes
Age Group					
8th Grade	1.4	—	4.5	8.3	14.6
10th Grade	2.5	—	2.6	23.5	23.9
12th Grade	2.6	3	2.2	32.3	31.4
College Students	2	1.1	0.9	—	28.2
Young Adults (19–28)	1.8	1.3	0.5	—	30.1

a. for 8th and 10 graders, use of narcotics other than heroin and barbiturates is excluded
b. only use not under doctor's prescription included
c. data calculated differently for 8–10th graders; see original for discussion
d. unadjusted for underreporting of PCP
e. unadjusted for underreporting of amy and butyl nitrates
SOURCE: National Institute on Drug Abuse, *Monitoring the Future, National Survey Results on Drug Use, 1975–2000*, Volume II NIH Publication No. 01-4925, Washington, D.C., U.S. Government Printing Office. 8/1/2001, pp. 40–44, Table 2.2.

Table 3.2 Substances Most Used Illegally, 2000 (other than marijuana, alcohol, and cigarettes)

Age Group	Rank				
	1	2	3	4	5
8th Grade	Inhalants[b]	Amphetamines[a]	Ecstasy (tie) Tranquilizers[a] (tie)		Cocaine (tie) Hallucinogens (tie)
10th Grade	Amphetamines[a]	Ecstasy (tie) Inhalants (tie)	Tranquilizers[a] (tie)	Tranquilizers[a]	Hallucinogens[b]
12th Grade	Amphetamines[a]	Ecstasy	Hallucinogens[b] (tie) Tranquilizers[a] (tie)		Inhalants[b]
College Students	Amphetamines[a]	Ecstasy	Tranquilizers[a]	Cocaine (tie) Hallucinogens[b] (tie)	
Young Adults (19–28)	Amphetamines[a]	Ecstasy	Tranquilizers[a]	Cocaine	Barbiturates[a]

a. only use not under doctor's prescription included
b. unadjusted for underreporting of PCP

focus, wants a fuller picture of the drug use phenomenon and therefore includes these drugs on its surveys.) This is not to say that interesting comparisons cannot be made among students taking the ESPAD. In Turkey, Iceland, and Sweden, inhalants are consumed as often as marijuana, whereas in Cyprus, the Faroe Islands, Malta, and Greece, inhalants are used more frequently than marijuana. In six countries—Turkey, Sweden, Romania, Poland, Lithuania, and Cyprus—surveyed students have used tranquilizers or sedatives without a prescription as often as they've used marijuana.[8]

The limited data for Latin American young people that is provided by the OAS school surveys attests to the prevalence of cocaine in local drug markets and the importance of inhalants and solvents. (See Table 3.3.) But note that, unlike the U.S. and European surveys, the CICAD survey does not report illegal use of prescription drugs in the same graphs as illicit drugs or even in the same units. Illicit drugs are presented for all grades together, whereas illegal prescription drug use is divided among the three groups. Extrapolating from the CICAD data, however, it appears that only in Panama was marijuana use higher than that of illegal use of tranquilizers, and only in Panama and Uruguay was the same true for illegal use of stimulants.[9]

Table 3.3 Last Year Prevalence of Use of Illicit Drugs among Students by Country (all grades)

	El Salvador	Guatemala	Nicaragua	Panama	Paraguay	Domin. Rep.	Uruguay
Marijuana	2.5	2.3	2.2	7.1	1.7	1.1	9.7
Hashish	0.1	0.2	0.1	0.1	0.1	0.2	0.4
Cocaine	0.7	1.3	1.1	1.4	0.6	0.3	1.9
Coca Paste	0.3	0.2	0.2	0.2	0.4	0.1	0.8
Crack	0.5	0.5	0.4	0.3	0.1	0.2	0.4
Solvents	0.9	1.0	0.9	2.6	0.6	1	1.4
Hallucinogens	0.5	0.3	0.2	0.1	0.3	0	0.8
Heroin	0.2	0.3	0.2	0.1	0.1	0	0.3
Opium	0.1	0.1	0.1	0.1	0	0	0.3
Morphine	0.2	0.1	0.1	0.1	0.1	0	0.3
Ecstasy	0.3	0.4	0.2	1.3	0.2	0.2	0.3
Other Drugs	1.8	0.8	2.4	4.5	0.6	0.8	2.8
Primo	-	0.4	-	-	-	-	-
Bazuco	-	0.1	-	-	-	-	-
Jarra Loca	-	-	-	-	2.1	-	-
Curitibana	-	-	-	-	0.1	-	-
Any	4.9	4.1	4.9	12.2	4.3	2.8	11.5

▨ = First most popular drug   ▉ = Second most popular drug
▩ = Third most popular drug
SOURCE: CICAD, p. 14

Who Consumes?

Illicit drug use is a popular pastime in the United States, judging by the fact that at some point in their lives almost 46 percent of the total population twelve years of age and older (94 million people) is estimated by government surveys to have used an illegal substance. Use is down from the peak years of the 1970s, but 19.5 million people in the United States aged twelve years or older were estimated to be current users in 2002. That represents 8.3 percent of the population in that age group. Changes in the methodology used in the 2002 NHSDA render comparison with prior years impossible,[10] but the 2001 figure represented a statistically significant increase over that of 2000 (7.1 percent compared to 6.3 percent). Table 3.4 gives a view of use, distinguished by any use during one's lifetime, any use in the past year, and any use in the last thirty days.

The 2002 NHSDA showed that 75 percent of current illicit drug users in the United States used marijuana, making it the most commonly used illicit drug. A little more than half of current illicit drug users consumed only marijuana (55 percent), and one-quarter of current illicit drug users did not use marijuana at all. Slightly more than six million people in the population aged twelve or older were current users of psychotherapeutic drugs, which were defined by the Substance Abuse and Mental Health Services Administration (SAMHSA) of the Department of Health and Human Services as "generally prescription medications."[11] Of those who reported current illegal use of any psychotherapeutics, 4.4 million used pain relievers, 1.8 million used tranquilizers, 1.2 million used stimulants, and 0.4 million used sedatives. Regarding use of the drugs generally seen as most serious, 2 million reported using cocaine, including 500,000 crack users; 166,000 people reported current heroin use.

The use and type of illicit drug used does vary by age. In the United States, use is a phenomenon of youth, almost half of current users are twenty-five-years of age and younger; use falls steadily after age twenty with a little blip in the early forties. (See Figure 3.1.) Overwhelmingly, use of hallucinogens and inhalants was concentrated among younger people, with 71 percent of users of both substances falling in the twelve- to twenty-five-year age bracket. In contrast, cocaine and nonmedical psychotherapeutics were used more by those twenty-five-years of age and older—62 percent and 57 percent, respectively. However, use of cocaine and nonmedical psychotherapeutics did not decline

Table 3.4 Use of Any Illicit Drug, 2002 (population aged twelve and older)

Measure	Lifetime	Last Year	Last 30 Days
Percentage of Total Population	46.0	14.9	8.3
Absolute Numbers (1,000s)	108,255	35,133	19,522

SOURCE: www.oas.samhsa.gov/NHSDA/2kSNSDUH/Results/2k2results.htm accessed 3/29/04.

Figure 3.1 Any Illicit Drug: Trends in Annual Prevalence among High School Seniors and Adults through Age 45.

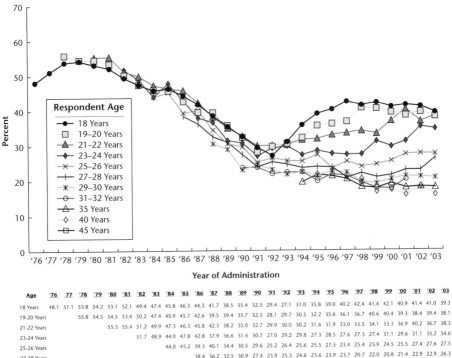

Age	'76	'77	'78	'79	'80	'81	'82	'83	'84	'85	'86	'87	'88	'89	'90	'91	'92	'93	'94	'95	'96	'97	'98	'99	'00	'01	'02	'03
18 Years	48.1	51.1	53.8	54.2	53.1	52.1	49.4	47.4	45.8	46.3	44.3	41.7	38.5	35.4	32.5	29.4	27.1	31.0	35.8	39.0	40.2	42.4	41.4	42.1	40.9	41.4	41.0	39.3
19-20 Years			55.8	54.5	54.5	53.4	50.2	47.4	45.9	45.7	42.6	39.5	39.4	35.7	32.3	28.1	29.7	30.5	32.2	35.6	36.1	36.7	40.6	40.4	39.3	38.4	39.4	38.1
21-22 Years					55.3	55.4	51.2	49.9	47.3	46.3	45.8	42.3	38.2	35.0	32.7	29.9	30.0	30.2	31.6	31.9	33.0	33.5	34.1	33.3	36.9	40.2	36.7	38.3
23-24 Years							51.7	48.9	44.0	47.8	42.8	37.9	36.6	31.4	30.7	27.0	29.2	29.8	27.3	28.5	27.6	27.3	27.4	31.1	29.6	31.1	35.2	34.6
25-26 Years									44.0	45.2	39.3	40.1	34.4	30.5	29.6	25.2	26.4	25.6	25.5	27.3	23.4	25.4	23.9	24.5	25.5	27.4	27.6	27.5
27-28 Years											38.4	36.2	32.5	30.9	27.4	23.9	25.3	24.6	23.6	23.9	23.7	20.7	22.0	20.8	21.4	22.9	22.9	26.3
29-30 Years													30.5	28.9	23.0	24.5	23.1	21.7	22.4	21.3	22.7	22.2	19.6	19.0	20.3	21.1	20.9	20.6
31-32 Years*															23.7	23.8	21.9	22.3	22.4	19.8	21.7	21.2	19.3	17.7	17.6	20.2	NA	NA
35 Years																			19.5	21.6	21.2	20.3	18.1	17.7	19.1	17.8	18.1	17.9
40 Years																							20.3	16.7	17.2	15.8	18.2	15.8
45 Years																												17.8

*Beginning in 2002, respondents were followed through age 30 (instead of 32, as in past years), then again at ages 35 and 40. The 45-year-olds were added in 2003.

as much with age. Inhalant use, assumed by many analysts to be a phenomenon of youth, was still 8.6 percent among persons aged twenty-five-years or older.[12]

Tables 3.5 and 3.6 provide some comparisons between the United States and other advanced industrialized countries. In the case of marijuana use by the general population (Table 3.5), the United States is second to Australia among countries surveyed. For cocaine (Table 3.6), the United States far outstrips other nations in lifetime use, but the significant decrease in current users has dramatically cut the nation's lead. A comparison of consumption habits by fifteen- to sixteen-year-olds provides an intriguing picture. Compared with their European counterparts, those in the United States smoke and drink less as well as less intensively, measured by six or more cigarettes per day and number

Table 3.5 Cannabis Consumption in Western Countries in the General Population

Country	Year	Ever Used	Used in the Last Year
Australia	1998	39%	18%
United States	1999	35%	9%
Denmark	1994	31%	3%
England and Wales	1998	25%	9%
Spain	1997	22%	8%
Ireland	1998	20%	?
The Netherlands	1997	18%	5%
France	1995	16%	5%
Germany (West)	1997	13%	5%
Greece	1998	13%	4%
Sweden	1998	13%	1%
Finland	1998	10%	3%
(Flemish) Belgium	1994	6%	3%

Percentage of users. Age limits vary between 14–18 (lower limit) and 60–70 years (upper limit) or 49 years (Belgium). Figures for the Netherlands: 15–70 years. No information was available for unlisted EU member states.
SOURCES: EMCDDA, SAMHSA, AIHW, as cited in Trimbos-Institute, Netherlands Institute of Mental Health and Addiction www.trimbos.nl/indexuk.html accessed 11/08/02

of times one got drunk, respectively. Use of cocaine, Ecstasy, and ampheta-mines, however, is significantly more frequent in the United States. Regard-ing marijuana, teenagers in the United States use at rates similar to those in the United Kingdom, France, and Ireland but at significantly higher rates than in the eight other European countries in the ESPAD.

Table 3.6 Cocaine Consumption in Western Countries in the General Population

Country	Survey Year	Ever Used	Used in the Last Year
United States	1999	12.0%	2.0%
Australia	1998	4.3%	1.4%
Spain	1997	3.3%	1.6%
England and Wales	1998	3.0%	1.0%
The Netherlands	1997	2.4%	0.7%
Denmark	1994	2.0%	?
Germany (West)	1997	1.5%	0.7%
Greece	1998	1.3%	0.5%
France	1995	1.2%	0.2%
Sweden	1998	1.0%	?
Finland	1998	0.6%	?
Flemish Belgium	1994	0.5%	0.2%

Percentage of users. Age limits vary between 14–18 (lower limit) and 60–70 years (upper limit) or 49 years (Belgium). Figures for the Netherlands: 15–70 years. No information was available for unlisted EU member states.
SOURCE: EMCDDA, SAMHSA, AIHW, as cited in Trimbos-Institute, Netherlands Institute of Mental Health and Addiction www.trimbos.nl/indexuk.html. Accessed 11/08/02.

The CICAD survey does not have comparative national data on consumption, although it does collect such statistics for trafficking and production in the Western Hemisphere. Chile has been collecting comprehensive data since 1994. The nation's 2002 national survey provides comparisons across socio-economic groups: past year use of any illegal drug was 5.01 percent for the upper class, 5.29 percent for the middle class, and 6.35 percent for the lower class (Table 3.7). While these numbers indicate differences in level of use, they also demonstrate that use of illegal psychoactive substances is not a phenomenon of the lower class. Consider that illegal use of prescription drugs is highest in the upper socioeconomic strata (5.56 percent), lowest for the middle class (3.73 percent), and second highest for the lower class (4.31 percent). It is clear that illegal consumption itself is similar across class in Chile. College students aged seventeen to twenty-five and twenty-six to thirty-four use illegal drugs at a higher rate than their peers who are not in school but are working; however, college students do use illegal drugs less than those unemployed or out of the workforce. Chileans, like their counterparts elsewhere, often begin their consumption of psychoactive substances with a licit one: Half of all users begin with tobacco at age fifteen or younger; consumption of marijuana and alcohol (illegal under age eighteen) begins at seventeen.[13]

The U.S., European, and Latin American data indicate that males and females differ in rates of use and types of substances used more frequently, but not in whether use occurs. In general, males use illicit substances more than females. Illegal use of psychotherapeutics is similar for males and females, although girls are more likely to use these at an earlier age than boys. In the twelve- to seventeen-year age group, boys use marijuana and alcohol more often than girls.

The U.S. surveys also break down use of illicit drugs by race and ethnicity. A few more stereotypes should be discarded by a look at the results. According to the NHSDA, of the 35.1 million users of illicit substances in 2002 (14.9 percent

Table 3.7 National Survey on Drug Use in Chile, 2002

Substance	Lifetime	Past Year	Past 30 days
Any illegal	22.9	5.58	3.17
Legal, but w/out a prescription	11.48	4.31	1.63
Marijuana	22.4	5.17	2.85
Cocaine	5.36	1.57	0.66
Cocaine paste	2.79	0.51	0.21
Inhalants	2.24	0.25	0.06
Halucinogens	0.94	0.12	not asked
Crack	0.12	0.01	not asked
Heroin	0.05	0.03	not asked
Ecstasy	0.17	0.1	not asked

SOURCE: Government of Chile, Consejo Nacional para el Control de Estupefacientes (CONACE), www.conacedrogas.cl/inicio/obs_naci_encu_tema1.php. Accessed 3/25/05.

of the U.S. population aged twelve and older), 24.6 million were white, 4.5 million were black, and 4.3 million were Hispanic.[14] Almost two-thirds of the users of illegal drugs in 2002 were non-Hispanic whites. Even when users are studied as a percent of their respective racial/ethnic groups and at current use (past thirty days) rather than use in the past year, minorities do not dominate the statistics (see Table 3.8). In the MTF surveys for 2000–2003, blacks have the lowest use rates for virtually all licit and illicit drugs, whereas whites have the highest use rates. Hispanics have the highest rates for lifetime use of crack, heroin with a needle, ice, steroids, and other cocaine, although only in the case of crack do they have the highest current use rates.[15]

The number of blacks currently using crack, popularly assumed to be a drug used by impoverished minority individuals, was 246,000 in the 2003 NHSDA compared to 281,000 whites listed as using.[16] Among inmates in state prisons, variations among whites, blacks, and Hispanics in three categories—use of illegal drugs at any time in the past, in the past month, and at the time of the offense for which they were incarcerated—were minor. At the federal level the percentages were similar for non-Hispanic white and black prisoners, but significantly lower for Hispanic prisoners.[17]

In addition to people currently incarcerated, the U.S. criminal justice system also includes those on probation and those on parole from prison. In the adult criminal justice system, all three groups are aged eighteen years and older. In 2001, 20.8 percent of the estimated 1.4 million adults on parole or other supervised release from prison were current illicit drug users. Of the estimated four million adults on probation at this same time, 24.4 percent were currently using illegal substances. These rates are substantially higher than the rate for adults not on parole or supervised release (6.5 percent) and not on probation (6.3 percent). The fact that 10.5 percent of prisoners in local, state, and federal prisons were found to be using drugs reveals the apparent inability of the criminal justice system to stop drug use.[18] That all of these users are under varying degrees of supervision, including incarceration, is a strong indicator of the challenge facing anyone who believes in a drug-free America or a zero tolerance future.

Table 3.8 Current Illicit Drug Users by Race/Ethnicity in 2003 (U.S.)

Race/Ethnicity	Percentage Using in Past 30 Days
American Indians/Alaska Natives	12.1
Black	8.7
White	8.3
Hispanic	8.0
Asians	3.8

SOURCE: Office of Applied Studies, Substance Abuse and Mental Health Services Administration, U.S. Department of Health and Human Services, "Results for the National Survey on Drug Use and Health: Detailed Tables," Table 1.28b, www.oas.samhsa.gov/nhsda/2k3tabs/PDF/Sect1peTabs28to32.pdf. Accessed 3/23/05.

As may already be clear, education does not determine whether or not one uses illicit substances; however, it does have an impact on lifetime patterns of use. In 2002, current use did not vary much among eighteen to twenty-two-year olds, whether they were enrolled in college full time or part time, were students in high school, or were not students. Expanding the sample to all adults eighteen years of age or older, college graduates had current use rates of 5.8 percent, whereas those who had dropped out of high school were using at a rate of 9.1 percent. However, lifetime use among people with at least four years of college was more than 30 percent higher than among those who had not completed high school—50.5 percent and 37.1 percent, respectively.[19]

Most current users of illicit substances, like most adults users in the United States, are employed. In 2002, 12.4 million, or 74.6 percent of the nation's 13.4 million illicit drug users eighteen years of age or older, were employed either full time or part time. The rates of current use do vary by employment status, however. Among those eighteen years of age or older who were employed full time, 8.2 percent were current users of illicit substances, with the rate rising to 10.5 percent for part-time employees and to 17.4 percent of those unemployed.[20]

Why Do People Consume Drugs?

The question of why someone consumes illegal drugs often conjures up images of despairing souls and addiction. But as the numbers show, and as discussed in earlier chapters, addiction is something that happens to a small percentage of those who use psychoactive substances. So it cannot be presumed

---

Box 3.2   **Zero Tolerance?**

"The FBI, which maintained a strict ban until 1994, now concedes that 'some otherwise qualified applicants may have used drugs at some point in their past,' according to official guidelines. Under the new rules, prospective agents are permitted to have smoked marijuana up to 15 times, though not within the previous three years; **hard drugs** (emphasis added) up to five times, though not within the previous 10 years."

" 'The general preference is still to hire someone who hasn't broken the law, but the harsh reality is ... there just aren't that many people,' said Jane Quimby, a spokeswoman for the FBI's Denver office who oversaw recruitment in the region from 1997 to 1999. Of the roughly 35 agents hired on her watch, Quimby said, one-third admitted to having smoked pot."

Jesse Katz, "Past Drug Use, Future Cops" *Los Angeles Times*, June 18, 2000, Part A; Part 1; Page 1 accessed via Lexis/Nexis 9/23/02.

that the factors that determine when someone falls into addiction are the same as those that determine why someone chooses to try a drug in the first place. Those who choose to drink alcohol are seldom asked why, despite the fact that it is a psychoactive substance that can lead to addiction and health problems that eventually result in premature death. The answer seems obvious: these individuals derive pleasure from their actions and don't believe that they will consume enough to threaten their health. Because society believes that answer, despite the data on the economic and social costs that say otherwise, the decision to drink is accepted within the realm of individual choice, and needs no explanation.

The risks posed by smoking have also become well known. Approximately 20 percent of my students at the University of California smoke. Students regularly indicate on my questionnaires that they are aware of the risks of smoking, but virtually everyone expects that they will be able to stop smoking when they want or that they'll be among those smokers who die from other causes. Everyone knows someone who lived to a ripe old age and smoked like a chimney, so many discount the risk of smoking. And statistics aside, it is absolutely true that no one can predict which specific individual will die of cancer, emphysema, or any other condition known to result from smoking.

The prevalence of drug use across all groups in society, including college students, clearly demonstrates that people who use drugs cannot be viewed as simply down and out. Scientific studies, as well as informal polls among friends, provide an infinite variety of reasons for consumption: mood (happy, bored, sad), future prospects (poor prospects as well as great ones), experimental interests, deprived or spoiled backgrounds, and peer pressure.

If, however, one believes that drug use is too harmful to ever result from free choice, one needs to find a reason why users would choose such a path. The pusher model of drug use emphasizes the causal importance of supply rather than demand. This view is particularly comforting to those who see users as victims worthy of rehabilitation rather than punishment. The decision to use is "wrong," but the responsibility lies with someone else; thus loved ones are still "good" even though they are doing something "bad."

Yet the supply and demand relationship is significantly more complex than this view allows. The commodity system approach illuminates the ways in which producers and suppliers, as well as all the purveyors of services to these two types of actors, including money launderers, gun dealers, and sellers of precursor chemicals, are linked to the consumer. Without a customer, however, it would be silly for producers to produce psychoactive substances and for sellers to attempt to sell them.

One model that tried to link supply and demand to explain use was the epidemiological model of heroin use developed in the 1970s by the man who would become President Jimmy Carter's drug czar. Peter Bourne argued that the civil rights movement and hippie phenomenon were sociological factors that decreased the perception of risk that had marginalized heroin users for decades; at the same time, an increase in supply made the drug readily available for experimentation.[21] The model postulated that as supply decreased because of law enforcement efforts and the perceptions of risk spread as addiction proliferated, heroin use would decline.

Despite such models and beliefs, the experience of the ten years from 1985–1995 for both cocaine and heroin use challenge the importance of supply in the model. In that decade, supply increased and prices decreased dramatically, yet consumption also went down; potential consumers perceived the associated risk to be greater for these than for other substances.[22] Even the federal government has recognized in its reports the chief importance of demand in understanding drug use,[23] although the federal budget continues to be overwhelmingly oriented towards the supply aspects of the trade.

This is not to say that there are not any examples of supply driving demand. The legitimate drug market is one such case in which aggressive marketing can stimulate illegal drug use. OxyContin was marketed in medical journals in ways that overplayed its benefits and understated its risks. Many doctors were happy to have a powerful new tool to provide relief for their patients. But OxyContin also found its way into the black market because a user who crushed a pill could get high from the sudden ingestion of an opiode designed for timed release. Young males suddenly began complaining to their doctors about back pain. The doctor could either prescribe the medication or lose the patient to another physician who would take the patient at his word. This process resulted in a dramatic increase in the overprescription of OxyContin, its increased diversion to the illegal market, and a new drug problem.[24]

Once pushers and peers are recognized as inadequate explanations as to why a good person would use illegal substances, it is still possible to articulate an argument for why users are mistaken in their choice. The claim is that they do not understand the risks associated with use. Perception of risk is affected by one's sense of vulnerability, and acceptance of risk is influenced by one's sense of responsibility and potential loss. Figure 3.1 demonstrates that use declines with age; presumably career, marriage, children, and recognition of one's own mortality affect this pattern. (Note, however, the mid-life crisis syndrome found in the early forties.) In fact, people who choose to use illegal drugs in their youth often counsel younger people against use.

All sides of the drug debate recognize that there are risks inherent in consuming substances that alter chemical and physiological processing within the human body. The debate is often over whether those risks are dramatically overstated for currently illegal drugs and understated in the cases of alcohol and tobacco. That debate will be evaluated later in the discussion of health and crime issues. For now, distinctions need to be made among effects caused by the substances themselves and those that result from the interaction among a substance, the personal and social characteristics of the users, and the rules of the legal system in which the substance is used.

The counterpart to overstating risk when discussing why someone uses drugs is underestimating the pleasure drawn from consuming them or defining that pleasure as sick or deviant. Those who overstate the risks believe consumption is illegitimate; therefore, the pleasures derived from consumption are not only dangerous but also illegitimate. If consumers don't see it that way, it is because they are unable to get similar pleasure in a legitimate manner, and thus are sick or evil. Consequently, for opponents of the use of currently illegal drugs, it makes no sense to consider these pleasures as a positive factor leading to consumption.

But for those who don't consider consumption to be socially deviant, considering the pleasurable side of consumption is fundamental because risk only matters in combination with expected benefits. A medium level of risk might easily be acceptable to someone who expects to get a very high payoff. And here is the dirty little secret about most drugs: the pleasure is certain and often highly valued.

Effects and Probabilities

The debate over the effects of illegal drugs is controversial because each side knows that support for its particular approach is dependent upon what the public at large believes about the consequences of using illegal drugs. The most vocal advocates for prohibition of these substances argue that "These drugs are illegal because they are bad, they are not bad because they are illegal."[25] Note the causal argument in the phrase; anyone agreeing with it should expect to see data that demonstrate that these substances induce personal and social consequences significantly worse than those produced by the legal psychoactive substances of alcohol or tobacco.

Antiprohibitionists need a stronger rebuttal to this claim than simply saying that currently illegal drugs are no worse than, and perhaps less harmful than, alcohol and tobacco. Most people are personally acquainted with drinkers and smokers and don't feel sufficiently threatened by them to support using the power of the state to suppress those behaviors. However, these same people generally do not know who among their acquaintances might be using illegal drugs. Because their personal awareness of illegal drug users is usually derived from the media, it is easy to understand why they associate such use with alarming criminal activity and are therefore resistant to the comparison of their friend the smoker or drinker with the drug user from the evening news.

This section tackles the major concerns people have about illegal drugs and discusses the evidence offered by competing policy advocates. Three concerns among many stand out: whether use of soft drugs leads to use of harder drugs, the health consequences to the user and society, and the impact on crime.

Gateways to "Harder" Drugs?

The term "gateway" is extremely popular, but it is rarely defined with precision. It is not scientifically acceptable to define it simply as use of a particular substance prior to the use of a different one, although many arguments about marijuana being a gateway to the use of harder drugs proceed in this fashion. Ascertaining the probability of moving on to another illicit drug requires more information. The percentage of marijuana users who turn to other drugs must be known, not the percentage of other drug users who began with marijuana. The percentage of those who have ever tried marijuana and are current heroin users, for example, is extremely small: 0.85 percent according to U.S. government estimates. But even that rate is an overestimation of marijuana's possible influence in promoting heroin use. One-third of illicit drug users have never used marijuana, so the realistic expectation is that some unknown percentage of marijuana users who consume other drugs would have consumed them even if they had not consumed marijuana.[26]

The gateway drug argument has another challenge. New studies from around the world indicate that young people who smoke cigarettes are significantly more likely to use illegal drugs than those who do not.[27] Youths who smoked were nine times more likely to use illicit drugs than those who did not—that's 48 percent of smokers compared with 5.3 percent of nonsmokers. Youths who were heavy drinkers (defined as five drinks in one occasion) were even more likely to use illegal drugs: 65.3 percent reported using compared with only 5.1 percent of nondrinkers. Given that the mean age of first use of cigarettes and alcohol is significantly younger than that for marijuana—15.4 and 16.1 years of age, respectively, compared to 17.2 in the 1997 NIDA study—any advocate of a gateway theory of drug use should identify tobacco and alcohol as greater threats than marijuana.[28]

Health Consequences? Addiction?

When discussing the health consequences of drug use it is important to distinguish between what are the results from the pharmacological properties of a particular drug and what are the consequences of the social and legal context under which it is consumed. Regulation of food and legal drugs by the U.S. Food and Drug Administration (FDA) protects the consumer from unscrupulous producers and venders who may adulterate products to make more money. But illegal substances are not officially regulated, leaving the consumer at risk. Historical data on alcohol demonstrate the importance of such safeguards: During Prohibition the mortality rate from adulterated or poorly made alcohol rose.[29]

Even with unadulterated substances the danger of overdosing exists because there are no scientific standards for dosages. Some have tried to deal with this in an informal fashion by publishing dosages appropriate to height and weight, but these, however well intentioned, are not reliable. Across Europe and the United States groups oriented toward harm reduction have surfaced to provide Web-based and on-site advice. Organizations like Dance Safe in the United States and Experience Amsterdam in Holland set up tables at clubs or provide kits to test the pills; but being on-site means that they can only evaluate whether Ecstasy is in the pill.[30] A complete analysis of all the substances in the pill requires work in the lab. (See Figure 3.2.)

Another danger related to overdosing is that the illegality of the substances makes some users reluctant to seek emergency treatment in a timely manner. Intravenous drug users also face risks from sharing needles, but these are not risks from the drugs themselves but rather from the means of use. As the legal availability of clean needles increases, the risks of AIDS and hepatitis decrease.

Image	Pill Name	Size (mm) Weight (mg)	Location Date Received	Contents	Marquis Reaction
	Mitsubishi	10.0 x 4.0 300mg	300 February, 2005	MDMA (100.0%)	Black/Purple
	Lacoste	8.0 x 4.0 207mg	207 February, 2005	MDMA (100.0%)	Black/Purple
	Armani	7.0 x 4.0 180mg	New Milford, CT February, 2005	MDMA (100.0%)	Black/Purple
	Triangle	8.0 x 4.0 178mg	Hollywood, FL February, 2005	MDA (83.3%) Methyl Salicylate (16.7%)	Black/Purple
	Alligator	8.0 x 5.0 275mg	Phoenix, AZ February, 2005	Caffeine (95.2%) MDA (4.8%)	Black/Purple (slow)
	Dolphin	8.0 x 4.0 250mg	Hollywood, FL February, 2005	Methamphetamine (66.7%) MDMA (33.3%)	Black/Purple

Figure 3.2 EXAMPLE OF LAB TESTS

SOURCE: Test results provided by EcstasyData.org, an independent project of which DanceSafe is a sponsor. http://www.dancesafe.org/labtesting/ accessed 3/27/05.

For instance, many of the health problems of heroin addicts come from the illegal context in which the substance is used. Heroin is so expensive because it is illegal. Given the cost, users want to minimize expense by using the drug as efficiently as possible. Needle injection is an efficient way to get high, but carries with it substantial risk of HIV and hepatitis C infections from dirty needles. Lack of regulation in regard to its manufacture and sale can result in adulteration of the heroin, as well as ignorance of the strength being used. A hard-core addict lifestyle, characterized by poor nutrition, inadequate health care, and violence is more likely within countries whose legal systems penalize addicts rather than promote policies of harm reduction. Heroin and morphine addicts who can maintain a middle-class lifestyle are reported to be as healthy as the general population.[31]

In the case of female users of psychoactive substances, these substances can impact not only the user, but unborn fetuses as well. The actual effect of drugs on fetal development is a major issue in the debate over drug use. By now the reader should not be surprised to discover that there is a significant disagreement over what, if any, harm is caused by the substance itself and what harm is caused or dramatically increased by the social and legal conditions under which the drug is used. One study found that "among the general population there has been no detectable increase in birth defects which may be associated with cocaine use during pregnancy."[32] Another study funded by the NIDA and the Albert Einstein Medical Center reports that

> Although numerous animal experiments and some human data show potent effects of cocaine on the central nervous system, we were unable to detect any difference in Performance, Verbal or Full Scale IQ scores between cocaine-exposed and control children at age 4 years.[33]

Instead, a number of studies point to the lack of quality prenatal care received by cocaine users as the real culprit in premature births, low birth weight, and fetal or infant death.[34]

Pregnant women seem to believe that there is likely to be a risk and adult women respond accordingly. The general rate of current use of illegal substances among women aged fifteen to forty-four is 10.3 percent. Based on the 2002 NHSDA samples, however, the rate of use among pregnant women is dramatically lower: 3.3 percent.

Illegal substances are not the only potential threat to pregnant women and their fetuses. A number of studies have demonstrated the negative impact of tobacco on birth weight and its contribution to premature birth, and it is suspected to increase the risk of both diabetes and obesity as well.[35] The U.S. government now mandates the labeling of alcoholic beverages as hazardous to pregnancy. SAMHSA reports that "Prenatal alcohol exposure is the most preventable cause of developmental disabilities. Yet 1 in 10 U.S. women drinks alcohol while pregnant."[36]

Undeniably, the ultimate negative health consequence of drug use is early death. Any drug is potentially dangerous, as evidenced by the number of people who die because of an adverse reaction to a drug prescribed by their medical provider—a yearly average of 32,000 people in the United States from 1982 to 1998—or to nonsteroidal anti-inflammatory drugs such as aspirin—7,600 in 1998 alone.[37] As mentioned, the possibility of an overdose or adverse reaction is higher for an illegal substance since its manufacture is not regulated and, consequently, users are rarely sure of what exactly they are consuming. Individuals are ingesting these powerful substances without detailed medical knowledge of dosage levels appropriate to their bodies' tolerance levels.

Data on emergency room visits and drug use are collected in twenty-one major U.S. metropolitan areas. DAWN estimates that there were 638,484 drug-related emergency room visits in 2001, with more than 1.1 million "mentions" of a drug (noncasual drug users often use drugs in combination). Of these mentions 16.6 percent were cocaine, 8 percent heroin, and 9.5 percent marijuana.[38] This means that two-thirds of the drugs mentioned in emergency rooms were not from the unholy trinity, another demonstration of the need to broaden the view of what drugs should be considered when the drug phenomenon is discussed.

Among psychoactive substances, tobacco is by far the leading cause of death in the United States, averaging 430,700 from 1990 to 1994; alcohol comes in second, with 110,640 deaths in 1996 alone. There were approximately nine thousand illicit-drug-related deaths in 1995. None of these were attributable to marijuana, the major illicit drug used in the United States.[39]

There are many more users of tobacco and alcohol than of illicit drugs, so using absolute numbers to compare mortality rates can only show that legal substances are dangerous as well. If drugs are legalized or use is otherwise tolerated, consumption may increase, perhaps significantly. So can it be assumed that mortality rates will rise to levels similar to those for tobacco and alcohol? Unfortunately, the data that would allow a definite answer is not available. The only case studied systematically is the Dutch experience with decriminalizing the use (but not the sale) of heroin and implementing a variety of harm reduction programs for addicts. The Dutch data indicate that drug mortality rates are low and falling.[40]

Chapter Two made reference to the dependency/addiction issue and it has been mentioned that dependency rates for marijuana are low, whereas those for heroin and cocaine are similar to those for tobacco and alcohol, respectively. The point to emphasize here is that the risks of dependency and addiction appear to be low enough to be acceptable to millions of people who willingly choose to smoke tobacco, drink alcohol, smoke marijuana, and use scores of different psychoactive substances that are currently illegal.

Drugs and Crime

The relationship between drug use and crime, not including the use of an illegal substance, is extremely complicated and has not been analyzed on a national level in such a way as to clarify the alleged causal links. The quick and dirty answer relies on surveys of those arrested for crime, in which high percentages answer that they were using illegal substances at the time of arrest. Ipso facto, the conclusion is reached that drug use leads to crime.

More than half of all prisoners report having a psychoactive substance in their body at the time of the commission of the crime for which they are serving a sentence. (See Table 3.9.) The one drug most used by these convicted prisoners is alcohol, however, not cocaine or heroin or any other illegal substance. In fact, it is most often alcohol that is closely related to violent crimes such as assault, murder, manslaughter, and sexual assault for both state and federal prisoners. For state prisoners, manslaughter and sexual assault were among the least likely to be associated with illicit drug use; for federal prisoners murder and robbery were most likely to be so linked.[41] Of course, the total number of people using alcohol is many times greater than those using the illegal drugs reported in the survey, so the percentage of users who commit property and violent crime is higher for the illegal substances than for alcohol.

These data do not support a conclusion that using these illegal drugs in and of itself produces property or violent crime; many other significant factors would have to be isolated before the contribution of substance use to crime could be determined. Alcoholics do not usually commit crimes to feed their habit, partly because they don't lose their jobs for getting drunk on weekends and in the evenings, and partly because alcohol is cheap. Illegal drugs are not only considerably more expensive than they would be if legal, but users can also lose their employment if the residue of Saturday use leads them to test positive for that use on Monday. In addition, one would need to know if the people who committed crimes after using illegal drugs also did so before using drugs. If so, subsequent crimes cannot necessarily be attributed to the drugs

Table 3.9 Illegal Drug and Alcohol Use at Time of Offense, Self-report by State and Federal Prisoners

	Percentage of Prisoners	
Self-reports	1991	1997
Illicit Drug Use at the Time of Offense		
State	31	33
Federal	17	22
Alcohol Use at the Time of Offense		
State	32	37
Federal	11	17

SOURCE: Bureau of Justice Statistics, "Substance Abuse and Treatment, State and Federal Prisoners, 1997," *Special Report*, January 1999, U.S. Department of Justice, Office of Justice Programs.

in a person's system. It also would be necessary to separate the crimes that can be attributed to the substances themselves and those that result from the social and legal context in which these drugs are purchased and consumed. During Prohibition, alcohol was associated with violent organized crime and corruption of police and public officials; but after Prohibition was repealed that was no longer the case.

Most users of psychoactive substances, even of heroin and cocaine, do not become addicts. Consequently, one cannot attribute the crimes to the drugs themselves. Rather, one must consider what it was that caused a particular user to first become addicted and then to commit crimes.

Summary

Despite decades of concern and hundreds of billions of dollars spent on the issue of drugs in the United States, the data are extremely inadequate to explain the two things that must be known about something almost half the population has done at some point in their lives: why do they consume and what are the consequences of that consumption? Part of the reason answers are elusive is the complexity of social reality: experiments to hold variables constant cannot be done, and separating the effects of genes, the environment, and the substances themselves is extremely complex. The problem is made even more difficult given the stereotypes that stand in the way of viewing the users themselves.

There is a huge misfit between who uses and who is thought to use. U.S. government statistics demonstrate that every category of class, ethnicity, national origin, gender, profession, and employment status, and even prisoners in federal and state prisons, includes consumers of illicit substances. The consumer is everywhere, consumes for every reason imaginable, and rarely becomes addicted no matter the drug. President Clinton, Vice President Al Gore, former House Speaker Newt Gingrich, and U.S. Supreme Court Justice Clarence Thomas have all admitted using an illegal substance.[42] President George W. Bush refuses to clarify whether he used illegal substances as a youth, but admits to having a problem with alcohol. The unmistakable conclusion is that the overwhelming majority of people who have ever used a psychoactive substance illegally have gone on to live normal lives, some with great responsibilities.

Use rates ebb and flow, partly influenced by philosophical, sociological, psychological, economic, and political factors. But what is abundantly clear from any historical or contemporary analysis is that drug free is a situation that is unattainable unless the problem is defined away by legalizing some drugs in the same manner that alcohol and tobacco are legal and ignoring the illegal use of other substances such as prescription medicines, paint, and glue.

How would the three analytic perspectives try to explain the gap between the reality and popular myths about consumption and the lack of proper scientific analyses of the consequences of drug use?

Constructivists would not be surprised at the inconsistencies in the claim that these drugs are illegal because they are bad and the willingness to accept promotion of alcohol and tobacco consumption as a legal and philosophical right of private enterprise. The logical and empirical inconsistencies are the result of entrepreneurs (politicians and the press) using ideas, not scientifically sound data, to build coalitions of voters and audiences, joined by norm entrepreneurs pursuing their own personal vision of the acceptable, for example, alcohol yes, marijuana no. Constructivists would note that citizens don't understand this phenomenon of illegal use and are frightened because it appears beyond their control; hence they fall back on socially constructed explanations such as stereotypes. Analysts using this perspective would argue that most citizens are not ready to paint alcohol manufacturers and liquor store and convenience store owners, as well as shareholders in these companies, with the brush of pusher or identify them as people willing to cause personal and social havoc simply to make money. But constructivists would also expect that advocates of change would bring more evidence to light about who consumes what and begin to disentangle the consequences of use from rhetoric. At some point in the future, these analysts would likely expect that the United States will follow many European nations along the path toward harm reduction for users.

Rational choice analysts would take the status quo of what is legal and illegal and expect people and politicians to defend it with power, influence, and easy to understand cultural cues (stereotypes). The existing legal institutions have privileged the consumption of some drugs, thereby pushing prohibition questions into the realm of taking something away from voters, many of whom drink and smoke tobacco. Realists and rational choice analysts would also note that drug companies can legitimately spend their money to influence election campaigns, thereby rendering it less likely that voters will elect politicians who advocate prohibition or strict regulation of alcohol and tobacco. They would also expect that as long as middle- and upper-class consumers do not have their houses and dorm rooms raided or vehicles stopped and searched in their streets, they will see the costs associated with drug wars as legitimate. Analysts in these traditions would not be surprised that research to question stereotypes is underfunded and that the NIDA provides no link on its Web site to the Institute of Medicine study on marijuana. Until users mobilize to articulate their position and put money and votes behind it, little will change. They would also point out that legalization is too risky for voters and politicians, given the inadequacy of the available data to support the view that consumption would increase slightly, health would improve, and crime would decline.

Social deviance analysts would seek to turn the tables against those who argue that the available evidence does not support the claim that consumption of these psychoactive substances is harmful and should be illegal. They would argue that since society accepts the consumption of alcohol and tobacco as a legitimate matter of individual choice—as evidenced by the large numbers who consume them and vote against strict regulation—it is the antiprohibitionists who are socially deviant in equating alcohol and tobacco with other psychoactive substances. For this group, the drugs that are designated illegal have been determined by society to be inherently bad and to pose a threat to society.

Each perspective generates big questions that have yet to be answered conclusively either in the United States or Europe, not to mention the rest of the world. At this point one is left knowing that use happens, but without any guidance at to what levels are acceptable. Given the human and financial costs of current policies, such a lack of knowledge is indefensible.

The following chapters look closely at the policy debate over what is to be done. But before one can fruitfully ask what can be done about consumption and the consumer, the rest of the psychoactive substance commodity system in which the user consumes needs to be studied. For consumers do not exist in isolation, nor are they without influence over the entire system that has developed to support their demand.

STUDY QUESTIONS:

1. Examine the following graphs: "Any Illicit Drug: Trends in Annual Prevalence among High School Seniors and Adults through Age 45" and "Any Illicit Drug Other than Marijuana: Trends in Annual Prevalence among High School Seniors and Adults through Age 45," 138–139 at www.monitoringthefuture.org/pubs/monographs/vol2_2003.pdf.
   - Beginning in 1985, what is the trend in overall drug use?
   - Beginning in 1976, what is the trend in overall drug use?
   - Beginning in 1992, what is the trend in overall drug use?
   - What year do you think should be the baseline for analysis and why?

2. Compare what NIDA (www.nida.nih.gov/ResearchReports/Marijuana/ and the Institute of Medicine (www.nap.edu/readingroom/books/marimed/Pp. 33–136) say about marijuana, including its use for medicinal purposes.
   - On what points do they agree and disagree?
   - What evidence do they present for these points on which they disagree?
   - Which do you accept and why?

3. Do you think that a focus on marijuana, cocaine, and heroin by U.S. officials and the public is effective? Why or why not? Support your answer, taking into consideration what you have already learned about the drug phenomenon that may have affected why such a focus was chosen and continues to be maintained.

4. Why do you think officials—and subsequently, policies—are often so slow to adapt to new or re-emerging drugs?

Chapter 4 **The Production of Psychoactive Substances**

"But the farmers feel misunderstood. 'Smoking is legal, it's freedom of choice and I think it's time for people to get off the companies' backs, to get off our backs and let us do what we do,' Mr. Ray says ... he pulls out a handful of seeds coated with a pink covering to distinguish them from the earth. 'When you can take a seed that you can barely see and in half a year produce a crop that will potentially make $4,500 to $5,000 an acre, it's pretty incredible.' "[1]

—*Mr. Ray*

"... our coca chewing is separate from all that. We are accustomed to it and have never had anything to do with cocaine. Why should we be deprived of our coca because of those narcotraficantes? There is no justice in this."[2]

—*Andean peasant*

The consumer cannot consume unless someone produces. In a relatively few cases, self-production is sufficient: meth labs in kitchens, marijuana plants in bathrooms. But virtually all users consume a substance that has been produced by someone else, usually because they do not possess the necessary ingredients for production (including climate), they do not want to run the legal and health risks associated with self production, or they just want to consume in the most effortless way possible.

The commodity system offers a way to think about the link between consumer and producer. Such a systemic approach reminds those interested that they cannot think of one without thinking of the other, that what affects one phase has an impact on the other. But a systemic perspective doesn't answer some fundamental questions: Why do some people decide to become involved in the production of psychoactive substances? Can the decision by tobacco and coca farmers to produce dangerous psychoactive substances be usefully distinguished simply by referring to their legal status? Why is the production of illegal psychoactive substances tolerated in some countries but not in others?

The four analytic perspectives provide different answers to each of these questions. Social deviance analysis looks to the failure of individuals to determine who is attracted to production of illegal psychoactive substances and to the faults of governments to explain this illegal activity. Constructivists look to the ideas people have concerning the substances themselves and the power of ideas against the reach of governments attempting to impose a distinct set of policies on individuals and subgroups. Rational choice analysts look to the profit motive and the ability of governments to impose a level of costs and an appropriate degree of risk to outweigh the attraction of profits derived from producing an illegal product. Realists look to issues of national security and strategic relationships among states to understand why production of illegal psychoactive substances is sanctioned in some countries and not others.

If it is known how and why production occurs and how it is linked to the consumer, then there is a better chance of devising strategies to influence what is produced, who produces it, and under what conditions. Interest in these latter questions can be driven by many different and even competing goals. For drug prohibitionists, the goal is to eliminate illegal production entirely. Others may feel the drug phenomenon will always be with us but seek to minimize the environmental and human harm that result from the toxic processes used to turn coca into cocaine or produce synthetic drugs like methamphetamines and that contaminate the product for the consumer. Still others may be interested in helping producers defend themselves against extortionists so that the producers get a greater share of the profits. Finally, there may be those who worry that producers may wind up being the unwilling or unwitting accomplices of organized crime, rebellions, and even terrorists.

This chapter begins with a discussion of the role that production plays in the psychoactive substance commodity system (PASCS) in order to keep the systems perspective front and center in the reader's mind. Indicative of the complexity of the drug use phenomenon, the ability of the producer to play an active role in promoting the product is also explored. Subsequent sections investigate the types of psychoactive substances produced and the geographic location of illegal production. A fourth section reviews the most popular arguments for why people choose to produce an illegal and dangerous product, and a fifth section looks at why illegal production happens. The conclusion briefly summarizes the chapter's main points and develops arguments from the four analytical perspectives to explain the production of illegal psychoactive substances.

The Role of Production in the Psychoactive Substance Commodity System

In the commodity systems framework, the production of psychoactive substances should be conceived as one phase in a multifaceted effort to supply the consumer. Production does not exist or function in isolation; hence, its role in the system and the nature of the links between producers and the other people operating in the system need to be understood.

Figure 4.1 illustrates the links that develop between producers of an illegal substance and others who facilitate or hinder their enterprises. It is already known that producers, whether of agricultural or synthetic products, create

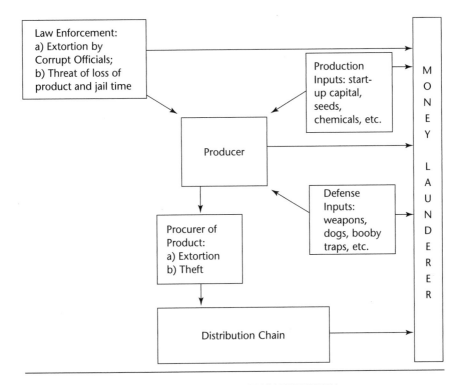

Figure 4.1 PRODUCER PHASE OF PSYCHOACTIVE COMMODITY SYSTEM

NOTE: Procurer of the product has to go between the producer and the distribution chain. The procurer is actually the first part of the distribution chain since he buys, steals or extorts the product from the producer and then moves it on to others (sells it or it gets stolen by others who then sell it) in the distribution chain

products that reach consumers through a distribution system. Production requires the standard items, or inputs, that producers of legal products need: start-up capital; seeds, if one is producing a hybrid crop; chemicals, if one is producing a synthetic product; and equipment. Producers also may deal with banks, merchants, and labor contractors.

Producers of illegal products, however, may need a distinct set of inputs avoided by their counterparts operating within a functioning legal system. The illicit nature of their work renders these producers vulnerable to extortion. Law enforcement threatens either their livelihood and freedom or their profits by demanding payment for looking the other way. Procurers of their products might actually steal it or threaten to harm them unless they lower their prices. Since it would be folly to call the police, the only protection producers have is created either through their own means or through playing one extortionist off another.

Playing one extortionist off another requires allying with one side either by selling the product directly to it or by paying a tax, or fee, for protection.

Peruvian coca farmers during the 1980s were confronted by the triple threat of corrupt government representatives, military personnel quite willing to use repressive and violent means to eradicate coca production, and increased pressure from the U.S. government against production. Growers responded by allying with the guerrilla group Sendero Luminoso against the government. The guerrillas offered to protect the crop if the peasants paid a tax and adopted the political and social philosophy of the Senderistas. Initially, the coca growers were willing to pay the tax, but they soon rebelled against the philosophical requirements. Meanwhile, the Peruvian military and government decided that fighting guerrillas was a more pressing matter than trying to eradicate coca production, so they offered to arm the peasants against Sendero Luminoso and ignore the illicit crop.[3] Once Sendero was neutralized, however, the Peruvian government relented to U.S. pressure and returned to actively pursuing the eradication of the coca crop.[4]

Given such possible ramifications, producers may try to protect themselves and their product on their own. Seeing a demand, businesses spring up to supply them with weapons, including pistols in remote mountains, or greater firepower in truly lawless zones like West Africa. Others supply dogs and booby traps in areas where the potential thieves may be chance passersby, as is the case of marijuana production in California's Sierra Nevada. (See Box 4.1.) The U.S. small arms market, as well as former soldiers and groups involved in recently resolved civil wars, feed the illegal arms market that supplies people involved in illegal activities around the world. In some countries like Mexico private ownership of nonhunting weapons is prohibited, but producers and others involved in the PASCS are well armed nevertheless.

As noted, some of the inputs necessary for production may be legally available, such as the provision of electricity and water to a home with greenhouse marijuana production. Other inputs may be illegal, including the precursor chemicals required for the production both of synthetic drugs and the processing of coca into cocaine. There are international conventions and national

---

Box 4.1 **Protecting Your Illegal Crop**

In Kentucky, police have encountered numerous means employed by producers to safeguard their marijuana patches. One crop was protected by steel spikes that were sharp and strong enough to pierce hard-soled boots; hidden bamboo stakes surrounded another pot crop. One of the most deadly traps was a group of copperhead snakes enmeshed in such a way that if the marijuana were disturbed the mesh would release the poisonous snakes. A police officer almost lost a hand as a result of a bite.

SOURCE: Shelly Whitehead, "Marijuana growers use tricks, booby traps against drug force." *Cleveland Plain Dealer* (Cleveland, Ohio) July 12, 2000: 2A.

laws that prohibit the illegal production or diversion of legal supplies to illicit activities. This aspect of production is a major issue for prohibitionists, as evidenced by the fact that the biggest drug bust in North America did not involve Mexican gangs and cocaine or heroin, but Canadian citizens providing ephedrine to methamphetamine superlabs in the United States.[5]

If producers make any amount above subsistence from their sales, they, like everyone they have dealt with, will need the services of someone who can disguise the illegal origins of this money and make it safe to spend. Thus pretty much everyone in Figure 4.1 has a link to the money-laundering phase of the illegal psychoactive substance commodity system. Not all individuals involved in the PASCS need to hide the origins of their money. Small local producers can commingle their illegal production with legitimate earnings. In remote areas, producers might spend all their illegal earnings with local merchants, who aren't prosecuted for providing them with goods and services. Small-scale extortion probably won't be noticed by superior officers in police forces. Large-scale producers, merchants who sell a great deal to illegal producers and corrupt politicians and police who extort large producers or many small producers, however, need the cover of a money launderer.

Is the Producer Limited to Just Producing?

The producer's role in the system may not be limited to simply providing a supply. Pharmaceutical companies and scientists are constantly producing synthetic drugs. In the case of new synthetic drugs approved for prescription use only, a pharmaceutical company interested in fomenting a demand for its particular drug advertises its benefits on television, recommending that viewers ask their doctors if the drug is appropriate for their particular ailment. Even something as ambiguous as social anxiety disorder can purportedly be overcome if viewers get their doctors to prescribe Zoloft. And if the TV viewers also read magazines, producers can try a different approach. Take for example, Budweiser, whose recent print ad campaign showed attractive young people holding beer bottles and interacting in a friendly manner with the words "Be Yourself" alongside the Budweiser logo.

Such advertising promotes the social norm of a pill for every ailment, alerts so-called deviants to new products, and helps generate an increased supply of psychoactive substances that can be diverted to the illicit market. Oxycontin is currently the most notorious example because the manufacturer chose a formulation that would give the pain reliever a competitive edge over competing synthetic opioids but that also made it more attractive on the illegal drug market.[6] Even when a new drug is not approved for prescription use, or a previously approved drug is decertified, the creators may have an incentive to promulgate the recipe. Timothy Leary went from legally experimenting with LSD for psychiatric purposes to advocating its production and use for counterculture experiences after it was removed from the legal prescription drug schedule.[7] Producers of legal psychoactive substances at times seek to market their product to those for whom consumption would be illegal, for example, alcohol and cigarette advertisements geared to underage consumers.[8]

What Types of Psychoactive Substances Are Produced?

The dorm party was a hit. The next day everybody marveled at how many people were able to dance late into the night. Of course, they also lamented that a few people drank too much and became obnoxious.

Most individuals have probably had an experience similar to this—a lot of fun, a little annoyance. That's just what's expected at that kind of party. And just as there are many types of parties, there are numerous ways in which one can classify types of psychoactive substances, including the alcohol just mentioned. The specific classification used, however, should be directly related to the question under discussion. The first two chapters should have presented a pretty convincing argument that there are too many dangerous substances that are legal for the issue of danger to be the dividing line between psychoactive substances whose production is taken for granted and psychoactive substances whose production individuals insist must be explained. Since this chapter examines the production of psychoactive substances in order to better understand this commodity system, it may be most useful to distinguish substances according to the precise laws that govern production and consumption.

There are three general categories of production: legal, illegal, or that inbetween territory of decriminalization, in which the act itself is not legal but the authorities either do not pursue it or provide for minor penalties. Consumption also can be legal, illegal, or decriminalized. The relationships among these six elements are illustrated in Table 4.1.

The table illustrates quite nicely that there is no simple relationship between production and consumption. The general public is most familiar with the extremes. However, when legal production and legal consumption are examined, it is discovered that even here there are limitations that can make production of legal substances illegal, including not paying taxes on its sale or not adhering to health and safety regulations. Consumption of legal substances can be rendered illegal as well, such as drinking alcohol while driving.

There are some surprising examples to illustrate different relationships in Table 4.1. Switzerland has heroin maintenance programs in which registered addicts can get prescriptions for heroin. This means that doctors and pharmacies have to have a legal source for the heroin they provide. Hence the government licenses a producer or importer to supply the requisite quantities. Britain once had a similar program but dramatically limited it in the 1960s after deciding that a few doctors were overly liberal with their prescriptions.[9]

Illegal production and illegal consumption may quickly bring Ecstasy and cocaine to mind. However, in Italy, Spain, Portugal, and Luxembourg, the

Table 4.1 Production–Consumption Relationships

	Production		
Consumption	Legal	Decriminalized	Illegal
Legal	Alcohol & tobacco consumed in legally-sanctioned place and by age; Medicinal marijuana produced under license in Canada; Licensed poppy cultivation for medicines (codeine, morphine, etc.); Medically supervised heroin maintenance programs in Britain[a] and Switzerland; Coca for domestic demand in Bolivia.	Marijuana production for private use in Belgium since January 2001.	Safe Injection Rooms (SIR) for heroin in parts of Australia, Canada, Germany; Medicinal marijuana exemptions in Canada during 1999.
Decriminalized	Use of prescription drugs without a prescription in Italy, Spain, Portugal; Underage smoking or drinking in countries with age limits.	Marijuana & hashish cafes with regulated consumption as well as private consumption in Holland; production for personal use in private in Belgium.	Illegal substances consumed in Italy, Spain, Portugal, and Luxembourg; first use of illegal substances in Belgium, Denmark Germany, and Austria; first and possibly second use of cannabis in Ireland.
Illegal	Solvents (paint, glue, etc.) that are sniffed; alcohol while driving; non-prescription use of prescription drugs.	Marijuana & hashish production for coffee houses that violate the ban on consuming alcohol & pot together.	Ecstasy, cocaine & non-licensed opiates; Coca in Colombia, Peru and beyond that needed to supply domestic demand in Bolivia.

a. British doctors who are licensed to do so may still prescribe heroin; few are now so licensed.
SOURCE: Drug War Facts, *International Facts, Policies and Trends: Data From Various Nations* http://www.drugwarfacts.org/internat.htm, accessed 8/29/03; European Monitoring Centre for Drugs and Drug Addiction, "Drug users and the law in the EU" Drugs in Focus series Briefing 2 March–April 2002, accessed 8/29/03; NORML, "European Drug Policy: 2002 Legislative Update" http://www.norml.org/index.cfm?Group_ID=5446, accessed 8/29/03

use of these substances has been decriminalized even as production remains illegal: one may face a fine and confiscation of the substance but can neither be arrested nor serve time in jail for such use. In Denmark, Germany, and Austria, the first time one is apprehended, use is decriminalized—and one might use multiple times before being caught.

Readers also will be familiar with some of the relationships among legal production and decriminalized or illegal consumption. Underage smoking or drinking itself brings no criminal action in the United States. The non-prescription use of legally produced prescription drugs, however, is illegal. Conversely, the use of psychoactive substances in Italy, Spain, or Portugal is not subject to criminal sanction, so the use of legally produced prescription drugs without a prescription is decriminalized there.

An exploration of the table reveals other variations. Perhaps the most interesting combination from the perspective of a reader in the United States is the case in which the use of a substance is legal, but its production, sale, or possession is either illegal or decriminalized. Where governments register heroin addicts and provide them with safer injection rooms (Supervised Injection Rooms, also known as SIRs) but do not supply the substance, production is illegal and consumption is legal for those registered addicts; Sydney, Australia began just such a pilot project in 2002.[10] And there's more. Since individual use in private is not an offense in Belgium,[11] and since the government decided in January 2001 not to prosecute cultivation of marijuana for personal use,[12] this represents a legal consumption-decriminalized production combination.

The decriminalized-decriminalized combination is currently found in Holland and Switzerland. The production of marijuana and hashish for sale in coffee-houses and for personal consumption is decriminalized in Holland, as is individual consumption. Decriminalized production and illegal consumption can be illustrated by patrons of Dutch coffeehouses who violate the ban on consuming alcohol in establishments that sell marijuana and hashish. A more familiar example is the U.S. tourist who brings her Belgian marijuana home.

Box 4.2 **The High Peaks of Europe: On the Ground in the New Stoned Switzerland**

At Growland, a two-story marijuana emporium in the up-scale shopping arcades of Bern, Switzerland, the product is remarkably inexpensive. Growland is one of fifteen stores here in the nation's capital that openly sell marijuana, and one of 250 nationwide. While it is technically not legal to deal pot in Switzerland, it is also not illegal. Store manager Peter Zysset has been in business for nine years and has only been visited by the cops once.

Whatever the Deadhead on your gift list wants, Growland sells, including ten sticky strains of marijuana—all grown in Switzerland, according to Zysett. "The product is 100 percent Swiss, mostly grown outdoors," he says. "Already some former vineyards here have turned to growing pot."

SOURCE: Media Awareness Project, "Europe: Europe Loosens Its Pot Laws" citing *Rolling Stone*, June 20, 2002: 55–57. www.mapinc.org/drugnews/v02/n1144/a01.html?2004. Accessed 8/30/03.

Where Does Production of Illegal Psychoactive Substances Occur?

A few party-goers tried to impress their companions by discussing the origins and merits of Ecstasy. The pills are marked to distinguish their manufacturing source. Producers must do this because users have preferences about the different sources of drug. During the pause in the music, the topic of conversation became whether Ecstasy produced in Holland, Germany, or Poland was better and if anyone could tell the difference. Someone also mentioned that Dutch coffeehouses have menus that offer marijuana from a variety of different sources, another indication that drug users care about their sources. And if they care that much, they tell their friends.

Many countries produce some type of illegal substance consumed for its psychoactive properties. None of the ready distinctions made in regard to rich and poor countries, nor developed and underdeveloped economies, nor corrupt or honest governments give any insight into where illegal production occurs. (See Table 4.2.) Certainly, Afghanistan and Bolivia are poor countries with economies based on agriculture; they have suffered under weak or corrupt governments for many years, and illegal crops, such as opium poppies and coca, are produced there.

But Holland and Germany, both highly developed countries, produce Ecstasy. In fact, a portable Ecstasy lab can produce up to twelve million tablets a day. Portability also contributes to concealment, since such a lab can be hidden on the back of a flatbed truck and be constantly on the move.[13] High-potency marijuana is produced in Canada and France. The United States is a cornucopia of illicit drug production, including regular and high-potency marijuana, methamphetamines, LSD, and heroin, and there have even been efforts to produce a synthetic cocaine.[14]

Production of illicit psychoactive substances boomed in the late 1990s as new markets opened in Japan, Asia, South Africa, and Russia. New production zones include West Africa for coca, sub-Saharan Africa for marijuana, and the Central Asian Caucasus, Balkans, and Ukraine republics of the former Soviet Union for poppies.[15]

The fact that legitimate production can be diverted to illegal trafficking, as in the case of legal pharmaceuticals sold without prescriptions, has already been discussed. What may be less familiar is that products ordinarily thought of as illegal, such as opium poppies, can be legally grown for such medicinal products as codeine and morphine. The UN International Narcotics Control Board oversees the legal market for narcotics. Under the Single Convention on Narcotic Drugs of 1961, the board requires countries that import such substances to estimate their need and exporting countries to report sales to specific countries.[16] Production and importation are done via regulated channels. Legal producers, except in India, harvest the entire poppy, including the stocks, and these are processed in factories to remove the alkaloids. This means of harvesting ren-

Table 4.2 Illegal Production of Psychoactive Substances: Some Comparative Evidence

Substance	Major Producers	Smaller Producers
Opiates (Heroin, etc.)	Afghanistan, Thailand, Myanmar, N. Korea, Colombia, Mexico	Russian Federation, China, India, Turkey, USA, France, Ukraine, Poland
Coca	Colombia, Peru, Bolivia	Africa
Cocaine	Colombia	Peru, Bolivia, Brazil, Argentina, Chile, Spain, Portugal, Italy
Ecstasy	Netherlands, Poland	USA, Canada, Belgium, Lithuania, Ukraine, Thailand, Indonesia, South Africa
Methamphetamines	USA, Myanmar	Slovakia, Mexico, China, Canada, Peru, Czech Republic, S. Korea, Egypt, Philippines, Malaysia, United Kingdom, N. Korea, Thailand,
LSD	USA	
Marijuana	USA, Mexico, Colombia, Kazakhstan, Kyrgyzstan, Philippines, S. Africa, Morocco	Jamaica, St. Vincent & the Grenadines, Guyana, St. Lucia, Trinidad and Tobago, Sub-Saharan Africa
High Potency Marijuana	USA, Canada, Netherlands	France
Hashish	Morocco	Afghanistan, Nepal, India, Netherlands

NOTE: Not all producing countries listed.
SOURCES: Elaborated from data from OGD, *The World Geopolitics of Drugs;* articles in *Current History* April 1998 issue on drugs; and List of Major Illicit Drug-Producing or Major Drug-Transit Countries, http://whitehouse.gov/news/releases/2001/11/20011102-13.html, accessed 8/16/05; Wikipadea, "Hashish" http://en.wikipedia.org/wiki/Hashish, accessed 8/16/05.

ders the product useless for the opium and heroin markets, as heroin and opium are produced by slicing the poppy bulb to harvest the sappy opium, which can subsequently be processed into heroin. India produces its legal alkaloids using methods that could lead to their diversion into heroin.

Turkish production of poppies has largely gone legal since 1974, when the United States helped it get certified for the legal market. But what had been a traditional crop in Turkey became an attractive industrial crop in France, Spain, and Australia. The resulting increase in supply drove world prices for the alkaloids down, thereby undermining the willingness of Turkish poppy farmers to remain within the legal regime. Responding to domestic pressure, an acreage of poppies beyond the UN licensed amount was authorized by the Turkish government in 1999.[17]

The decline in Turkish production for the illegal market prior to 1999 was offset by increases elsewhere. Afghani production was among those on the increase. After consolidating its domestic hold on the country, the Taliban government instituted a ban on poppy production that was extremely successful because the government was willing to tolerate a dramatic decline in the standard of living of already poor farmers and demonstrated that it would deal harshly with those who questioned its policies.[18] Opium production, however, has thrived under U.S. occupation as soldiers ignore crops and supplies in their pursuit of al Qaida terrorists and the U.S.-supported government tries to maintain its support among regional war lords deeply involved in the heroin trade.[19]

Why Do People Produce Illegal Psychoactive Substances?

Four empirically driven factors dominate most explanations for production: tradition, poverty, profits, and rebellion and terrorism.

Tradition

Psychoactive substances harvested from natural products have been used for religious, medicinal, and culinary purposes for ages. Peyote harvested by the North American Church, under protection of the U.S. Constitution, is legal but limited to traditional religious use by members of the church. Coca production is legal for traditional chewing, as well as for the teas and soups recently developed to help tourists deal with the effects of altitude in highland Bolivia. Although used in the Andes by non-indigenous people (tourists) in these forms, this use remains consistent with a traditional purpose and context (to deal with altitude sickness).

The argument that focuses on tradition to explain production cannot account for the expansion of that production by traditional producers who then sell their product to nontraditional buyers or who produce substances for new uses in new places. An example of this is Turkish opium produced for use as heroin in Europe. Nor can it explain the decision of new producers who

---

Box 4.3 **Paris Cannabis Market**

Utilizing indoor production using high-pressure sodium lamps and hydroponics watering systems and importing seeds from the Netherlands, United Kingdom, Switzerland, Germany, United States, and Canada, suburban "farms" in Paris can produce up to five hundred grams per square meter of plants three to four times a year. Local cannabis clubs hold fairs to compare varieties.

SOURCE: Observatoire Geopolitique des Drogues (OGD), *The World Geopolitics of Drugs 1998–1999*, p. 101–102.

move into new areas to produce traditional crops for nontraditional markets. If production of coca and opium poppies were limited to their traditional purposes in the developing world, citizens of Europe and the United States would not be consuming heroin or cocaine. They would, however, still have large illegal markets for the many drugs produced in laboratories and modern kitchens: painkillers and tranquilizers without prescriptions, methamphetamines, Ecstasy, LSD, and GHB (gamma hydroxybutyrate).

Poverty

Many producers of coca and opium poppies are mired in poverty. For some— opium growers in Afghanistan, coca growers in Bolivia—the production of illegal psychoactive substances provides an escape from this poverty or an opportunity to improve their children's future. For others, however, such as opium growers in Myanmar's (Burma's) Shan State, production brings little relief. How much illegal activity of this sort is able to ease the conditions of poverty depends less on the value of the production than on the local conditions under which such production occurs. The two key items here are infrastructure and the degree of control the nonproducers involved in the illegal trade have over producers. Bolivian coca growers in areas with good infrastructure probably benefit the most, whereas Myanmar growers, physically isolated and in the middle of a civil war, benefit the least.

Poor farmers who are poor because they have land that is marginally fertile may relieve their poverty by planting hardy but illegal crops. Other farmers may have fertile land but little effective access to the inputs necessary to produce high-value licit crops because local monopolists keep prices of inputs and transportation exorbitantly elevated. Despite such setbacks, these farmers might still be able to sell illicit crops and purchase electricity, potable water, telephone and television, health care, and education for their children, thereby finding a path out of poverty.

Many poor farmers in the developing world, however, live in regions characterized by a total lack of infrastructure: no highways, no electricity, no local health care, no potable water or sewage, and only limited access to formal education opportunities. For these farmers, higher prices for illegal crops do not translate into higher standards of living. Leaving the area most likely means losing the ability to earn an income above the one they can earn doing irregular work in the informal and unskilled economy. These farmers may have bank accounts in the regional cities, but the lack of infrastructure can still mean living below the poverty line.[20]

Profits

Unemployment is not necessarily indicative of poverty, but it does contribute to the same type of argument about why people produce illegal crops: their economic condition forces them into it. Producers may move in and out of production depending upon their legal job situation. In Paris, some people use their involuntary free time when unemployed to grow high-potency marijuana to tide them over until they can find employment in the legal economy again.[21] Still others might give up legal jobs because producing illegal products is more remunerative, as in the case of Bolivian miners who moved to the jungles to grow coca at the height of the cocaine boom in the 1980s.[22]

Rebellion and Terrorism

Rebels are ordinarily at a financial disadvantage against established governments that can tax legal activities to recruit, arm, train, and mobilize police and the military. Traditional sources of income for rebellions have been kidnapping; extortion, such as levying their own taxes in territory they control; and contraband sales of natural resources and commodities under their control, such as timber or diamonds. During the cold war many rebel groups garnered important financial and military support from either the United States or the Soviet Union; but with the end of the superpower rivalry such free money and weapons became harder to come by.

Terrorists and rebels who use proceeds from contraband trade are most likely to tax or traffic that production rather than use their soldiers to produce it. The reason they are included here is the claim by some analysts and policymakers that producers may be forced to produce illicit substances by rebels who want to tax the production. The rebels in Myanmar's Shan State coerced farmers into expanding their opium production in the 1970s. The Fuerzas

In 2003 a coalition of groups, including NORML (National Organization for the Reform of Marijuana Laws) began a billboard campaign to support medical marijuana. The girl is the 8-year-old daughter of Brian Epis—who grew marijuana under California's medical marijuana legislation but was sentenced in federal court to ten years for violating federal marijuana laws.

Armadas Revolucionarias de Colombia (FARC) guerrillas in Colombia and Sendero Luminoso in Peru initially moved into areas already producing cocaine to collect taxes. But with U.S.-supported eradication programs making progress in Colombia, the FARC has since offered protection to growers who move into areas better controlled by the guerrillas.[23]

Summary

Production of psychoactive substances occurs because the consumer exists; the relationship between producer and consumer is symbiotic and reinforcing. The conditions under which production occurs, as well as the physical location of production, are determined by the particular characteristics of a substance as well as by those of the national market. These factors, rather than whether a government is corrupt or weak, contribute to an understanding of why large amounts of illegal psychoactive substances are produced not only in countries like Afghanistan and Colombia, but also in the United States and Holland.

Each of the three analytic frameworks attempts to explain the production of psychoactive substances. The reader should notice that each explanation looks to different causal factors; any effort to combine explanations will need to justify which factors are chosen and how they interact to produce the hypothesized outcomes. After reviewing each of the four analytic frameworks, one possible way in which they can be combined to explain production is provided as an illustration.

Social deviance analysts would argue that production of marijuana and other psychological substances is illegal because society has adopted norms against the consumption of those products. Although sociologists and psychologists may question the appropriateness or consistency of these norms as they are applied to different psychoactive substances, criminologists and prohibitionists would not. It is not the harms per se that matter, but society's decisions about which harms are acceptable or not. This latter group of analysts, therefore, does not believe that asking why someone would choose to produce a legal psychoactive substance that contributes to addiction and death would help increase understanding of illegal drug markets.

Producers of illegal psychoactive substances are expected to be people who cannot attain the social or economic achievements that would make them feel successful in mainstream society. They turn to the production of illegal products because it generates wealth and perhaps even prestige among a subgroup with whom they interact now that they have chosen this job. They may even be able to pass themselves off as successful in mainstream society if they can disguise the source of their income. The deviant producer's motivation can be acted upon because the legal authorities—police, judiciary, or politicians—are either absent, as in weak or failed states, or are deviant themselves, that is, corrupt.

A constructivist looks for explanations other than the deviance of producers without denying that some producers might be people unable to achieve success within the dominant social norms. For constructivists the phenome-non is too big to be adequately understood in deviant or materialist terms. This perspective recognizes the potential clash between belief systems that see particular (or all) psychoactive substances as acceptable and those that do not. Hence the constructivist would look to the norms of the producers, not to the laws, to understand why some people might choose to produce psychoactive substances associated with addiction and death.

Traditional production is a legitimate enterprise in the eyes of people whose ancestors have carried it out for centuries. These people have experience with the psychoactive substances in religious, health, and culinary activities. Such legitimate uses convince them that the production of a particular psychoactive substance is not inappropriate and shouldn't be illegal. Producers may even know that harmful psychoactive substances are legal and perhaps subsidized by foreign governments. They may find it self-serving when these foreign gov-ernments seek to eliminate production of different psychoactive substances in other countries. For example, the U.S. government subsidizes tobacco pro-duction in the United States even as it pressures other governments to elimi-nate coca production. Another set of producers may defend their actions with the precepts of the dominant value system—individuality and freedom—and see the prohibition of their chosen psychoactive substance as an unacceptable intrusion by the state into private affairs.

To make the transition from motivation to behavior, the constructivist argues that the clash of norms around the issue of producing psychoactive sub-stances would be greater than the ability of any government to control. These ideas are internalized by individuals; no government is powerful enough to control ideas, nor can it be omnipresent and thus preclude individuals from acting upon their beliefs.

Rational choice analysts assume that producers of psychoactive substances choose these products because the profit generated by them, minus the eco-nomic or legal risk, is greater than what they could earn producing a legal product or engaging in legal employment. For the rational choice analyst the important distinction between legal and illegal products is not normative but economic. Therefore, these individuals do not spend time on questions of soci-etal values and mores. They instead focus on the fact that these substances are illegal, and as such, that the risks associated with supplying them produce retail prices that are particularly high relative to the costs of production. Conse-quently, profits are expected to be attractive; only the credibility of the legal risks, that is, the likelihood of arrest and punishment, can deter production.

Under this view, no attempt is made to identify which individuals have pref-erences for wealth sufficient to lead them into illegal production. Advocates instead would argue that some individuals in every society are tempted and the chief determinant of how much is produced is the ability of social, political, legal, formal, or informal institutions to generate risks that significantly drive down the enjoyment producers get from the fruits of illegal production. Rational choice analysts expect some production of illegal products everywhere, but they expect more production in countries with institutions incapable of increasing the risks associated with such production through police and judicial means.

Realists have little to say about where production occurs. They expect governments to decide that production of illegal psychoactive substances constitutes a threat to national security when a country has been diverting a great deal of economic and human resources to dealing with the various issues caused by drug consumption, whether those were of a criminal or medical nature. Realists also expect that more powerful countries push the costs of combating production to the weaker nations. A realist argues that not all weak countries have the same strategic value. A weak country, for reasons having little to do with drugs, might not be forced to pay the same costs associated with eradicating production as another weak country. For example, the current Afghan government benefits from U.S. national security concerns about international terrorism in a way that the Peruvian government does not.

The four analytical perspectives can also work in complementary, albeit hierarchical, fashion. For example, rational choice analysts can argue that the costs and benefits of profit seeking in the illegal drug market drives producers. While expecting that most producers are not deviant or normatively driven, they could still accommodate them within their argument. Advocates of the social deviance theory and alternative thinkers, in their argument, assign a lower cost to absorbing the obstacles created by illegality, such as isolation, fear, and the threat of arrest and incarceration. These producers can also rationally provide a higher value to production than a simple monetary calculation might provide. Consequently, the cost-benefit analysis performed by deviants and alternative thinkers does not differ significantly from that undertaken by a rational materialist-motivated producer.

Given the low probability of getting caught and the relatively high monetary value generated by illegal products, a rational choice analyst finds little need to look for deviance or alternative norms to explain the proliferation of production around the globe. The discrepancy between a government's policies toward illegal production at home and abroad is explained by the different costs to the politicians of addressing that production. Citizens at home can vote politicians out of office; hence the politicians want to demonstrate that they are doing something about drugs but not increase the immediate costs of those policies on their constituencies. Citizens of foreign countries are not part of these politicians' constituencies, so violating or systematically diminishing their civil rights is unlikely to be very costly to these politicians. For the rational choice analyst, the strategic value of a foreign country is important only if the electorate at home is willing to subordinate the issue of illegal production of psychoactive substances to other matters, such as international terrorism.

Once again, evaluating the different hypotheses one can develop to explain production requires that relevant evidence be collected. This chapter provided some basic facts about the role of production in the drug phenomenon.

Although producers of illegal psychoactive substances can be found in virtually all countries, most consumers and producers never meet in a face-to-face transaction. A distribution phase, consequently, is necessary to link consumer and producer.

STUDY QUESTIONS:

1. Would you use a deviance, constructivist, or rational choice approach to understand Mr. Ray, the tobacco farmer cited at the beginning of this chapter? Do you interpret the decision of a coca farmer in the Andes in the same way? Why or why not?
2. What are the strengths and weaknesses of an argument that the illegal production of opium occurs in Afghanistan because the government is corrupt and weak?
3. The production of marijuana for medicinal purposes is licensed by the Canadian government but prosecuted by the U.S. government, even in states that have approved its use. How would social deviance, constructivist, realists and rational choice analysts attempt to explain the difference between the two national governments? Which argument do you believe is most useful? Why? Which do you believe is least useful? Why?
4. A farmer in Bolivia, a chemist in Belgium, and a renter in Canada all produce illegal psychoactive substances. Do you need different explanations to understand the actions of each? Why or why not? What explanation(s) do you think best help you understand illegal drug production? Why?

Chapter 5   **Distribution: Linking Producers and Consumers**

"You know, I've seen a lot of people walkin' 'round
With tombstones in their eyes
But the pusher don't care
Ah, if you live or if you die
God damn, The Pusher
God damn, I say The Pusher
I said God damn, God damn The Pusher man"

—Lyrics from "The Pusher" by Steppenwolf

The young woman had plenty of contacts on the college campus. She was after all a student at the school herself, and that gave her some measure of credibility in the eyes of those who wanted to party all night. It also deflected the attention of the authorities. There was little worry among her customers that her Ecstasy could be tainted or that she would rip them off with placebos. Why, she was as trustworthy as the older students who bought booze for the underclassmen in the dorms.

—Compiled from several actual events

Most people who consume psychoactive substances, just like most people who consume pasta for dinner, need to find someone who will sell them the product. And usually the producers of the product aren't interested in selling their wares only to individual consumers. Hence, the distribution phase of the psychoactive substance commodity system (PASCS) develops.

The distribution of legal psychoactive substances is regulated by law and varies from country to country. In the United States, consumers of alcohol must be at least twenty-one, whereas in Germany the minimum age is sixteen. Even the distribution of illegal substances can be legally regulated if their consumption has been decriminalized, as illustrated by Dutch policy toward coffeehouses: they are licensed, limited in number, pay taxes, cannot advertise, and may sell a consumer only five ounces of cannabis per visit.

The distribution of those psychoactive substances still subject to criminal penalties doesn't have these legal constraints. Nonetheless, it turns out not to be a very chaotic process despite their absence, because even illegal markets have dynamics that impose at least some order. Once again, an examination of the empirical evidence in regard to who traffics, why they engage in such illegal activities, and where such behavior occurs, shows some important stereotypes to be dramatically mistaken. The errors embodied in these stereotypes make it impossible to understand why trafficking occurs not only in poor countries with weak and corrupt governments but also in stable democratic countries in the advanced, industrialized world. Among the ironies of the trafficking phenomenon is that while the United States targets traffickers in Colombia, Mexico, and Afghanistan, the trafficking network in the United States is probably the most extensive in the world and penetrates even into the federal prison system.

This chapter begins with a discussion of the role of the trafficker in the PASCS, illustrating the variety of ways that illegal drugs are distributed. The discussion then turns to the argument that traffickers play a fundamental role in pushing the product onto consumers, and finds it wanting. A subsequent section addresses the question of why someone would sell products that are considered dangerous. The discussion demonstrates that distributors of these substances are neither homogenous nor adequately described or understood by the overarching label of "pushers." The conclusion summarizes empirical findings about the trafficking phase and presents distinct ways in which the four analytical frameworks can be used to understand the existence of purveyors of illegal psychoactive substances.

The Role of Traffickers in the PASCS

Jeffrey had heard about Oxycontin via the Internet. He knew that it was available by prescription for pain relief. He'd read that some people got theirs from elderly women who sold their prescribed pills to supplement their meager Social Security checks. While he didn't know any of these women, he was sure that he could find a doctor to prescribe it, since he knew that doctors often have little understanding of pain, particularly back pain in young men.

Whether through elderly women intentionally selling their prescriptions or via physicians just trying to relieve a patient's suffering, drugs find their way to consumers. Traffickers serve a fundamental purpose in the illegal psychoactive commodity system, just as wholesalers, distributors, and retailers do for legal psychoactive substances and every other legal commodity. The retailer of cigarettes and alcohol provides consumers who want to light up or enjoy a cold one with their smokes and their liquor. Similarly, the role of a distributor of illegal substances is best understood as that of a facilitator of a market transaction waiting to be made between the consumer and the producer. Without a trafficker, consumption becomes more problematic for both the user and the producer. The trafficker, in short, creates a more efficient link between the other two parties. This description holds whether the trafficker is viewed as a deviant, a freethinker, or a profit seeker.

Some substances, such as methamphetamine and marijuana, are easy to produce, yet production not only takes time but increases the risks to consumers that surround purchasing the necessary ingredients, having evidence of production in their homes, creating toxic residues, and ultimately, perhaps producing a dose that is either too strong or contaminated. The increased number of deaths from drinking contaminated beer produced in home bathtubs during the U.S. Prohibition era attests to the validity of this last risk.[1]

Establishing direct contact with a producer of an illegal product is invariably risky, since potential consumers must seek the person out and travel with the substance back to where they wish to consume it. Such a search entails time and monetary costs for travel, which individual consumers must pay for entirely, while traffickers spread those costs among their clientele.

Producers also face increased risks and costs in the absence of people who specialize in the distribution of their products. To sell directly to consumers, producers must find them, thereby increasing risks and travel costs. The alternative is to wait for consumers to find them, which means a smaller market and a dangerous one—they don't necessarily know if the person is just a consumer looking for a fix, an undercover agent, an informer, or a thief.

Because of the functional link they create between consumers and producers, traffickers are the people casual consumers are glad to see, whereas antidrug warriors and many addicts see them as embodying unmitigated evil (see Steppenwolf's lyrics at the beginning of the chapter). Prohibitionists may be able to conceive of consumers as misguided or depressed and producers as forced by poverty to produce illegal substances, but traffickers are a whole different story. They are perceived to be getting rich on the misery of others. Even those advocating legalization often believe that traffickers have no socially redeeming value. Libertarians, who support the right of individuals to decide whether or not to consume, emphasize the replacement of drug selling, violent gangs by respectable businesspeople as a benefit to a legalization policy.[2] The very word "trafficker" was created to normatively distinguish the seller of illicit products from those who sell legitimate commodities.

The term actually covers a number of people who play different roles within the distribution phase of the illegal commodity system. This phase is multilayered and specialized, although an individual or group of traffickers might span several tiers. Analysts distinguish various layers and label them differently, but in general, one can characterize the distribution phase of the commodity system as similar to that shown in Figure 1.2 (see page 15).

Each layer of the trafficking system complements the others and each has its own inherent risks as well as profit level. Those college students who consume Ecstasy in the United States are at the end of a distribution chain that includes exporters and importers because there is virtually no production of the drug within the country. Dutch students, on the other hand, are likely consuming domestically produced Ecstasy and hence have less need for importers. Meth produced in the kitchens of private homes in the United

States is distributed locally without the participation of the importers of precursor chemicals, wholesalers, and regional distributors required by the distribution chain of the superlabs in the California's Central Valley. Someone who gets Oxycontin directly from a doctor has no need to buy from elderly women supplementing their Social Security checks. In short, it is not the drug per se that determines the characteristics of its distribution structure, but rather the interaction among social, legal and economic contexts.

How Is Trafficking Conducted?

At first glance, the distribution phase of the PASCS appears to be the ideal embodiment of organized crime. The concept actually predates the official and popular concern with the drug trade. Many illegal activities, whether gambling, prostitution, kidnapping for hire, or drugs, may have inherent characteristics that propel actors toward organization. There have even been efforts to accuse legal businesses of operating in ways that transform them into institutions of organized crime.[3]

Government officials, the media, the entertainment industry, and plain old common sense all agree on the characteristics of organized crime in the drug trade, whether it is called the Mafia, the Mexican or Russian Mafia, the Cali or Medellín Cartel, or the Israeli Crime Syndicate. It is large, rich, and violent; male-dominated; controls vast percentages of the drug trade in a hierarchical organization; and has a constant desire to expand. For example, the U.S. Department of Justice reports that Mexican cartels "control" methamphetamine in the U.S. market.[4]

In the United States the stereotype is also that one step below these infamous crime organizations are ethnically based gangs, such as the Bloods, Crips, Jamaican Posse, and MS-13, whose centralized control of membership, violent tactics, and increasing wealth make them formidable competitors even to the Mafia.[5] In Italy, the stereotype suggests Mafia control.[6] Each of these groups certainly does exist, and in regard to some products they have had substantial influence for particular time periods at different levels of the distribution phase.

However, many of these crime syndicates have been destroyed, yet the availability of illegal psychoactive substances continues to be extremely high, with commensurately lower prices since the early 1980s. This, after thirty years, hundreds of billions of dollars spent on the drug war worldwide, and the spectacular elimination of numerous crime syndicates.[7] The phenomenon of destruction of stereotypical supply sources in tandem with continuing abundant supply and low prices should speak volumes about the fact that focus on these groups is so misleading as to render this understanding of how consumers get their substances virtually useless.

For a variety of reasons having to do with the physical characteristics of psychoactive substances and their illegal nature, it turns out that the most useful way to understand drug markets is as competitive markets in which a variety of different organizational types, most of which are quite small in size, serve distinct market segments. This is true even in regard to the same drug and in the same neighborhood. Distributors rarely clash violently. The attraction of the business crosses racial, ethnic, and class divisions and has become less male-dominated than stereotypes suggest. And, despite the fact that some individuals make a great deal of money, most people involved in the business make relatively little from selling drugs.

To understand why this alternative view more accurately describes how organized crime operates, one needs to first investigate the interaction between the physical characteristics of the substances and the legal regime regulating their distribution; then one can turn to the relationships among distributors within the drug markets.

Psychoactive substances tend to come in easily concealed packages, whether this means cartons of cigarettes on which someone wants to avoid taxes, small plastic bags of heroin, or Ecstasy tablets. This makes them relatively easy to smuggle; even alcohol and marijuana can be hidden if one is satisfied with moving small amounts, as anyone knows who has exceeded the one liter limit on free importation of alcohol into the United States at the customs declaration point. The profit associated with just a toiletries-size bag of Ecstasy pills that cost $.20 each to produce and sell for $20 a piece can entice many individuals to move the product into or across the country.[8] Considering the value that illegal psychoactive substances have in the markets of rich countries, and the low barriers to entry into that market, one might naturally expect a decentralized and unorganized system for their sale. The sort of "every man for himself," "looking out for Number One" type of attitude that's often found around other get-rich-quick schemes. However, this is not the case for several reasons.

Given the easy availability of supply, the primary challenge for would-be sellers is to limit their exposure to legal authorities as much as possible. One of the few studies to involve high-level cocaine and marijuana traffickers in federal prison suggests that trust, reliability, and concealment are strategies that limit size of operations. The researchers suggested that "Successful operation does not require the creation of a large or enduring organization.... Some supplier/customer relations last a long time, but they are rarely exclusive, and those that are exclusive are voluntarily so."[9]

A study of heroin dealers found that lower-level dealers prefer to service a known client base of five to twenty customers because it limited the number of sales, reduced the probability of information leaks, allowed for the surveillance and discipline of customers if necessary, and permitted dealers to adjust their behavior relatively quickly without a great deal of planning and negotiation if risks suddenly increased.[10] Cocaine dealers from the middle-class also minimized the risk of arrest by explicitly limiting sales to people they knew and trusted. This strategy is less likely to be followed by dealers who sell in bars and on the street; consequently, these individuals are the most likely to be apprehended by the authorities.[11]

In the case of heroin and cocaine, the two most lucrative substances in the illegal drug market, one study of trafficking groups in New York City found that only one of the thirty-nine groups investigated (the study specifically eliminated sellers who had no ties to anyone else in the distribution chain) was involved in all the phases of the PASCS from manufacturing to retail. The majority of the groups engaged in only one level of distribution in the commodity system.[12] Multiple empirical studies in Australia, Italy, the United States, and Britain also call into question the notion that a few large criminal organizations control the market for illicit drugs.[13]

The preceding paragraphs should have demonstrated that the organized crime recognized as the Medellín Cartel or the Arellano Felix Mafia is not the norm in the trafficking phase of the PASCS. In addition, the material should have at least hinted at why interactions among participants in all illegal markets are not simply free-for-alls. Yet the perception remains of an extremely violent business.

The illegal nature of many psychoactive substances provides a powerful incentive for some type of order no matter the size of the enterprise. Even small traffickers run the risk of having their supplies seized and therefore seek costly information about when and where to move their product. And every trafficker of illegal products is vulnerable to theft and extortion to a degree that someone who can appeal to the authorities and the legal system is not. However, order in the illegal drug trade arises not from an organization instituting control over the system, but rather through the process of separate actors interacting with each other and adhering to mutually beneficial norms of behavior, some of which have already been alluded to.

Because the distribution system is multilayered, participants need to interact across the levels in order to move product to the consumer. The relationship among people in the distribution phase of the PASCS can be usefully placed into five distinct categories. Freelance is the most independent of these because the individuals cooperate without hierarchy, division of labor, or future expectations of working together. Some individuals, however, seek the greater level of trust that is found in family businesses. Others try to make the relationships binding by creating communal businesses based on ethnic, religious, or nationalist ties. Street-level dealers may try to limit their exposure by working exclusively within a small area, creating community-based businesses. Still other traffickers seek the efficiencies of greater divisions of labor and the sense of control provided by hierarchy and operate as a corporation.[14]

The corporate type of structure provides the most control for those at the top because reporting channels are clearly established and everyone in the organization understands the general layout of authority. Peter Reuter and John Haaga, two RAND scholars who study public policy and drugs, didn't find a need for specialization among the various levels of trafficking, except for the actual smuggling of a substance across international borders.[15] However, the few super-rich traffickers in existence may have need of special bodyguards, lawyers, and money launderers whom they would wish to keep tabs on by having them in the organization. A downside of corporately organized control, however, is an increase in vulnerability. If moles (undercover agents) penetrate the organization or an informant is developed, law enforcement can go right to the top, arrest the leadership, and dismantle the organization.

Just as there are relations among individuals in this market, there can be relations among the distinct groups formed by these individuals. A freelance relationship in which organizations come together on an ad hoc basis for a specific transaction is one example. Organizations engaged in exporting an illegal substance may have an incentive to cooperate with each other on a longer-term basis. A cartel among distinct organizations is one such way to pool resources—the shipments contain product from each of the members—as a form of insurance.

Insurance well worth its deductible, considering that most estimates put the United States at intercepting only 10 to 20 percent of shipments of illegal substances at its borders.[16] Given the vast resources and passion with which the United States pursues its drug war, which puts it on the extreme end of the spectrum, other countries are likely to stop a comparable or perhaps slightly lower percentage, so the success rates for international traffickers tend to be high. The earnings from successful shipments are divided among the cartel members. Each party can also contribute in order to increase the resources available to purchase information and offer bribes. But with success also comes some risk; cartels have the same vulnerabilities as corporations.

Box 5.1 **The Underpublicized Career of John Gotti Sr., U.S. Drug Lord**

You've probably heard of Pablo Escobar and Arellano Felix, heads of infamous Colombian and Mexican drug cartels. But you're probably not as familiar with the name John Gotti Sr. He is the reputed head of the New York-based Gambino crime family.

Three criminal trials ended with hung juries and freedom, earning him the nickname "Teflon Don." A fourth trial on murder and racketeering charges sent him to federal prison for life in 1992. Although confined to a federal maximum-security prison in Illinois, the FBI reported years later that he still managed the Gambino crime family by speaking to his brother in code.

SOURCE: Adapted from Associated Press, "Gotti's Brother Likely to Take Reins of Mob Family, Paper Says" *Buffalo News*, April 19, 1999: 6A.

For years the major traffickers in Colombia experienced the benefits from organizing themselves in corporate forms and developing the Medellín and Cali Cartels. Yet ultimately they were destroyed because of the risks inherent in corporations and cartels with defined and widely known hierarchies. The remaining Colombian traffickers learned these lessons well and reorganized themselves into discreet units. These networks

> ... are a series of connected nodes ... can be individuals, organizations, firms, or even competitors ... vary in size, shape, membership, cohesion, and purpose. They can be large or small, local or global, cohesive or diffuse, centrally directed or highly decentralized, purposeful or directionless.

Their cores are small, composed of tightly connected members who have bonded together in some fashion. Networks also have peripheral elements engaged directly in the activities that entail contact with members outside the network. Because of these variations, networks resist disruption better than hierarchically organized structures.[17]

There is no necessary correlation between the degree and formality of organization and the level of distribution. Cocaine smuggling/importation seems to be more organized than heroin smuggling, perhaps because of the limited area in which coca currently is grown. But once the cocaine has entered the U.S. market, the barriers to entry for traffickers at even a high level of dealing are low, resulting in a proliferation of people seeking to profit from its sale.[18]

The highest levels of cocaine trafficking still have a constant competitive dynamic at work, often fueled by successful legal efforts against large crime syndicates—"successful" in that they managed to dismantle some organizations. However, they did not affect availability or price in the medium or the long term. The decision by the United States to increase resources to customs facilities and personnel and to incorporate the military into intercepting suspected shipments before they got to the country dramatically raised the risk of shipping cocaine directly from Colombia through the Caribbean to the United States.

To get around this obstacle, Colombian cartels made deals with Mexican small-time criminal organizations to develop new routes to the U.S. market. As a result of this collaboration, the Mexican organizations gained the wealth and power to become major players, forcing their one-time Colombian masters to make room for new independent associates. The Colombians acquiesced, but also began to develop new routes via the small islands in the Caribbean where the United States had not yet had an effective presence.[19] As the current U.S. effort to disrupt the cocaine traffickers in territory held by Fuerzas Armadas Revolucionarias de Colombia (FARC) guerrillas in Colombia progresses, not only is new production moving to areas held by different guerrillas, but manufacturing is also developing in Bolivia for the first time.[20]

There is also a darker side to trafficking that can motivate those involved to organize. This side is closer to that portrayed in the public eye and by the media. As with any product, the degree to which someone can monopolize supply is the degree to which they can influence price. Would-be monopolies have a difficult time in a free market guided by antimonopoly legislation and laws that limit the incentives one can offer competitors to turn over their supply. But in an illegal market, competitors cannot complain to the law if one party threatens them with force. This fact produces a situation in which extortion of competing traffickers can produce violent competition and, at the very least, oligopolies in which products with high value are held by a small group of traffickers. When violence is used, it can be used by distributors against local suppliers or even by suppliers against customers who would steal the product or pay with counterfeit money.[21] Box 5.1 illustrates that even traffickers of marijuana, a drug not known for violence, can find themselves in violent conflicts over sales territory.

Yet, even though "the threat of violence ultimately underlies the power of dealers and distribution heads,"[22] a number of studies of sellers find that it rarely materializes and doesn't even seem to be part of the daily calculations of the sellers. Among those incarcerated in U.S. federal prison for drug offenses, only 12 percent had known histories of major violence. Among the prisoners interviewed by Reuter and Haaga, there was a perception that Colombian drug dealers stood out from other traffickers for their willingness to use violence.[23] Most traffickers seem to prefer to stick to the business of making money by expanding within known territory and investing excess profits in other businesses, including legitimate ones.[24]

One of the major reasons for the low level of violence that actually erupts in the drug world, is that there is not "a" drug market, but multiple markets, even for the same substance. Multiple markets, even within a small area, may each be serviced by different types of dealers. In one four-block area in Brooklyn researchers found an ethnically based market, another market geared towards working persons, users/dealers selling to other users/dealers, and prostitutes hustling sex for drugs for themselves and their partners. Many consumers

---

Box 5.2 **Marijuana Violence in New York City**

High potency marijuana, grown in the United States, now sells for $300 to $600 an ounce in New York City. As a result, groups that had trafficked in crack are turning their attention to marijuana, producing an increased level of violence in the trade.

SOURCE: Kevin Flynn, "Violent Crimes Undercut Marijuana's Mellow Image," *New York Times*, May 19, 2001: 1.

are willing to buy from sellers representing different markets, but sellers "prefer to define a market and to locate and retain repeat customers [in order] to increase business and reduce the probability of arrest."[25] The competition that could produce violence in this illegal realm is thus constrained by this diversity of the markets for drugs.

Marketing

The pusher model suggests that traffickers are aggressive marketers, constantly seeking out new users. Yet, as shown in the prior section, virtually all scholarly analyses of trafficking find that, whereas buyers may be willing to purchase from multiple sources, most sellers tend to avoid new faces not vouched for by existing customers.

Although traffickers may not be best understood as pushers of drugs, some traffickers are innovators on a quest to create greater demand. One of the roles of the distribution system is to convince consumers that the way in which they should satisfy their demand for an artificial boost is to use their product. Availability does not seem to be the issue; drugs are widely obtainable in all major markets.

Innovators in the distribution system seek ways to make their particular product more enticing by decreasing the cost, combating the social stigma, and reducing the associated health risk. Thus, heroin with higher purity makes it snortable. This creates a less stigmatized way of using it than injecting and makes it more tempered and safer (no dirty needles means less chance of AIDS or hepatitis C transmission). Snorting also means lowered chance of overdose, and the powder can be sold in small bags.[26] Crack cocaine was developed not in Colombia but on the West Coast of the United States. It was the result of a search to create a more potent, smokeable form of cocaine that sold for less.[27] LSD is also now marketed in less potent doses than in the 1960s when it first became popular and developed a reputation that many people willing to experiment with psychoactive substances found too threatening.

Consumers respond to these invitations and, as seen in Chapter Two, over time can evaluate whether the hype of the new drug or the new form of use is worthwhile. This learning may help explain the shifts in popularity of different drugs over time.

Why Is Someone a Trafficker?

Although traffickers serve a function in the PASCS, one cannot deduce from that fact why people become traffickers, especially in light of the job's illegal nature. So the question needs to be: "Why would someone sell substances known to have potentially negative consequences to both the user and to the seller if the seller is caught?" Dominant answers from the public perception

---

Box 5.3   **Phillip Morris Tries to Convince Czech Government It Is Better Off Financially If People Smoke**

The Czech Parliament was considering raising taxes on cigarettes. Fearing a reduction in demand as a result of the increased price, Phillip Morris hired a consultant to evaluate the true economic costs and savings of smoking. The study found that the government saved more money by the early death of smokers (decreased costs in the areas of health, welfare, and housing) than it might get through instituting a tax. Phillip Morris apologized for any suggestion that it was better for people to die younger, insisting this was simply an economic analysis of policy alternatives.

SOURCE: BBC News, "Smoking is cost-effective, says report." July 17, 2001. http://news.bbc.co.uk/hi/english/world/americas/newsid_1442000/1442555.stm.

---

include unemployment, the attraction of easy riches, the traffickers' own addiction to drugs, and prior criminal activities. Unfortunately, none of these answers adequately explains the choice to become a purveyor of illegal psychoactive substances. Yet no other explanation seems to offer a comprehensive picture either.

One stereotype is that minorities sell drugs because they are at the bottom of the social scale and either have no alternatives or have become socialized into having less respect for law and social order. In this view, suburban, white, middle-class users drive to depressed, inner-city areas to purchase drugs.[28] Yet middle-class and suburban dealers have already been noted in comments in other sections of this chapter. More evidence contradictory to this stereotype can be gleamed just from scanning the headlines: Hassidic young men moving drugs and money in and out of New York, doctors in Appalachia arrested for writing Oxycontin prescriptions for street dealers, Canadian military vehicles discovered with 240 pounds of high potency marijuana at the U.S. border, a U.S. colonel's wife using a diplomatic pouch to transport cocaine to New York from Colombia.[29] Several British diplomatic staffpersons have also taken advantage of this method of transport.[30]

New studies have found that even street-level dealers are not especially likely to be unemployed. A RAND study of male street-level sellers of crack in Washington, D.C., in the mid-1980s found that dealers did not have higher unemployment rates than people arrested for nondrug-related crimes and that 75 percent of dealers had been legitimately employed at some point when they were dealing. Legitimate employment provided these drug dealers with a median monthly income of $500. Ironically, among those employed, those who were better paid were more likely to sell more and to do so more often.[31] In other words, dealers tend to have legal employment, and more successful dealers tend to also earn more from their legal employment than do less successful dealers. Drug dealing tends to be a supplement to income rather than a primary income.[32]

Another, related myth associated with trafficking is that everyone involved in it, including street-level dealers, makes large sums of money, more so than they could get in legitimate jobs, especially those individuals with no high school diploma or job skills.[33] The reality is that most people involved in selling drugs make very little money doing it—if they work many hours trafficking their average wage mirrors that earned from minimum-wage jobs. If they only work a few hours a week it is because they have a regular job and are engaging in drug sales only when the time and context is particularly advantageous, say a Friday night. Multiple studies suggest that selling drugs is more akin to moonlighting than a regular job.[34]

Still, as Table 5.1 demonstrates, there is a great deal of money in the system and some people do get very rich. The wealth is just not widely distributed.

Clearly, some traffickers of illegal psychoactive substances are attracted to the business because it is one more way to make money and they are already criminals. In a study of the Italian drug market, Vincenzo Ruggiero and Nigel South note that in Italy the Mafia and the Camorra (the Neapolitan criminal network) invested their profits from cigarette smuggling into establishing operations for smuggling hard drugs. But this study also reports that a number of other studies in Italy found no prior involvement in criminal activity among heroin distributors, whether they were low-, middle-, or even high-ranking distributors.[35]

Users who see the consumption of a particular psychoactive substance in ideological terms, for example, as a counterculture, may engage in selling or exchanging drugs among themselves without a focus on profit. Ruggiero found such users/traffickers in the early development of the cannabis and heroin user groups in Turin, Italy.[36] Cannabis, homemade meth, LSD, and hallucinogenic mushrooms are the most likely drugs for which one might find these types of traffickers, although ideology would not characterize the majority of the people distributing these substances.

Another preconception regarding why traffickers do what they do is that it's a means of supplying their addiction. There is certainly a great deal of use

Table 5.1 Heroin Prices throughout the Psychoactive Substance Commodity System, 1994 (US$ per Kilogram)

Pakistani farmer (raw material)	900
Wholesale Pakistan	2,870
Wholesale U.S.	80,000
Retail 40% purity U.S	290,000
Retail 100% purity U.S	725,000

SOURCE: Peter Reuter and Victoria Greenfield, "Measuring Global Drug Markets," *World Economics* 2: 4 October–December 2001: 166, citing unnamed 1994 United Nations Drug Control Program study.

among traffickers at all levels of the distribution chain, although use and trafficking are not perfectly correlated. In the case of crack "most (probably
70 percent or more) crack sellers and low level crack distributors ... support a
compulsive crack use pattern...."[37] But the RAND study in Washington,
D.C., suggests caution in jumping to causal connections. Most sellers in this
study reported selling first and subsequently becoming users. The researchers
found further corroboration of this separation between the decision to sell and
the decision to use in a survey of D.C. high school students aged 15.5 years
to 17.5 years. In this group, 16 percent were selling illegal drugs, compared
with 11 percent who were using them. Since the two groups had little over-
lap, people appeared to sell drugs as a way to earn money, not in order to get
drugs. And, in a strong illustration that drug selling had not become a norm
among black youth in D.C., 80 percent of respondents reported that they did
not admire someone who sold drugs.[38]

One of the most popular answers to why people sell drugs links it to gang
behavior. The question of gang participation in the drug trade can be
approached in two ways. Do gangs dominate the drug trade? And, if not, do
most gangs nevertheless become involved with it, perhaps dominating sales
on their home turf? In summarizing the empirical studies of the crack market,
which is most identified with gangs in the popular perception, one study
found that "some gang members sell drugs, many do not, and many crack sellers have never been gang members." This study also cites a symposium of
experts in the late 1980s, the heyday of crack consumption, in which the consensus was that youth gangs and drug distribution groups were relatively independent phenomena.[39]

It's not just academics who dispute the popularly accepted link. The 1998
national survey of youth gangs undertaken by the U.S. Department of Justice found that only 34 percent were "drug gangs."[40] In 1995 the chief of
police of Pomona, California (a suburb of Los Angeles known for gang activity), concluded that the connection between gangs and drugs was overstated.[41] Research in the early 1990s suggested that the majority of local
drug selling arrests involved people without gang affiliations.[42] Yet gangs
continue to be a convenient scapegoat for many people worried about the
drug phenomenon.

Another popular argument emphasizes females being forced into selling
drugs either by their husbands, boyfriends, pimps, or by their economic condition. Perhaps most female traffickers studied in the past fell into at least one
of these categories. More recent studies, however, are demonstrating that
women, including middle-class women, can operate their own trafficking businesses without being subordinate to anyone. One study in Australia found
women excelling in family business organizations in which their familial position helped them benefit from "close and long-term kin ties bound even more
tightly together by norms of reciprocity, expectations of personal gain and perceived moral duty to support blood relations." The family provided support

even when the women were serving jail time.[43] One high-level cocaine dealer in Michigan sold to four female friends from high school who ran their own local distributing businesses. These

> divorced suburban mothers … had children to raise, rent to pay, and reputations to protect, and were not participating in other crimes. They were not part of the local bar or street scenes; the women themselves had stable contacts for sales in local businesses.

And a widow of a high-level cocaine dealer recruited one of his male clients to take over the business and received regular payments from him for setting it up.[44]

Summary

The distribution of illegal psychoactive substances is a ubiquitous phenomenon: traffickers can be found in most societies and across class, race, and gender boundaries. New evidence about how illegal drugs are sold suggests that traffickers tend not to seek out consumers and are not necessarily consumers themselves. Once again, the empirical reality of this phase of the PASCS is found to be quite complex. Understanding the phenomenon of distribution requires systematically thinking about these data; consequently, it is necessary to turn to the four analytical perspectives.

For analysts using social deviance frameworks, societal norms have determined that an illegal psychoactive substance is appropriately prohibited and the trafficker is violating these norms. Once again, this perspective places more emphasis on the norms about the substance rather than the actual harm it creates. Hence, a social deviance analyst would reject any efforts to compare the seller of marijuana, Ecstasy, or cocaine with the companies that retail the legal but dangerous psychoactive substances tobacco and alcohol. The deviancy of the trafficker takes on an added dimension for those who view the consumer as a victim of the pusher man or of peers.

Deviance-focused arguments about trafficking aren't limited to the analysis of individuals. Press accounts and politicians often blame the corrupt political systems of certain other countries to explain why the United States consumes illegal drugs. These claims apply social deviance concepts to groups of individuals guided by the norms of their groups; in these arguments the international norms proscribing the sale of these psychoactive substances constitute the norms from which these groups are deviant.

Constructivists look not to societal norms alone, but also to the social reality of high use rates of legal and illegal psychoactive substances in societies that prohibit some, but arguably not even necessarily the most harmful, of these substances. These revealed norms help constructivists to understand why some people choose to distribute illegal substances. Since norms are in constant competition, and policies have varied over time and place, some people can be expected to believe that if consumers demand these drugs, it must be okay to sell them. Constructivists can accept that some dealers are sociopaths, but they would argue that the fact that millions of people who otherwise lead unexceptional lives also periodically sell illegal psychoactive substances is evidence that the norms of prohibition are contested.

Rational choice analysts prefer to conceptualize the suppliers of illegal substances as akin to businesspeople surveying markets for opportunities and weighing risks and benefits of investing their time, money, and energy in this particular market. The individuals who supply illegal substances evaluate the positive and negative incentives created by social, legal, economic, and political institutions that affect profit and risk. Low barriers to entry— a small investment that can produce large profits, established dealers who prefer not to seek out new buyers, substances that are easy to store and move—facilitate replacement of those caught. From this perspective, distributors of illegal substances exist not only because demand exists but also because the level of profit is sufficiently high to outweigh the relatively small risk of getting caught.

Realists understand that markets exist and aren't surprised that traffickers operate both across and within national boundaries. Analysts using a realist perspective argue that not all sellers of illicit drugs pose national security threats and that prudence determines how nations respond to traffickers at home and abroad. Some traffickers may be linked to foreign governments or other actors who seek to threaten specific governments; these traffickers need to be pursued as a matter of national security. If the drug trade has been identified as a threat, a realist expects governments to underplay the importance of national, and overplay the impact of international, factors in the distribution of illegal drugs domestically.

Analysts who seek to understand drug trafficking and advocate appropriate public policy can combine the four analytical perspectives in a variety of ways. The following is an example outlined from a realist viewpoint that demonstrates how the other perspectives could play subordinate roles in this comprehensive explanation. Readers can use this as a model for developing their own arguments by integrating factors from the different perspectives.

Realists might argue that the distribution of illicit drugs is unlikely to reach proportions that threaten the ability of a nation to protect itself from foreign threats or to project its influence internationally. They would not deny that people are selling illegal psychoactive substances and could accept that traffickers come from all walks of life: deviants, profit seekers, and those advocating alternative norms about drug consumption. To deal with the deviants, realists would advocate either incarceration or treatment; they would want to evaluate the possibilities of diminishing the number of deviant dealers before deciding how to allocate the nation's resources. A realist could see a potential threat from profit-seeking or alternative thinking traffickers if the consumption of psychoactive substances were to produce severe economic or health costs the remedy for which diverted economic, political, and human resources away from growth and security. But once again, realist analysts would want to see the evidence that such a situation was developing before investing important national resources in combating these alternative thinkers.

STUDY QUESTIONS:

1. Do you think the distributor of illegal substances is best understood as a supplier or "pusher"? Why? What evidence would you need to have more confidence in your view?
2. Is the violence associated with drugs better explained by the drug itself, the characteristics of people involved in the psychoactive substance commodity system or the fact of illegality? Defend your answer. What evidence would you need in order to have more confidence in your view?
3. Is corruption essential for the distribution phase of the psychoactive substance commodity system to function? Defend your answer.

Chapter 6 Money Laundering: Money Makes the World Go 'Round

From 1992 to 1995, Raul Salinas, brother of then Mexican president Carlos Salinas de Gortari, laundered approximately US$100 million through Citibank accounts that went from Mexico City to New York, then to London, from there to Switzerland, and, ultimately, to the Caribbean. Citibank vice president Amy G. Elliott violated bank policy by not filing a standard financial profile or financial background check and by not asking for a waiver of these requirements. Instead Ms. Elliott devised a system that entailed using a disguised name, hiding the money's origins by combining it with deposits from other banks and customers, and sending it to the accounts of a shell corporation. Citibank earned US$1.1 million in fees. No U.S. laws were broken, but Citigroup chair John S. Reed conceded that the bank had made mistakes in defending against money laundering.[1]

—Adapted from news stories by Tim Golden and Nick Anderson

The fact that many psychoactive substances are illegal creates a sense of having norms and values distinct from the mainstream for those participating in the psychoactive substance commodity system (PASCS). These people may produce and distribute these illegal substances simply because they want others to share the benefits, such as enjoyment or pain relief, that they experience. But the overwhelming majority of people involved in the PASCS, whether poor or well-off, expect to make money.

As the war against drugs has progressed globally, however, it has become riskier to use the proceeds of producing, distributing, or supplying illegal drugs. International and domestic legal authorities worldwide now pursue the profits of this illegal enterprise.

However it is gained, "money" is simply a store of value and as such it makes multiple transactions among people more possible than if these people had to barter goods for everything they wanted. If you can't use money it has no value; illegal money that is pursued by the authorities becomes dirty and is hard to use without drawing unwanted attention. Money laundering is the process of hiding the ownership and origins of this dirty money and converting it into currency that can be used to purchase legitimate goods.

Laundering money is not a phenomenon limited to drug trafficking, although drug trafficking does constitute a major source of dirty money. Other sources are prostitution, the illegal arms trade, corruption, kidnapping, illegal gambling, tax evasion, insider trading, and computer fraud. As with most statistics dealing with illegal activities, it is hard to know how much money is being laundered; in 1996 the International Monetary Fund (IMF) suggested that the amount could range from US$590 billion to US$1.5 trillion.[2]

In its simplest form, money laundering involves two main actors. The first is the one with the ill-gotten gains. The second is the one who accepts them in exchange for some good or service or who agrees to mix the dirty money with clean money and thereby hide the fact that it is dirty.

There has been a tendency to assume that people are not engaged in money laundering if they do not explicitly recognize that the money they're working with was derived from illegal sources. Indeed, one of the major problems in cutting down on money laundering is the fact that people involved in the legitimate channels through which it flows don't see themselves as part of the process. Recently, however, legislation in countries and organizations around the globe has moved in the direction of holding people accountable if they *should* have known that it was of a suspicious nature. Yet as this chapter will show, deciding what is suspicious is not easy to do and bumps up against privacy laws in many countries, including those of the United States.

This chapter has three sections and a conclusion. The role of money laundering in the PASCS is the focus of the first section. This examination illustrates the importance of hiding the origins of earnings generated through illicit activities. A subsequent section introduces the process of money laundering, highlighting the multiple means for mixing bad money with good and making it all come out smelling like roses. The final section is a brief description of the four major strategies used by the U.S. government, the chief proponent of anti–money laundering legislation both domestically and internationally, to combat money laundering at home. The conclusion summarizes this empirical discussion, provides arguments from each of the four analytical perspectives about why money laundering happens, and ends with an example of how an analyst can combine insights from the four in one general argument.

The Role of Money Laundering in the PASCS

If the origins of money earned through an illegal activity cannot be hidden, spending that money significantly increases the likelihood of getting caught. Assume that your neighbor earns $70,000 a year. Suddenly, he's driving a $100,000 sports car. You might think he inherited some money or just maxed out his credit cards, but should the police get a call from someone who is simply curious or has a grudge against that neighbor, he may suddenly become the object of an investigation. And if the police cannot quickly find a reasonable explanation for his sudden wealth, your neighbor may become a prime suspect and his activities may be scrutinized, perhaps even by a grand jury.

Most people engaged in an illegal activity would not relish becoming the object of any investigation, whether by the police, the press, or just nosy neighbors. Consequently, the number of people engaging in illegal activities would decrease if they couldn't explain why they are purchasing items and vacations well beyond what appears to everyone to be the expected earnings associated with their jobs, even with a good line of credit at the bank.

Now think about that same hypothetical neighbor. He takes a few water-color classes in the evenings then invites the neighbors over for a party. You think his paintings are awful, but he tells the assembled group that he has created a business on the side to sell his work on the Internet and even provides everyone with a business card with the Web site address. Over the next few weeks you notice that UPS trucks stop regularly to pick up packages at his house. A month later the nosy neighbor tells you that the "artist" is so successful that he has rented a studio somewhere in the city to handle his business. Two months later you notice a $100,000 sports car in his driveway. And in three months he takes his family on a trip to Europe "to look for artistic inspiration."

"Dang," you think, "this is what happens when cultural education falls victim to budget cuts in public schools! People just don't have any appreciation for real art."

But unbeknownst to you, your neighbor simply shipped his paintings to an associate in his illegal activities. He has stopped painting and doesn't have a studio somewhere in the city. However, because he didn't actually set up a company nor rent a studio nor get receipts for alleged sales he has not engaged in money laundering. What he has done is create an explanation to preempt casual curiosity about his newfound wealth.

If his illegal activities continue and are generating significant amounts of income, your neighbor will need to conceal himself from the attention of not just the neighbors but also of the tax authorities and the narcotics squad trying to track down the local cocaine distributor who emerged after the woman who ran the action was arrested the previous year. For these purposes, your neighbor would want to legally establish his company, actually rent a studio, and generate real sales receipts. Now he has entered the realm of money laundering.

The Process of Money Laundering

The Republican-majority of the Montana state legislature believed that it had found a way to eliminate state taxes and still provide state government with the necessary funds to carry out its tasks: it would create "offshore" banking in Montana. By federal law only people with residency outside the United States could deposit in such banks, but that didn't faze legislators. Minimum deposits were to be US$200,000 and a service fee of 1.5 percent would provide the depositor with the protection of the strictest privacy and confidentiality laws in the United States. State officials expressed confidence that they could keep dirty money out of the system. Despite such self-assurance, in February 2002, a federal court convicted the founder of the company Montana hired to promote the program of money laundering.[3]

It can be carried out in many ways, but the purpose of money laundering is always to service the needs of illegal activities and to help those activities flourish. Money laundering surfaces wherever illegal activities generate significant amounts of income. While cocaine and heroin production and distribution became illegal in the United States in 1914 and the focus of the federal government in the 1950s and 1960s was on illegal gambling, prostitution, and extortion, money laundering itself has only been a crime in the United States since 1986. Why so much later? In part because it is an activity that benefits from specific social, political, and economic characteristics that render authorities reluctant to pursue it with vigor.

The money to be laundered in the PASCS originates with the consumer. Like most illegal activities, illegal drugs are a cash business. Consumers prefer cash because it severs the paper trail between user and dealer as soon as the transaction is completed. Distributors and producers, as well as corrupt officials and most everyone else who has a business relationship to the system, also prefer cash. Not only does it provide anonymity, but it also offers an important degree of security for those receiving payment. Money can be counterfeited, but it cannot bounce like a check nor can it have payment stopped as with a stolen credit card.

It has already been shown in previous chapters that there are multiple layers of distributors for an illegal psychoactive substance. In major consuming societies, the process of hiding the origins of illegally made income begins with the local-level dealer. The cash must get from the local dealer all the way up the system to the producer. As one moves up the ladder of dealers the money pile to be sent to the next level—virtually all of it beginning with the $5s, $10s, and $20s that consumers use to purchase drugs—grows geometrically. As Table 6.1 illustrates, in 2001, just one kilo of cocaine could generate up to $150,000 for retailers.

The process by which drug money is amassed and distributed among those involved in the PASCS suggests that most of the people involved in laundering the money are found in the major consuming centers. Thus one might hypothesize that the greatest number of money launderers will be found in the richest market for psychoactive substances—the United States. This is indeed

Table 6.1 Cocaine Price Breakdown, 2001

1 kilo costs $1,500 in Colombia; transport to Mexico costs $1,000–$1,500 kilo
1 kilo costs $7,000 in Mexico
1 kilo costs $16,000 at U.S. border
1 kilo costs up to $30,000 in major U.S. cities
1 kilo mixed with other substances can generate up to $150,000 on the street

SOURCE: The Americas Foundation, Victor Pinzon. Based on data from Geraldo Reyes, *Miami Herald*, March 2001. www.theamericas.org/cocaine_huge_profit_margins.htm. Accessed May 2001.

the case, but before it ever leaves the major consumer societies to be deposited in offshore banks, a great deal of this cash is shipped within the United States and out of the United States in its physical state. Trucks, boats, and people crisscross the country moving stacks of currency to areas far from where the money was accumulated. One of the important ways in which dirty money leaves the United States is via international mail: "A single four-pound letter-class parcel can accommodate approximately $180,000 in $100 bills."[4]

Things weren't always so big time. The traditional process of money laundering utilized small businesses to mix bad money with good to conceal its illegal origins. Many readers today would be surprised to learn that up to the early 1970s most people did not have credit cards and small businesses were leery of accepting checks. This made restaurants, jewelry stores, pawn shops, and dry cleaners ideal candidates to launder money: a successful operation could deposit hundreds of dollars in small bills into its bank account every day without raising

---

Box 6.1 **The Black Market Peso Exchange System**

The Black Market Peso Exchange (BMPE) is the primary money laundering system used by Colombian narcotics traffickers in repatriating perhaps as much as $5 billion annually to Colombia. This is how it works:

First, a Colombian drug cartel arranges the shipment of drugs to the United States. The drugs are sold in the United States for U.S. currency, which is then sold to a Colombian black market peso broker's agent in the United States. The U.S. currency is sold at a discount because brokers and their agents must assume the risk of evading the Bank Secrecy Act (BSA) requirements for reporting large deposits when later placing the U.S. dollars into the U.S. financial system.

Once the dollars are delivered to the U.S.-based agent of the peso broker, the peso broker in Colombia deposits the agreed upon equivalent in Colombian pesos into the cartel's account in Colombia. The cartel has now laundered its money; it has successfully converted its drug dollars into pesos, and the Colombian broker and his agent now assume the risk for integrating the laundered drug dollars into the U.S. banking system. This is usually accomplished through a variety of surreptitious transactions.

Having introduced the dollars into the U.S. banking system, the Colombian black market peso broker now has access to a pool of laundered U.S. dollars to sell to Colombian importers. These importers then use the dollars to purchase goods, either from the U.S. or from other markets, which are transported to Colombia, often via smuggling, in order to avoid Colombian laws and customs duties.

SOURCE: Department of the Treasury, *The National Money Laundering Strategy for 1999*, 35. www.treas.gov/press/releases/ps113.htm. Accessed May 10, 2000.

suspicion. Once the money was in the bank, checks could be drawn on it, it could be used as collateral to borrow more money, and it could be transferred to other bank accounts, effectively hiding its origins to an even greater degree.

With the increasing popularity of high-value drugs like cocaine and the creation of new higher value versions of old drugs, such as high-potency marijuana, the value of illegal drugs increased further and the money to be laundered exceeded the capacity of the traditional system. Small businesses had to become large operations to channel such considerable sums. For example, between 1995 and 2001 a Brooklyn ice cream shop allegedly laundered $20 million to accounts in China, Thailand, Italy, Switzerland, and Yemen.[5]

Besides the mail, money launderers also have begun to take advantage of traditional systems used by migrants for sending money back home. Whether called *hawala* (Islamic world), *fei ch'ien* (Hong Kong), *padala* (Philippines), *hundi* (India), or *phoei kwan* (Thailand), the general pattern is the same. An individual provides cash to someone in a small office, who faxes notification to someone back home, and the money is quickly dispatched. The transaction leaves little paper trail, as code words are often used in place of names to generate even more uncertainty for those who manage to peek inside the system and try to distinguish legal from illegal transactions. The participants ensure fairness and credibility through trust and a bond of ethnic relationships.[6]

The purchase of goods and their subsequent sale is another means of laundering money. If I buy a house in New York with money made selling illegal drugs in San Diego, I can subsequently sell the house in New York, open a new bank account in San Diego, and have the escrow company in New York transfer the proceeds from my sale in New York directly into my San Diego account. Anyone who looks into this San Diego account would see that I made my money by selling a house in New York—a quite legitimate source.

In addition to these almost common sense approaches to money laundering, continued evolution of the U.S. financial system regularly offers new opportunities. The 1970s saw the creation of "non-bank banks," or financial institutions that provided traditional banking services, such as checking or loan services, as a means of attracting investments and deposits or of selling services. As a result, money began flowing more widely into such institutions as brokerage firms and insurance companies.

Traditional banks responded to this competition by offering services that made it easier for people to access their money directly (longer banking hours, ATM machines) or leverage their accounts into credit (proliferation of credit cards). All of this served to increase the opportunities for mixing dirty money with clean and increased the circulation of the money, making it more difficult to track once the dirty money got into the system.

The integration of national financial systems everywhere into the process known as globalization, in turn, has created still more new opportunities for money laundering and made prosecution more difficult. Globalization refers to the reach that economic processes have attained. Usually it is thought of in terms of production: a design originates in one country, is manufactured in another with materials brought from still other countries, and is sold to consumers in yet another country. In the financial arena, globalization refers to the ability of money to move quickly—perhaps even in "real time"—across multiple national boundaries, either in the form of investment or simply as payment for goods and services.

Figure 6.1 presents a hypothetical process of money laundering, based upon the experiences of Citibank noted at the beginning of this chapter. The process could begin in any country and could involve financial institutions from any country.

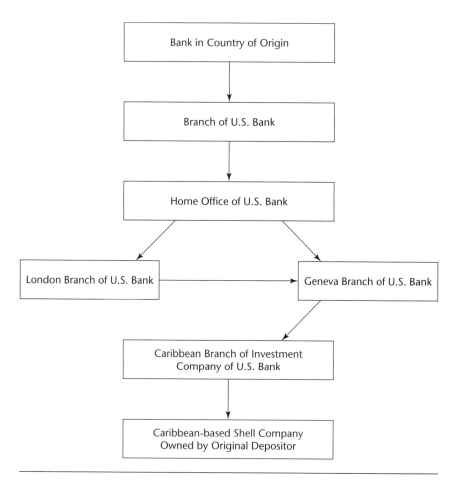

Figure 6.1 Hypothetical Process of Money Laundering by Foreign National Using U.S. Bank
NOTE: Inspired by the Citibank-Salinas case.

International business wants money to move quickly and easily between banks and even across national borders because time is money: often, goods cannot be moved nor paperwork submitted until a payment order comes through. Business also wants secrecy in the movement of money. For example, a company that wishes to buy another may need to make a "good faith" deposit to begin negotiations, but doesn't want competitors to know it's done this because they may try to buy the company also, thereby raising its purchase price.

The desire of business and individuals for secrecy for legitimate reasons, the quantity of clean money involved, and the speed with which money moves around the international financial system all facilitate the hiding of money's origins. Even if we accept the IMF's upper estimate of the quantity of dirty money laundered in 1996 ($1.5 trillion worldwide), it is a drop in the bucket compared to the legitimate flows of money (Fedwire alone transferred $249 trillion) recorded that year.

U.S. banks primarily use two wire services, Fedwire and the Clearing House Interbank Payments System (CHIPS), to transfer money from one bank to another within the United States. Fedwire is operated by the U.S. Federal Reserve and is the primary U.S. wire service. The system is designed to

> handle large-value, time-critical payments, such as payments for the settlement of interbank purchases and sales of federal funds; the purchase, sale, and financing of securities transactions; the disbursement or repayment of loans; and the settlement of real estate transactions.[7]

In 2003, Fedwire processed 123,280,721 transfers, for a total value of $437 *trillion;* daily volume averaged almost a half million transfers with an average daily value of $1.7 trillion.

In 1970, banks worldwide joined together and created their own wire service, CHIPS. In 2002, it had fifty-nine members, among them the largest U.S. banks and U.S. branches of foreign banks. CHIPS serviced more than 240,000 transactions a day in 2002, and those transactions were worth about $1.2 trillion. To provide privacy for its corporate customers, CHIPS sends the transactions using only Universal Identification Numbers and the bank name rather than bank account information.[8]

Most international transactions, even those using CHIPS, are transmitted via the Society for Worldwide Interbank Financial Telecommunication, appropriately known as SWIFT. Created in 1973, SWIFT is based in Belgium and overseen by the central banks of the Group of Ten (G-10) countries.[9] The service is used in more than two hundred countries, and can send more than nine million messages a day; in 2003, SWIFT sent more than two billion messages for financial transactions.[10]

Searching for dirty money within this huge and complex international financial system is difficult, but not impossible. Any efforts to track the origins of money more carefully, however, will clearly increase the cost of transferring money, legitimate or otherwise, and slow down the speed at which it moves through the system. The financial institutions and the people or corporations who use them have been opposed to increasing the cost of their businesses for the uncertain payoff of making money laundering more difficult.

Pursuing Money Launderers

Sometimes money launderers operate because the government of a developing country is corrupt or weak. Certainly, high-ranking officials in many countries have been found to be willing to accept bribes to ignore suspicious financial transactions. Money laundering, as demonstrated, also can be a very sophisticated process that requires great knowledge of how financial institutions operate; some governments simply don't have that type of expertise. So, they rely upon the expertise of the institutions involved in money laundering, with the result that loopholes in regulations are created that permit the financial institutions to continue laundering money.

But since money laundering also happens in developed countries with great expertise in the financial sector, weakness and corruption may not be the true source of money laundering's ability to function. A look at the history of the pursuit of money launderers in the United States can provide insights into why money laundering persists despite being the target of a powerful legal system.

In general, there are four means by which the U.S. federal government has attempted to put an end to money laundering. The first effort was to deter depositors by monitoring their activities. Since dirty money is the result of an illegal activity, those who want to launder their money prefer not to leave any

---

Box 6.2 **Example of CHIPS Transaction**

- Manufacturer of toys in Hong Kong gets an order from a retailer in France, to be paid in U.S. dollars.

- Hong Kong company tells its French warehouse to fill the order.

- French retailer receives the goods and tells his Paris bank to pay the Hong Kong company in U.S. dollars.

- Payment is sent via CHIPS from New York office of the Paris bank to New York office of Hong Kong bank used by the Chinese company.

- New York office of Chinese bank notifies its Hong Kong office that payment has been received.

- Hong Kong bank credits the toy manufacturer's account.

SOURCE: Adapted from the New York Clearing House Association, "Clearing House Interbank Payments System," 1995.

paper trail of their financial activities at the start of the laundering process. Beginning with the Bank Secrecy Act of 1970, banks were required to report any cash deposits of $10,000 or more to the Treasury Department through documents known as Currency Transaction Reports (CTRs). This legislation was of limited value in combating money laundering, however. It only covered cash transactions; depositing more than $10,000 using money orders, checks, securities, or other financial interests did not have to be reported. In addition, only banks were subject to reporting requirements; consequently dirty money could be mixed in with clean money through a variety of other financial institutions such as insurance companies or stock brokers. State privacy laws made state-chartered banks leery of reporting information about depositors. And, by making multiple deposits of less than $10,000—a process known as "structuring deposits" that was carried out by multiple depositors known as "smurfs"—a depositor and the holder of the account could avoid the CTRs.

It took sixteen years for Congress to address the limitations of the 1970 legislation. The next strategy was to deter money launderers by government regulation of financial institutions. The Money Laundering Control Act (MLCA) made money laundering illegal, broadened the definition of transactions to include financial instruments other than cash, and exempted banks from some secrecy laws if they were reporting information to the police. The 1986 act made it a crime to engage in monetary transactions of more than $10,000 if the person knew that the money came from an illegal activity, even if he or she did not know the specific illegal act. This covers not only banks, but also "currency exchangers, securities brokers, insurance companies, dealers in precious metals, real estate brokers, casinos, and car, boat, or airplane dealers."[11] Structuring transactions also became illegal.

Six years later, the Annunzio-Wylie Money Laundering Act of 1992 created a new means of gathering information about clients, Suspicious Activity Reports (SARs). The legislation authorized the Treasury Department to promulgate rules for minimum anti–money laundering programs at financial institutions. It also added a civil penalty for negligence, thereby further reducing the ability of people engaged in monetary transactions to simply claim, "I didn't know." Now, if individuals should have known, they can be fined.

Still other laws followed in 1994, 1998, and 2001, all designed to plug loopholes in existing legislation that allowed money laundering to thrive in the United States. The 2001 legislation was significantly influenced by the USA PATRIOT Act. In its efforts to put a stop to money laundering used to fund terrorist activities, Congress instituted new reporting requirements even down to the level of the local pawnbroker.

These legislative changes have made catching money launderers easier. From 1987 to 1995, 7,300 defendants were charged in U.S. courts with money laundering. However, the government was able to win convictions in only 580, or 8 percent, of those cases, and those convicted were mostly small

---

Box 6.3 **Who Is a Money Launderer?**

Sherrie Miller Daly, who married golfing major champion John Daly in 2001, and her parents, pleaded guilty to federal money laundering charges stemming from a larger investigation of their role in buying and selling cocaine, methamphetamine, and marijuana between 1996 and 2002. The three maintained their innocence. Sherrie and her mother received probation for five years along with six months home detention rather than the five years in prison they might have received had they been found guilty after a trial; her father received a two-year prison sentence. John Daly stood by his wife's claim of innocence but advised her to make a deal with prosecutors, noting, "You don't beat a federal court, a federal judge and the FBI."

"Daly's wife pleads guilty in drug case," *St. Petersburg Times,* (St. Petersburg, Florida) April 6, 2004: Sports, 11C.

---

operators.[12] The number of arrests and conviction rates increased dramatically from 1994 to 2001. Yet even in 2001, with 18,500 defendants brought to trial and conviction rates of 90 percent, only 17 percent of these convictions involved drug trafficking.[13]

A third strategy used to deter money launderers is self-policing by financial institutions. U.S. companies are leery of government regulation because it adds to the cost of doing business and may be developed by someone with little understanding of business. Hence, when faced by great pressure for regulation, companies often propose self-regulation. In the banking industry, these regulations have become known as "Know Your Customer" (KYC) rules.

Under KYC rules, financial institutions create financial profiles and check their potential customers' business dealings and credit backgrounds. Ironically, Citibank was one of the chief proponents of KYC self-regulation; com-

---

Box 6.4 **U.S. Bank Fined $25 Million for Lax Money Laundering Efforts**

Riggs National Corporation, owner of Riggs National Bank, was fined for omitting information on Suspicious Activity Reports forms for accounts held by the Embassy of Saudi Arabia, personal accounts of the Saudi ambassador, and personal accounts of citizens of Equatorial Guinea. Tens of millions of dollars in cash were withdrawn without the bank reporting any suspicions of improper behavior. Regulators called Riggs' behavior "willful" and "systematic." Riggs consented to the fine without admitting guilt.

SOURCE: Kathleen Day, "Record Fine Levied for Riggs Bank Violations," *Washington Post*, May 14, 2004: A01. www.washingtonpost.com.

pany policy also called for visiting clients up to twelve times a year.[14] Vice president Elliott, known for her involvement in the Salinas case, had earlier testified as a government witness against another banker (not a Citibank employee) whose defense had been that he was unaware that the money deposited was of questionable legitimacy. But all in all, and perhaps not surprisingly, given the fees earned by banks on large transactions and the legal ambiguity of what it means to "know your customer," self-regulation has not been sufficient to eliminate money laundering.

Since it is clear that dirty money is still successfully laundered despite legislation and self-policing, the next logical step in fighting it is to go after its benefits. These assets—stocks, houses, cars, boats, etc.—are targeted because they either allow the facilitation of crime or have been purchased with laundered money. At the height of the war on drugs in the United States, Congress passed the Comprehensive Crime Control Act of 1984, which expanded the government's ability to seize property. This civil asset forfeiture (CAF) legislation made those who possessed the suspected assets guilty until proven innocent.

Criminal procedures in the United States normally are based on the concept that one is innocent until proven guilty, but the standard for determining guilt is lower in civil procedures. Given this, civil suits appeared an excellent means to make it difficult for people engaged in illegitimate activities to enjoy their money. Individuals did not even have to be charged with a crime for their assets to be seized. Congress saw an additional benefit in going after the assets: these ill-gotten gains could be auctioned off to fund the drug war. And the law enforcement agency that seized an asset was authorized to receive half of the proceeds when the ownership of the asset went uncontested or the owner was found guilty.

The CAF law produced significant seizures and funds for law enforcement. The billions of dollars generated were so unexpected that it created management and oversight problems for the government.[15] Many civil libertarians, however, were concerned that the law made it difficult for legitimately purchased assets to be contested in court since the owners had to post a bond, hire a lawyer, and go to court to prove that the assets were purchased with money made in a legitimate fashion. In addition, there was a concern that the incentives for law enforcement to be overzealous in pursuing allegedly ill-gotten gains were too strong to protect citizens from unreasonable seizures. After years of debate and some high-profile abuses, Congress amended the law in 2000 to require law enforcement to prove the illegitimate origin of the assets before they could be seized.

Summary

Money laundering is necessary for the PASCS to function beyond a rudimentary barter/philanthropic scope. Deviants, alternative thinkers, and those driven by the profit motive all want to be able to enjoy the fruits of their labor.

Box 6.5   **Pursuing Suspicious Assets**

Federal agents and Los Angeles County sheriffs arrived, with a search warrant and prepared to confront violent criminals, at Donald Scott's multimillion-dollar ranch in 1992. When Mr. Scott heard noises, he came out of his bedroom armed with the gun he legitimately owned and believed would protect his property. Upon seeing the occupant brandishing a weapon the sheriffs opened fire, killing Mr. Scott. No drugs were found and the property was deemed lawfully his. Seven years later, the authorities settled a suit filed by Mr. Scott's survivors for his wrongful death, paying $5 million.

"Illegitimate gains; Bill would reform civil asset forfeiture rules," *San Diego Union-Tribune,* April 6, 2000, B-12.

To avoid the increased risk of spending money that could link them to their illegal activities, they need to hide the origins of that money. Significantly decreasing opportunities for money to be laundered, therefore, would probably have the greatest impact—after significantly reducing demand—on reducing the trade in illicit substances.

So why hasn't more progress been made in curtailing this phase of the PASCS? The four analytic perspectives again offer differing explanations for why people engage in money laundering and why they are able to get away with it.

The social deviance analyst expects money launderers to have some type of individual flaw that accounts for their illegal behavior. These individuals may possess reasonable lifestyle desires but perhaps they never developed the educational or vocational skills that would allow them to earn income legitimately. Or perhaps they suffer from chemical imbalances or genetic defects that make them unable to achieve success via legal means. Deviance analysts would also argue that some of these people have unlimited appetites for the good things in life and do not see anything illegal that they do to pursue those needs as their fault (i.e., they are sociopaths).

Social deviance analysts wouldn't necessarily label as a money launderer the real estate agent who facilitated laundering by not reporting large cash purchases as suspicious in the period before such activities became illegal. The fact that it was not against the law to engage in such transactions meant that society either had no consensus on it or was willing to leave it up to individual norms to determine whether the individual should take on some of the burden of combating the illegal drug trade. But once the activity becomes illegal, a social deviance analyst expects that only social deviants will continue with such activities.

Rational choice analysts see rational and egoistic individuals seeking to reap the large profits associated with money laundering as the perpetuators of the process. These analysts are also aware that the legal institutions for discovering and prosecuting money launderers lag considerably behind the ability of individuals to devise schemes for mixing bad money with good, to a great extent because the legitimate and politically influential financial system seeks to avoid the economic costs that a sufficiently invasive legal framework would impose.

Therefore, these analysts expect money launderers to be cognizant of the fact that few money launderers get caught. They can't tell you which individuals will be attracted to this activity, but they are confident that some unknown percentage of entrepreneurial individuals will find the relatively low risk acceptable in the face of the large profits to be made.

For the constructivist, money laundering can represent one of the major points of contention between societal and group or individual norms. If there are societal norms that say that people and financial institutions should not facilitate profit making by those in the illegal drug trade, there are also norms among financial and other profit-making institutions and their stockholders that place the importance of making a legal profit above those societal norms. In this scenario, the challenge of ensuring that the money one handles is not dirty and of not discouraging clean but private transactions is often addressed by erring on the side of money laundering.

Constructivists could accept that some deviants may flaunt the law. But they will likely argue that the very experience of U.S. anti–money laundering legislation and its enforcement demonstrate that most people involved in accepting dirty money separate their activity from that of the people who earned the money illegally. The money takes on a life of its own as "me generation" values and strict adherents to the right to privacy ally to facilitate a rationale of "it's not my business to find out where people make their money."

Realists look to political power under the auspices of anarchy to explain money laundering behavior. In most countries, and particularly in stable, democratic nations, domestic politics is not anarchic. Consequently, realists couldn't say much about the internal aspects of money laundering except to subordinate the economic and political resources devoted to combating it to the demands necessary for securing a country's security and promoting its international economic, military, political, and diplomatic prosperity. If money laundering were identified as a threat to national security, a realist would expect a strong nation to shift the costs of fighting money laundering to weaker nations that were not themselves important to national security for other reasons.

An example of this for a realist would be Panama. Although the country's leader, General Manuel Noriega, had been involved in money laundering (and drug trafficking) since the 1970s, the U.S. focus on combating the Sandinista government in Nicaragua meant that the United States did not pressure Panama on drugs. When the cold war and Central America's civil wars wound down and the drug war heated up, Noriega became a target of U.S. policy, and the United States ultimately invaded Panama in 1989 to seize the general for his crimes.

As with each of the other levels of the PASCS, the four perspectives can be combined in numerous ways to develop hypotheses about why money laundering prospers. Here, a priority should be given to a deviance perspective, illustrating how aspects of the other perspectives can be integrated in a subordinated fashion.

The social deviance analysis of money laundering would begin by emphasizing the primacy of the societal norm against money laundering. These analysts would note that it took time and multiple efforts to arrive at the recognition that money laundering could only be mitigated by adopting broader and more intrusive laws. They might draw from the constructivists by seeing the advances in legislation over time as indications of the creation of a societal norm that even those indirectly involved in the illicit drug trade had to be held responsible. Competing norms would be identified as a sign of deviance, since societal norms are assumed to be reflected in the laws of a democratic nation. The emphasis of the rational choice perspective on the importance of legal institutions in shaping individual behavior would explain why not all deviants who could launder do. But, the deviance analysts could argue, the institutional constraint of illegality is sufficient to deter nondeviants from money laundering; the calculations of costs, benefits, and probability of being caught are relevant only to deviants.

STUDY QUESTIONS

1. If it were possible to eliminate weak and corrupt governments, would you expect the amount of money laundered to decrease significantly? Why or why not?

2. How do privacy concerns affect the ability of the government to patrol money laundering?

3. Many people in developed countries now earn salaries and have investments that permit them to pay tens of thousands of dollars for cars, hundreds of thousands for homes, and even millions for companies. Should they be willing to have their financial transactions scrutinized as a contribution to the war on drugs? Why or why not?

4. If I am a real estate broker and someone wishes to buy a house from me for $2 million cash, why should I report her to the money laundering authorities? If I choose not to report the potential purchase as "suspicious," should I be held responsible for facilitating money laundering? Why or why not?

Chapter 7

The Political Economy of International Drug Strategies
Going It Alone or Working Together

The Commission of the European Communities currently has projects related to drug issues in one hundred countries with a total value of more than € 100 million. The projects cover a wide range of activities, including prevention, treatment, social, and professional reinsertion for drug users, epidemiology, alternative development, controls on chemical precursors, customs and police cooperation, institutional support for the development of national policies, money laundering, and drafting new legislation.[1]

—*Adapted from the Communication from the Commission to the Council and the European Parliament on the Implementation of the EU Action Plan on Drugs (2000–2004)*

Looking at the international politics of illegal drugs from a Latin American perspective, European governments seem much more willing to fund a wide variety of programs that Latin American governments say are necessary to confront illicit production and trafficking than does the government of the United States. Rather, the United States has a reputation for imposing its view on how the drug issue should be addressed and what Latin American governments must do to avoid punishment by the United States over drug policy. There is plenty of evidence to demonstrate that the Latin Americans are at least partially correct in these evaluations. That said, what accounts for this difference in the European and U.S. approaches? Put another way, what accounts for cooperation and conflict in international drug policy? Not surprisingly, each of the analytical perspectives answers this question differently.

This chapter applies the lessons learned in Part II about the substances themselves and the psychoactive substance commodity system (PASCS) to analyze the international politics of drug policy. First, the general concepts of cooperation and conflict in international affairs are examined and related to the drug issue. Then the discussion turns to decisions not to cooperate, that is, efforts to undertake unilateral policies in the international arena to solve one's national drug problem alone. The section illustrates the strengths and weaknesses of this approach and is followed by another that focuses on cooperative international policies. This section explores the benefits of such efforts as well as the fact that cooperation doesn't mean an equal split for everyone. The final section is a mini–case study of Plan Colombia and why it generated both cooperation and conflict within the Western Hemisphere. The chapter ends with discussions of how each of the analytical perspectives approaches the issue of international cooperation and conflict in the policy arena of drug policy.

Cooperation and Conflict

Why states cooperate on policy is not immediately clear because all interactions between countries are accompanied by disagreements over the goals, the means, and the distribution of costs and benefits generated by the interactions.[2] Countries may disagree on goals, but even when agreeing that all of them are important, they may prioritize them differently. Peru and the United States can easily agree that both supply and demand factors should be addressed. The Peruvian government, however, understands that if demand for cocaine is reduced in the United States, then there will be fewer incentives to attract individuals in Peru to produce illegal drugs. Reducing supply in this case is easier for Peru than if the United States attempts to limit supply without there being a significant reduction in demand. In this latter case, prices would rise as supply fell but demand did not and more people would be attracted to produce in Peru, thereby presenting the Peruvian government with a more difficult task.

Even when parties agree on priorities, they can still disagree about the means to pursue them. For example, do governments reduce demand through education and social welfare programs or do they pursue punitive policies? And finally, parties can agree on priorities and means, but disagree vehemently over the distribution of the costs of implementing those means.

Cooperation doesn't require agreement on goals; however, the goals just need to be complementary, not contradictory. For example, the goal of the U.S. government when it decided to participate in Plan Colombia was limited to reducing the supply of cocaine and heroin coming into the United States. The overarching goal of a string of Colombian presidents, however, has been to deprive domestic guerrilla and paramilitary groups of the finances that enable them to maintain well-equipped forces to compete with the national government for control over significant parts of the country. Although these goals are quite different, it is easy to see how they can become complementary.

To cooperate means to adjust one's policies to take others' interests into consideration. Essentially, a nation cooperates because it can get something better than if it goes it alone. Cooperation differs from both imposition, in which a nation is not allowed to make a decision, and harmony, in which a perfect compatibility of interests guides states' behavior.[3] It is particularly relevant on issues like drugs, for which the commodity system spans international borders, making it less likely that any one country, even a powerful one like the United States, can control both supply and demand.

The specific costs that each party will pay for cooperating depend upon the negotiating power of the parties involved. All policies carry costs and benefits and rarely are these costs and benefits naturally distributed equally. Consequently, much of the bargaining over cooperation has more to do with how costs and benefits will be distributed than over the actual goals of the cooperation.

States cooperate on policies and strategies, not on outcomes or results. Outcomes may not be entirely foreseeable or may depend on what those outside of the agreement also want. In this context, the desires and behavior of producers, distributors, money launderers, and consumers of illegal substances are fundamental determinants of outcomes. For example, the U.S. and Canadian governments work together to keep illegal drugs and precursor chemicals from crossing into the United States, yet the substances continue to move across the border. Where there is a will (and a demand), there is a way.

Unilateral International Policies

One of the earliest and most violent expressions of unilateral behavior in the international politics of drugs was the Opium War of 1839–1842 between China and Great Britain. The war was precipitated when China attempted to prohibit the importation of opium. The British, whose citizens largely controlled the opium trade from British India, responded with military force. They quickly defeated China and forced it to make numerous concessions, including continuation of the opium trade.

The dramatic increase in drug use and violence within the United States starting in the 1970s provoked a number of unilateral actions by the U.S. government. A case of unilateral international violence occurred in 1989 when, despite opposition from the Organization of American States (OAS), the United States invaded Panama with more than twenty thousand soldiers to apprehend strongman General Manuel Noriega for, among other crimes, protecting drug traffickers and money launderers.

Another way in which the U.S. government has unilaterally dealt with participants in the PASCS when their home governments do not cooperate with U.S. criminal proceedings is to kidnap the suspects and bring them to the United States to stand trial. The U.S. Supreme Court has ruled that agents of the U.S. government have "the unilateral authority to seize foreign nationals on foreign territory." Not surprisingly, the policy has been condemned by many nations.[4]

At the other end of the unilateral action spectrum are diplomatic threats. President Bill Clinton's point man, Bob Gelbard, on international drug policy flew to Tasmania, Australia, to warn the state government that should it adopt a heroin maintenance program the United States would seek to revoke the UN license for the state's $81 million legal opium production.[5] More recently, U.S. ambassador Paul Celluci told the Canadians that all tourist and commercial traffic into the United States from Canada could be severely slowed if the

United States had to increase vigilance as a result of Canada's approval of a marijuana decriminalization bill pending in its congress.[6]

Invasions and kidnappings aside, the U.S. Congress is also quite willing to take less dramatic unilateral action. As part of the Anti-Drug Abuse Act of 1986, believing that other governments were being too lax in the war on drugs, Congress sought to score political points with voters by mandating that the executive branch compile a list of major producing and transit nations for marijuana, cocaine, and heroin (note the focus on the unholy trinity). The president was to certify whether each country was cooperating with U.S. antidrug policies. The United States would then be required to vote against loans from international financial institutions (IMF, World Bank, etc.) and suspend U.S. aid to any decertified countries. Congress did provide a huge loophole by which the president, in the name of national security interests, could avoid decertifying a country that was not cooperating. Even countries that were "certified" were offended that the United States would unilaterally evaluate their efforts in fighting drugs and yet not subject its own efforts at controlling drug use to scrutiny by an impartial third party.

Congress approved a pilot modification of the certification policy in 2001 after the OAS created the Multilateral Evaluation Mechanism (MEM) in 1999 to objectively evaluate what hemispheric governments are doing to fight drugs and encourage cooperation. Under the new waiver, the president no longer has to certify those countries that cooperate with U.S. policies but still must decertify non-cooperating ones. This waiver has been extended indefinitely, but at Congress's discretion. In 2003, Myanmar (formerly Burma), Haiti, and Guatemala were decertified; only Myanmar (whose military government is considered by the United States to be a pariah and who has no national security value for the United States) failed to receive a national security waiver.[7]

General Problems with Unilateral International Policies

It is impossible for any country that has any contact with the outside world to convert itself into a fortress to keep out drugs. The expectation that a country such as the United States could create something akin to a "Fortress U.S." and seal its borders against penetration by couriers with illegal drugs or laundered money is simply not credible. The United States has almost one hundred thousand miles of coastline and nearly six thousand miles of borders. In 2000, the United States legally received "477 million people, 127 million automobiles, 11.5 million trucks, and 5.8 million maritime containers.... People and goods arrive daily at more than 3,700 terminals in 301 ports of entry."[8] And, as seen in Chapter Four, even if foreign drugs could be significantly reduced, national production of illicit substances would still be a significant threat to a country that seeks to be drug free.

The evidence presented in Part II of this text clearly demonstrated that drugs are transported by people from all walks of life; drugs are easily hidden, and thus take a great deal of time and manpower to detect; and money moves easily and quickly from place to place. Unless taxpayers are willing to pay the economic costs and accept the social frustrations to search every individual, every vehicle, and every container that crosses a U.S. border, drugs will find their way in.

In a globalized and decentralized market like that for illicit drugs, effective policy requires that all countries efficiently implement policies that have a reasonable chance for success. The imposition, coercion, and bullying inherent in punitive and deterrent unilateral strategies only work as long as the powerful country has intimate knowledge of what is going on in the foreign country and is willing to devote the necessary resources to constantly monitoring it and following through on threatened sanctions. Because other foreign policy concerns, including national security, usually have greater priority than illegal drugs, in most cases the credibility of the coercion begins to dissipate shortly after the unilateral policy has been announced. Even in the case of Panama, which the United States ostensibly invaded in 1989 to clean up the drug trade, the threat of U.S. punitive action has not been sufficient to dramatically reduce its attractiveness to drug traffickers and money launderers. It remains on the list of countries that are problematic and subject to the certification threat every year.

One attraction of prohibition and deterrent strategies is the greater ease of blaming another country for the drug problem. Yet these policies are inherently unlikely to produce much decrease in drug consumption. More than likely, they will only serve to maintain the high value of the commodity and therefore contribute to attracting newcomers to replace those that are arrested, killed, or retire from the business. Latin Americans have long believed that the violence and corruption associated with the drug trade that wracks their countries is fundamentally the result of the riches to be gained from selling these products in the Untied States, not in Latin America. As Colombian author and Nobel Laureate Gabriel Garcia Marquez noted, the best hope for Colombia is that American chemists synthesize cocaine and thus take the market away from Colombia.[9]

Cooperative International Policies

Cooperative international policies to deal with the PASCS can take a variety of forms, from bilateral cooperation between two states to regional cooperation involving a geographically defined set of countries (e.g., "inter-American," meaning states in the Western Hemisphere) to truly global cooperation as in the case of the UN or other international institutions.

Bilateral cooperation may be the best for preserving the specific bargaining strengths of the two parties. Both sides must prefer bilateral cooperation, however, or the situation will switch to either unilateral imposition by one country or multilateral negotiations as other parties become involved. Such coalition building against stronger nations is not always desirable. Adding more parties does allow one side to beef up its bargaining power, but it also lessens the potential benefits a member of the alliance might receive. This is because any benefits won in the bargaining must be divided among all members of the alliance and because the bargaining itself may yield more costs than if the cooperation had remained bilateral.

An example of just such a situation is the bilateral relationship of the United States with individual countries in Latin America, despite the fact that an alternative cooperation vehicle is available in the OAS, of which all Latin American countries, Canada, and the United States are members. The Latin American governments criticize U.S. pressure on them to adopt punitive measures to deal with illegal drugs. Yet most continue to bargain bilaterally with the United States even though they might be able to bargain more effectively if they presented a united front. When they do choose to cooperate amongst themselves to oppose the U.S. approach, the agreements generally are not followed through, mostly because the major producing and trafficking countries seek to use the threat of collective Latin American action to benefit from direct bilateral negotiations with the United States.

Most Latin American nations also choose to continue bilateral negotiations because they perceive that they have special bargaining chips with the United States. For instance, Mexico is an immediate neighbor, Bolivia is the poorest South American country, Peru was battling a radical insurgency in the 1980s and early 1990s, and Colombia is a long-standing democracy and home of the cocaine trade. These nations feel that the impact of these bargaining chips would be diminished in a general alliance.

Box 7.1 **Andean Cooperation Plan for the Control of Illegal Drugs and Related Offenses**

"The Andean Community Member Countries have committed themselves to take the necessary measures to come to grips with the world drug problem, bearing in mind the principles of shared responsibility, non-conditionality, and prioritization of alternative development, which require comprehensive and balanced management of both the control of the supply and the reduction of the demand.

"This war on the production, trafficking, distribution and misuse of psychotropic substances and related offenses is being waged in keeping with the principles of international law, particularly those of full respect for the sovereignty and territorial integrity of the States, non-intervention in their internal affairs, human rights, basic freedoms, and the rejection of unilateral actions detrimental to the course of relations between countries."

SOURCE: Andean Community, General Secretariat, Common Foreign Policy, www.comunidadandina.org/ingles/common/drugs.htm.

Another interesting subregional relationship is that among Holland and France, Germany, and Belgium, again within the context of a multilateral relationship, the European Union. The Dutch decriminalization policy for marijuana irritated the French government, which believed that French youth traveled to Holland to buy drugs and bring them home. France demanded that the Dutch repeal decriminalization and threatened not to implement the EU treaty on opening borders unless the Dutch responded. Holland's government refused to repeal a policy—harm reduction and separating the soft and hard drug markets (see Chapter Nine)—it believed worked. The Dutch did, however, remain open to talks with their French counterparts. In the end the Dutch dramatically decreased the amount of marijuana that could be sold in cafes from thirty grams to five grams and the French eased up on border controls.[10]

Europeans have not only sought cooperative solutions to their internal disagreements over drug policy, they have been very cooperative with Latin American drug control efforts as well. These cooperative efforts usually avoid the punitive measures favored by the United States, especially that of using the military for crop eradication and interdiction efforts. Instead, the two groups of nations find common ground in pursuing increased information on drugs, nonpunitive demand reduction, and harm reduction, as well as concrete efforts to promote cooperative efforts at the city-to-city level.[11]

One might hypothesize that because the Europeans understand the limits of a government's ability to "control" the drug trade, they do not view the fact that illegal drugs continue to be produced in and exported from Latin America as grounds for questioning Latin America's interest in cooperating to decrease the drug trade as much as possible. The United States, on the other hand, believes that a total victory over the drug trade is possible—"Drug-Free America!" and "Zero Tolerance!" are its battle cries. Consequently, the United States sees the continuation of the drug trade as a result of a combination of lack of political will, weak state authority, and corruption. The U.S. response, therefore, is to pressure for more political will, build up the police power of governments and sanction corruption; the resulting ill-will with Latin America is perceived to be just a short term cost on the road to victory.

Whether (or how much) nations agree or disagree, global cooperation on drugs has been around since the 1909 Shanghai Convention brought thirteen nations together to discuss regulating the opium trade. (See Box 7.2.) Today, the UN provides the best international forum for drug policy cooperation because of the large number of countries represented and the ability of the organization to collect information, evaluate it, and make recommendations regarding policy. In the area of psychoactive substances, the UN has been a player since 1946, when the organization created the UN Commission on Narcotic Drugs (UNCND) to coordinate its efforts. Its role was further enhanced when the General Assembly established the Fund of the United Nations International Drug Control Programme (UNDCP). European countries provide the majority of funding for the UNDCP, with Italy being especially generous.[12]

Further development proceeded in the wake of a booming international trade in illegal substances. In 1997 the UN Office on Drugs and Crime (UNODC), headquartered in Vienna with twenty-one field offices around the world, was created to deal not only with drugs but also with international crime, specifically terrorism and human trafficking (e.g., international prostitution and illegal migration). The office takes a prohibitionist approach to drugs, which is conveyed through reports about the dangers of illicit drugs and the extent of the drug trade. The Commission on Narcotic Drugs (CND) is under its purview; its chief task is to keep abreast of developments in the drug trade and present proposals for fighting drugs to the UN General Assembly.[13]

Although Europeans are very active internationally, they do not always agree with each other. During the 1990 World Ministerial Summit, the Dutch pushed for a reduced focus on law enforcement and increased attention on self-control and social control policies. In particular, they advocated decriminalization of marijuana as part of a drug control strategy. At that time the Dutch were largely abandoned by their European counterparts, who preferred an approach more in tune with the U.S. position focused on legal deterrents and punishment.[14] Today, the Dutch have the pleasure of seeing a large portion of Europe moving in their direction as domestic political forces tire of the costs of a prohibitionist strategy and instead seek ways to reduce the harm associated with the ubiquity of illegal psychoactive substances.

The International Politics of Plan Colombia

"Plan Colombia: Plan for Peace, Prosperity, and the Strengthening of the State" illustrates both bilateral and multilateral forms of cooperation and reveals some strengths and weaknesses of each.[15] The United States has a long-standing interest in Colombian drug production as it was a major source of first the marijuana, then the cocaine, and now the heroin consumed in the United States. Europe has had less interest in Colombia: Europeans view marijuana as a less threatening substance than other psychoactive substances, Europe's heroin comes largely from Asia, and Europeans came later to the cocaine market than did U.S. consumers. Latin American countries have long viewed Colombian drug production and trafficking as something best ignored, lest its destabilizing aspects spill over into neighboring countries.

During the 1980s and 1990s, the Colombian government essentially was involved in two civil wars, a long-standing one against leftist guerrillas and a more recent one against the Medellín and Cali drug cartels. Over the years, the Colombian government has participated in a variety of international efforts to control exports of illegal drugs from its territories as well as to solve its civil war. It has also been subject to unilateral action by the United States, which decertified Colombia in 1996 because of links between President Ernesto Samper's electoral campaign and drug barons. In 1989, Colombia successfully

Box 7.2   **Some Major International Conferences and Conventions**

1909 Shanghai Conference: involved 13 countries; call for control of opium and derivatives

1911 Opium Conference at the Hague: drafted first treaty attempting to control opium and cocaine through worldwide agreement

1912 Hague Opium Convention: parties agreed to limit the manufacture, trade, and use of opiate and cocaine products to medical use; to cooperate in order to restrict use and to enforce restrictions efficiently; to penalize possession; and to prohibit selling to unauthorized persons; also called for study of "Indian hemp" (marijuana)

1925 Second International Opium Convention: became effective in 1928; established a system of import certificates and export authorizations for the licit international trade in narcotic drugs

1931 Convention for Limiting the Manufacture and Regulating the Distribution of Narcotic Drugs: introduced a compulsory estimates system aimed at limiting the world manufacture of drugs to the amounts needed for medical and scientific purposes

1946 United Nations Commission on Narcotic Drugs: creation of the central policymaking body within UN, which "analyses the world drug situation and develops proposals to strengthen the international drug control system to combat the world drug problem"

1948 Paris Protocol: ceded to the World Health Organization the power to determine which new drugs should be treated as "dangerous drugs" for the purpose of the 1931 Convention

1961 Single Convention on Narcotic Drugs amended by 1972 Protocol: stress placed on the need for treatment and rehabilitation services; involved 180 countries; consolidated and further extended control over the international and domestic drug trades; limited possession, use, trade, distribution, import, export, manufacture, and production of drugs exclusively for medical purposes; combated drug trafficking through international cooperation

1971 Convention on Psychotropic Substances: involved 175 countries; extended international controls to broad range of synthetic behavior- and mood-altering drugs

1988 United Nations Convention against Illicit Traffic in Narcotic Drugs and Psychotropic Substances: involved 169 countries; addressed money laundering and precursor chemicals

1990 World Ministerial Drug Summit: sponsored by the United Kingdom and backed by the UN; 112 countries attended

protested U.S. plans to station a naval task force off the Colombian coast to monitor and intercept ships and planes heading for the United States.

With the peace process stagnating, the drug trade booming, and violence escalating, incoming president Andrés Pastrana developed a new vision for tackling the challenge. Plan Colombia was a complex and balanced strategy to bring peace and prosperity to the country by promoting alternative development, reforms of the Colombian government and judicial system, and the eradication of illegal drugs. The plan foresaw a budget of US$7.5 billion, of which Colombia committed to providing US$4 billion and appealed for international support for the remainder.

The Clinton administration and the U.S. Congress held discussions to determine how the United States would participate in Plan Colombia. Congress was more leery of becoming involved in Colombia's civil war than was the executive branch, but it did wish to fight illegal drug production and trafficking. Ultimately, the United States created its own vision of Plan Colombia and funded it with US$1.3 billion. Rather than equal funding to each area of the plan, the U.S. version provided 81.5 percent of the money for counternarcotics efforts (74 percent in Colombia and 7.5 percent in neighboring countries) and only 18.5 percent for human rights and humanitarian assistance, alternative development, and judicial reform. The U.S. version of the plan also included funding to help neighboring countries deal with any potential spillovers of the fight against drugs in Colombia.[16] The Colombian government, recognizing that the bulk of any international funds would come from the United States, acquiesced and adopted a Plan Colombia that was significantly more punitively oriented than originally conceived.

The European Parliament discussed and opposed the U.S. version of Plan Colombia by a vote of 474 to 1, with thirty-three abstentions. Most of the European governments involved believed that the U.S. drug war approach had greatly influenced the strategy, skewing it toward a militaristic focus that not only would not produce peace nor eradicate drugs in Colombia, but would become a potential threat to the stability of Colombia's neighbors. Leery of U.S. confidence in a military solution, the Europeans chose to fund the nonmilitary and nonpolice aspects of Plan Colombia, sending aid for social and economic assistance projects and insisting upon respect for human rights.[17]

Latin American governments criticized the U.S.-modified Plan Colombia but were very silent on how they could cooperate with the Colombian government. Some, like Ecuador and more recently Panama, immediate neighbors of Colombia, accepted U.S. military aid as a means of diminishing the "threat" from Colombia. Most have preferred to discuss demand reduction and small arms regulations at international conferences rather than become directly involved in the standoff between the Colombian government and guerrillas.[18]

The debate about what Plan Colombia has actually accomplished still rages. Its supporters note that thousands of acres of coca have been sprayed, there is at least a temporary decline in acreage devoted to coca in the targeted zones of Putumayo, Caquetá, and Guaviare, and the paramilitaries are close to negotiating a peace with the government.[19] Detractors point out that coca production is climbing back up in Bolivia and Peru and has extended into new areas in Colombia. Cocaine labs also have been found in Bolivia, which had previously only been a supplier of raw material. Peace negotiations with the main rebel group, the Fuerzas Armadas Revolucionarias de Colombia (FARC), are not back on track, and the paramilitants might not be tried for their human rights violations, even as they appear to maintain their involvement in the drug trade.[20]

Summary

Why do countries cooperate on international drug policy or choose to go it alone? The harms inherent in the substances cannot answer this question, as it is political. The four analytical perspectives provide ways of explaining that international policy choice.

From a social deviance perspective, deviant countries are not able to advance their interests by playing by the rules and violate those international norms in the expectation that they will be able to achieve their goals. Analysts using a deviance perspective could focus on governments as the deviants or look for the fault in a national culture.

With respect to the question of international cooperation, social deviance analysts could accept that nondeviant countries will not necessarily cooperate with others internationally—they might be able to accomplish their goals acting alone. But if a nondeviant nation cannot succeed alone, it should be able to cooperate easily with other nondeviant countries because their word and signature are true representations of their intentions. No one has to worry about anyone shirking responsibility or cheating on the agreement. Whether deviant countries are able to cooperate depends on whether their deviancies are complementary or competitive. But one should not expect to see cooperation between deviants and nondeviants. By their very nature, deviants constitute a threat to the norm. In addition, nondeviants seek to behave in nondeviant ways and accomplish nondeviant outcomes; consequently, nondeviants can't agree to behave deviantly nor can they trust the deviant to behave in an acceptably nondeviant manner.

Constructivists would hypothesize that the ideas a policymaker's constituents hold about the advantages of cooperation will be the fundamental determinant of whether a state pursues unilateral or cooperative international policies. If people perceive that illegal drugs are an international phenomenon and that solutions will require cooperation, a country will cooperate—even if acting unilaterally could provide short-term benefits or there is a chance that a partner might engage in small-scale cheating on the agreement. Alternatively, a constructivist could argue that if people believe that national security takes precedence over cooperation and see drugs as an issue of national security, cooperation with others will be very difficult, because of the competitive nature of traditional views of national security.

Rational choice analysts see cooperation as a second-best solution: they believe that the international realm contains many potential points around which states can fruitfully cooperate, but also many obstacles that must be overcome even among countries that desire to cooperate. Because of all of the potential points of disagreement among countries and the accountability of policymakers to their constituencies, the ideal policy for political leaders would be the one they have developed to meet their constituencies' needs.

Working with others at the international level necessarily implies becoming involved in a two-level game in which political leaders try to negotiate compromises with their international counterparts that are acceptable to their domestic constituencies. Each of these adjustments entails, by definition, a move away from a leader's ideal policy. Hence, cooperation is not a first choice. If the desired outcome is unattainable acting alone, however, a leader is expected to seek out cooperation with other states. Leaders who fear constituents' response if cooperation fails to yield promised benefits or generates unforeseen costs may still cooperate if unilateral action is difficult or costly and international institutions provide a framework to facilitate cooperation.

As noted in Chapter Two, realism assumes that international politics occurs in a context in which no set of rules is binding on all states—a condition of anarchy—and thus subjugation or elimination of states is a constant possibility. This context forces states to mistrust each other on matters that could affect their ability to survive, thrive, and make policy decisions that respond to their own best interests. As a result, power is the chief currency in international politics, and cooperation on important matters will be limited to immediate self-interest and therefore be short-lived and unlikely to be fully adhered to by any nation. From the realist perspective, cooperation should be rare and often merely rhetorical.

These hypotheses are summarized in Table 2.2, found on page 33 of Chapter Two.

STUDY QUESTIONS

1. What goals would you have for international policy on psychoactive substances? Why?
2. Identify some unilateral policies and their goals. Did they make progress toward achieving those goals? Why was it possible or not possible to make progress acting unilaterally?
3. Identify a cooperative international policy on some aspect of the trade in illicit drugs. Reference the table of hypotheses for international policies in the introduction to Part II. Which hypotheses do you think best reflect the logic of that cooperation? Why? Which do you think is least useful? Why?

Chapter 8 **The United States**
From Crime Reduction to
Drug War, 1968–1982

Summary

In the 1960s a number of factors jolted the country's psyche: the civil rights movement, the "hippie" counterculture movement, the Vietnam War, race riots, and a rise in crime. In this context, drug use became an issue of public policy. President Lyndon B. Johnson created the Bureau of Narcotics and Dangerous Drugs (BNDD) in 1968 to spur cooperation among the disparate federal agencies responsible for various aspects of drug control. The Johnson administration, however, was unable to incorporate the FBI in the new efforts because J. Edgar Hoover worried about the corrupting influence so much cash might have on agents working undercover.[1]

When Johnson decided not to run for reelection in the wake of the Tet Offensive, a major setback in Vietnam, he left it up to his successor to address the public's new concern over illicit drugs. Richard Nixon focused on heroin and its relationship to crime; his administration implemented an important methadone program that provided benefits for both crime and harm reduction. The administrations of Gerald Ford and Jimmy Carter continued such programs and started moving toward a harm reduction focus by advocating the decriminalization of marijuana. In this policy development the federal government was following the lead of a number of state governments.

By the end of Carter's term, however, policy had shifted toward a strategy that emphasized interdiction. Ronald Reagan pursued this change vigorously, focusing on prohibition and targeting producers, suppliers, and users. He promoted a punitive policy that culminated in a drug war strategy, expanded efforts to control supply from foreign sources, and limited government responsibility for reducing harm to users and society.

Background

Prohibitionist strategies for dealing with psychoactive substances have a long history in the United States. Originally focused on alcohol, prohibitionists at the local level were expressions of nineteenth-century social reform movements that included antislavery and women's rights. Because alcohol was blamed for such social ills as unemployment, poverty, slums, insanity, crime, and violence, the major movement of the emerging middle class was alcohol prohibition.[2]

Although a number of state governments, beginning with Maine in 1847, outlawed alcohol, the U.S. federal government maintained a laissez-faire policy toward psychoactive substances until the early twentieth century. The Anti-Saloon League and the women's temperance movement combined efforts to help propel the nation to alcohol prohibition in 1919. Advocates expected Prohibition to reform the morality of drinkers, improve household economies, bring families closer together, and remove the influence of the alcohol industry on politics. Until its repeal in 1933, the Eighteenth Amendment banned the production, distribution, and sale of alcoholic beverages, except for that contained in patent medicines, prescribed by physicians and hospitals, or used in sacramental wine.[3]

Prohibition can be considered a mass movement; the outlawing of opiates (including heroin) and cocaine by the 1914 Harrison Act cannot. Rather than being domestically driven, this prohibition was sparked by a desire to align U.S. policy with the growing international movement to outlaw these substances.[4] It was also spurred by the personal commitment of Henry Anslinger, a man who would dominate U.S. drug policy for almost half a century.[5]

Marijuana was effectively banned in 1937 when high taxes were imposed at each stage of the psychoactive substance commodity system (PASCS). The level of taxation priced the drug out of the market while allowing the federal government to pursue the drug's adherents for tax evasion. State governments had already taken this step by 1936.[6] What all of this meant was that, for the next thirty years, drug policy receded into the background of national politics, largely perceived by mainstream America as a problem of minority youth that was being taken care of by law enforcement.

The Context for Modern U.S. Drug Policy

Social and Economic Characteristics. The United States is a geographically large country with a large population spread across cities and towns and everywhere in between. This large population is also ethnically diverse; yet for years, the racial classification of "white" continued to dominate the public consciousness. The 1954 Supreme Court decision that "separate but equal is inherently unequal" combined with social and economic changes produced by economic growth in a modern economy to create dramatic social instability in the form of the Civil Rights Movement during the 1960s. The southern states, where a social caste system had existed for centuries and continued even in the wake of the Civil War and Reconstruction, experienced the violent disruptions first. Racial violence soon followed in the states of the North and West, which had supported civil rights in the South, when the Congress and courts ordered racial desegregation to be applied in regard to education and housing nationally.

The pace of change experienced in society was matched by the rate of economic change. The economy had developed rapidly after the Second World War, creating a large middle class yet leaving a sizeable group in the lower working class and below the poverty line. In the 1960s, the economy began to experience inflation as a result of large federal expenditures for the maintenance of a global U.S. military presence to contain communism. Money was also being committed to support the Vietnam War and fund Johnson's "Great Society" social welfare programs, which were designed to assist the large portion of the population below the poverty line. In order to diminish opposition to these national policies, they were not financed by tax increases. Instead, the government printed and funneled more money into the economy. Soon, the value of the dollar fell, and it took more and more money to buy the same amount of product. Ultimately the U.S. dollar would devalue by 10 percent in 1971; convertibility of the dollar into gold would also end in 1973.

Political Characteristics. The United States is a constitutional democracy, with power divided among three branches of government: the legislature, the executive, and the judiciary. The legislature is divided into two houses. Members of the House of Representatives are elected by local district, whereas members of the Senate are elected by state. Because even the least populated states have two senators whose votes count equally with those of senators from densely populated states, the system overrepresents the interests of local voters in sparsely populated states while underrepresenting the interests of voters in large cities. Only presidents are elected by national vote, yet not even they are chosen directly. The delegates in the electoral college actually choose the president. The United States is a decentralized polity, with some powers explicitly granted to the federal government, and the states retaining all other powers. The winner-take-all electoral system influences voters to support the two parties most likely to win, which currently are the Democratic and Republican Parties. This creates a fairly stable two-party system at the federal level.

Distribution of Political Power. In the 1960s, the Democrats achieved their greatest influence at the federal level since Franklin D. Roosevelt's New Deal days in the 1930s. They controlled both houses of Congress and Johnson had won in a landslide in 1964 against Barry Goldwater, a Republican perceived by many as a right-wing radical. But the quagmire of Vietnam, the expense of the Great Society programs, the political and cultural rebellion of middle-class youth, and race riots were frightening the large middle class. Richard Nixon rode this angst of the "Silent Majority" to the presidency in 1968, but Democrats retained control of the Congress.

Pyschoactive Substance Use. The social norms against illegal drugs were breaking down amid the social upheavals of the 1960s. Marijuana seemed to be everywhere, from rock concerts to college dorms to high school dances. LSD and methamphetamines were popular among subgroups, with heroin beginning to attract more users as the decade closed.

Crime Reduction: 1970–1974

The drug on most people's minds in the 1960s was marijuana, and it was largely associated with counterculture youth in the big city; "hard" drugs were generally associated with the poor and minorities. However, the fall of 1969 brought big news on the drug front when the daughter of Art Linkletter, a major TV personality in Middle America, killed herself while on LSD. The Nixon administration held a bipartisan meeting at the White House with Linkletter in attendance. At the meeting, the president announced that drugs were no longer a menace simply to the poor. Linkletter declared that his daughter "was not a hippie ... was not a drug addict ... [but] a well-educated, intelligent girl from a family that has traditionally been a Christian family and has been straight."

Richard Nixon had campaigned in 1968 as a Republican and won the support of mainstream America with his simple promise to end the Vietnam War with "peace and honor." He loathed the counterculture movement, and was not beyond slighting blacks and Jews if he saw it as necessary. But he was also a realist, a political leader who believed in the national interest and was willing to take bold measures to promote it. To further those goals, he and his secretary of state Henry Kissinger opened relations with Communist China and widened the Vietnam War to Cambodia in an effort to "bomb the Vietnamese communists to the negotiating table."

Nixon also campaigned as a "law and order" candidate. He argued that crime had been allowed to rise because Democratic policymakers focused on the underlying societal causes of crime rather than the actual behavior of the criminals. To that end, his camp began dispensing data that linked drugs and property crime; no matter that these figures were substantially higher than those collected by the Department of Justice and as such were little more than political rhetoric. Nixon promised a new approach, one in which criminals would be held accountable for their actions. He vowed to increase the ability of law enforcement to fight illegal drugs at home and abroad.

The Democratic Congress was not willing to let Nixon get all the credit for being tough on crime. Working with the White House, it passed a new bill that gave law enforcement additional tools to go after illegal drugs. The Comprehensive Drug Abuse Prevention and Control Act of 1970 placed narcotic and other drugs under federal jurisdiction. It closed a loophole in previous marijuana legislation by outlawing it directly. Alcohol and nicotine were omitted from the bill, presumably because their legal status kept their health-related issues off the crime policy agenda. Per the act, a drug was to be regulated according to five criteria: pharmacological actions, other scientific knowledge about it and related drugs, risk to public health, dependence (psychological or physiologic) potential, and whether the drug was a gateway to other drugs listed.

As the federal drug war stepped up a notch, the United States was entering one of its periodic heroin epidemics. Heroin was beginning to command national attention. Although it had traditionally been perceived as a drug used by poor black males in major urban areas with few repercussions for the middle class, the press, both print and television, began to carry stories about a growing heroin menace. The medical profession was increasingly turning its attention to the drug as well; it was during this period that Peter Bourne, a psychiatrist and Jimmy Carter's future drug policy chief, published his analysis of the process by which college students in Middle America were becoming attracted to the drug.[7]

When Nixon's staff discovered a study that reported that 44 percent of those incarcerated in Washington, D.C., jails had been using heroin at the time of their arrest, the Nixon administration used this as further evidence that drug use produced crime. No one seemed to care that correlation and causation had not been distinguished in the article.[8] Washington, D.C., was not the murder capital of the country in the 1960s and 1970s, but there was a great deal of other crime. Since the District of Columbia is under the jurisdiction of the federal government, federal policy could be quickly implemented and experimented with there. (Most crime falls under state, not federal, jurisdiction).

There was no question that crime and drugs were intimately connected in Nixon's mind and in that of a majority of the U.S. public. A June 1971 Gallup poll placed drugs third on the list of most serious problems, after Vietnam and the economy.[9] Nixon believed that rhetoric and seizures of drugs were not sufficient to produce a real difference in the status quo. Once, when briefed about the amount of drugs seized coming into the United States and the number of people arrested, Nixon inquired, "Let me ask you this, are we taking one step forward and two steps back? Is there any less narcotics coming into the United States? Are we solving the problem?"[10]

Despite Nixon's fierce opposition to drugs and generally prohibitionist orientation, his administration's approach to heroin modified after Republican representative Robert Steele of Connecticut and Democratic representative Morgan Murphy of Illinois returned from Vietnam in 1971 with horrifying stories of soldiers addicted to the heroin that was readily available throughout the region. Nixon worried that the country would now add addiction to the threat of dying in battle and would demand an immediate end to the war. (U.S. involvement in the war would not come to a negotiated end until 1973.) The Pentagon dealt with this problem by effectively decriminalizing consumption in order to encourage soldiers to undergo treatment at the end of their tours of duty and before returning to the United States.[11]

Nixon created a new group of agencies to develop and implement the primary focus of his administration's drug strategy: reduce crime associated with heroin. At the June 1971 press conference announcing the creation of the Special Action Office for Drug Abuse Prevention (SAODAP), he declared that drugs were America's number one enemy. His advisors were professional medical people; his drug chief and the head of SAODAP were both psychiatrists. They were to examine the drug issue from a medical perspective of associated harms, while Nixon and his political advisors considered its political ramifications.

The result of such federal activity was that crime associated with drug activity did fall dramatically. After having risen nearly 30 percent from 1969 to

1971, in 1972 the national crime rate fell by 3 percent, with declines of 27 percent in Washington, D.C., and 18 percent in New York. Death, emergency room visits, and cases of hepatitis C related to drugs were all down as well. Arrests fell as crime rates fell and treatment numbers rose.[12]

Treatment proved to be an answer from which both crime- and drug-focused groups could benefit. During the Nixon administration, 67–80 percent of the drug budget was spent on treatment and rehabilitation; the nonpunitive harm reduction aspects of U.S. drug policy have not been as favored since.[13] In New York, a new treatment for heroin addicts—methadone—was being promoted. Researchers found that when the synthetic drug was administered orally to addicts their cravings subsided, permitting them to function as normally as they had before becoming addicted. Methadone also was dispensed in professional medical settings in which trained personnel could provide counseling to those in need. It quickly became an important means of addressing the heroin problem. Unfortunately, two-thirds of the federally funded slots in treatment programs were drug-free, not maintenance programs; consequently, only a small part of federal treatment funding could be used to support methadone treatment.[14]

Treatment was not Nixon's only policy for drugs. He promoted the interdiction of supplies of marijuana and heroin in Turkey, Europe, and Mexico. Providing extensive aid to the military government in Turkey and working with the French virtually eliminated the flow of heroin from Turkey to France to the United States. His administration almost closed the border with Mexico (Operation Intercept) to force the government to spray Mexican poppy fields with the herbicide paraquat.

In 1971, Nixon appointed a presidential commission to advise him on national marijuana policy; the perception among his nonmedical advisors was that the commission's report would end the nonsensical talk of legalization/decriminalization. Chaired by retired Republican governor Raymond Shafer of Pennsylvania, its members were perceived to be drug hawks. Rumors, however, leaked that the commission would recommend legalizing marijuana, and Nixon told the press that he would ignore such a recommendation. Later, when the director of the National Institute of Mental Health suggested in a speech that marijuana offenses should get minimal civil penalties, Nixon fired him. Notwithstanding the president's views, the commission's report concluded that the harm caused by making marijuana illegal outweighed the harm caused by the drug. Nixon, true to his word, ignored the report.

Nixon's marijuana commission and his drug policy leaders weren't the only people considering the need to reform the marijuana laws in regard to consumption. State governments were adopting harm reduction policies on marijuana use. Decriminalization was adopted in eleven states between 1972 and 1978. Another thirty-three states replaced imprisonment with probation, permitting arrest records to be erased after as few as six months.[15] Traffickers, however, were still seen as criminals to be punished.

The increasing legitimacy of the idea of legalizing marijuana not only spurred a national commission, it also generated a new lobby in Washington.[16] The National Organization for the Reform of Marijuana Laws (NORML) became a major participant in policy debates, even testifying before Congress and Nixon's special committee. The press often went to NORML for a reaction whenever opponents of marijuana legalization produced a new study or policy proposal.

Studies and reports cost money to generate, but the money diverted to these was tiny compared to that spent on drug programs as a whole. In 1973, federal spending on treatment and prevention totaled $420 million. Granted, this is a drop in the bucket when placed against the $18–20 billion the federal government spent annually on drug programs beginning in the late 1990s. Nevertheless, it was still an increase of more than 800 percent from the amount spent in 1969. At least two-thirds of the federal budget went toward reducing demand.[17]

But the beginning of the end to this crime reduction merged with harm reduction strategy showed itself at the height of the Nixon administration's successes on the drug front. Despite the dramatic decrease in crime rates, voters continued to worry. New York's Republican governor, Nelson D. Rockefeller, announced in his annual address the need for measures he described as "drastic" to fight drugs, such as mandatory minimum sentencing for drug dealing, including life in prison. The federal government had just repealed mandatory minimums in 1970, but with two-thirds of New Yorkers supporting the governor's proposal, politicians took notice.[18]

Harm Reduction Stillborn: 1975–1980

In the end, the same traits that got Nixon elected contributed to his eventual downfall. He perceived his 1972 reelection to be so important to the nation that he committed criminal acts to ensure it. What came to be known as the Watergate scandal would shake voters' confidence in political figures to an unprecedented degree that is arguably still felt today.

Gerald Ford assumed office when Richard Nixon resigned. Ford made an important shift in Nixon's national drug strategy: instead of being a means to reduce crime, treatment for heroin addicts became the goal. His drug policy advisors produced a 1975 review (known as a "White Paper") on drug abuse in the United States. This review called for a "realistic" drug policy that focused on heroin and large-scale traffickers while arguing that "We should stop raising expectations of total elimination of drug abuse from our society."[19] The president subsequently delivered a special message to the Congress on drug abuse, in which he called for increased and mandatory penalties against drug traffickers but ended by describing drug abuse as "an enemy we can control, not as one that we could defeat."[20]

In the same report, cocaine was discussed, prophetically, as relatively unharmful "as currently used...." Limited to those with extremely high incomes who could afford it—it cost around $1,000 an ounce at the time—cocaine was perceived more as a rich person's plaything than as a threat to the United States. Wealthy individuals wouldn't lose their jobs simply because they used it, and they were able to afford expensive rehabilitation if they slipped into dependency.[21]

Following the review of drug strategy in the 1975 White Paper, the 1976 Federal Drug Strategy report set the administration's direction for the drug issue. The report distinguished between the reality of drug use and the perception of how much of a problem an individual's drug use is for society. For the first time in federal drug policy since the end of Prohibition, alcohol was discussed. It was called "the most widely used drug in the United States today" and was charged with "more deaths and injuries than any other drug."[22] The report also called for "seriously studying" marijuana decriminalization, a policy option previously recommended by Nixon's national commission on marijuana, but rejected by Nixon.[23] Despite acknowledging that alcohol, a legal drug, harms and kills more people than illegal drugs, and despite adding study of decriminalization of marijuana to the drug agenda, the Ford administration's report outlined plans to enhance vigorous enforcement of drug laws and punishment of traffickers.

Consistent with a primary focus on enforcement, funds for treatment did not increase. Nixon had used the drug budget to treat heroin addicts because of the linkage between veterans and heroin use; the Ford administration increased the enforcement budget in order to put more effort into the interdiction of heroin before it arrived in the country. In 1976, the money spent on enforcement equaled that spent on treatment and prevention for the first time.[24]

Despite the growing focus on enforcement, marijuana decriminalization continued to be a legitimate topic during the Ford administration. Robert DuPont, drug chief and director of the National Institute on Drug Abuse (NIDA) during the Nixon administration, speaking at NORML's annual convention in 1974, proclaimed law and health to be two separate issues and advocated the end of incarceration of marijuana users. John Erlichman, one of Nixon's closest advisors, told a congressional committee that the federal government's "massive war ... on narcotics is only going to be effective at the margins.... Maybe we can use the money some other way." The chief counsel for the Drug Enforcement Agency (DEA) provided an opinion that the United States could decriminalize marijuana without violating any international treaties against drugs. The *Washington Post* wrote an editorial favoring the reform, and presidential candidate Jimmy Carter spoke out in support of it.

After winning the 1976 election, President Carter shifted the focus back on treatment and rehabilitation in his national drug strategy. Psychiatrist Peter Bourne, who had also earned a Bronze Star in Vietnam and been a founder of Vietnam Veterans Against the War, became his drug czar. Bourne perceived few health-related dangers in marijuana or the new drug making the rounds among moneyed circles, cocaine. Like his predecessors, he thought heroin was the main threat and that harm reduction was the path to take. He did, however, worry about the potential impact of cocaine if its price became low enough to make the drug widely accessible.

Bourne favored legalizing marijuana; while campaigning, Carter had raised the concern that the penalties for using it were worse than the drug itself. Once in office, however, Carter worried that legalization might signal that using was okay. Others did not share his misgivings. Not only were states decriminalizing marijuana, the drug had spawned a business boom in which marijuana use was indirectly promoted. Shops on main street marketed associated paraphernalia, board games were developed in which players used marijuana, and comic books included it. Hollywood and the record industry were using the drug's popularity to promote new stars, including Cheech and Chong. In this context, Carter favored civil, rather than criminal, penalties for users while maintaining the tough policies on traffickers.

Undeniably, marijuana was getting some good press. Alcohol and prescription drugs, conversely, took it on the chin when former First Lady Betty Ford revealed in 1978 that she needed professional help to deal with her dependence on prescription drugs and alcohol.[25] Once again, drug addiction, not simply use, revealed itself as a problem of the elite, not simply the poor or rebellious youth.

The Carter administration did not ignore interdiction or enforcement issues. Nixon and Ford had scored successes against the heroin supply coming out of Turkey and Mexico. But other countries stepped in to fill the shortfall in U.S. supply, particularly Burma (today known as Myanmar), where a military government was fighting an ethnic insurgency. Both sides taxed the opium growers and traders. The insurgents, however, approached the United States with an intriguing proposition: if the United States would pay for the unprocessed opium, the rebels would burn it all before it got to market and was refined into heroin. But Peter Bourne refused to move in this radical new direction; instead the Burmese military government was provided with more military aid to fight drug trafficking and the insurgents.[26]

Carter's 1978 crime legislation significantly enhanced the ability of the police to fight illegal drugs by making the assets—bank accounts, boats, cars—procured with money made from crime subject to forfeiture and auction by the federal government. By making this a civil and not criminal provision, the assets could be constitutionally assumed to be ill-gotten until the owner proved the legitimacy of the funds used for purchase. Although the Carter administration did not pursue the full impact of this law, its mere passage was indicative of a changing attitude toward drug policy, one that would support increasing police powers as a means of protecting the nation against the drug threat.

Carter's efforts to maintain a drug policy that balanced decriminalization and treatment with interdiction and enforcement received a serious blow in 1978. Earlier that year, Bourne had been asked by an assistant for prescription medicine to relax because she was going through a personal crisis. As a psychiatrist who had criticized the easy availability of prescription drugs, Bourne worried about the negative publicity if the press discovered that he was writing prescriptions for coworkers. He provided a prescription for Quaaludes but told the woman to use a false name; when an auditor who happened to be at the pharmacy asked her for identification and she had none in the name of the prescription, the police were called.

Not surprisingly, the press had a field day when the story broke. To make matters worse, Bourne and other White House staffers were accused of smoking marijuana. The final straw came when the founder of NORML confirmed to the *Washington Post* that Carter's drug czar had snorted cocaine at the group's annual party. Bourne resigned, and Carter insisted to his entire staff that, if they wished to remain at the White House, the drug laws had to be obeyed even if one disagreed with them.

The Road to the Drug War

While Carter's drug policy team was self-destructing, a new social movement was fomenting in homes nationwide. It began when two parents in Atlanta, Georgia, became enraged when they discovered that their young children were smoking marijuana and that the social support system for youth, including school principals and counselors, classified such behavior as normal rebellion. The parents also became aware of the business world that thrived on promoting drug paraphernalia, stories, and games to young children.[27]

National surveys of school-age children and young adults now showed a major increase in marijuana use, as well as an increase in overall drug use. The annual Monitoring the Future (MTF) survey of high school students undertaken by researchers at the University of Michigan found that in 1978, 10 percent of seniors were smoking marijuana every day. It also reported that 72 percent of seniors had consumed alcohol within the past month, and that 40 percent had engaged in binge drinking (five or more drinks consumed in less than two hours). Both figures were far higher than the corresponding numbers for marijuana, but parents focused on the marijuana use as the primary problem.[28]

Parents across the nation rallied to protect their children against the specter of drug use and abuse. For many, the right of adults to use marijuana was an issue that had to be subordinated to shielding children from temptations they were too young to understand. These parental concerns spread like wildfire, producing a national movement that demanded health care professionals be stripped of their influence over national drug policy and be replaced by people who focused on the moral questions concerning drug use and the vulnerability of children, regardless of their professional training.

Parents Resource Institute for Drug Education (PRIDE) began collecting and disseminating information about the dangers of drug use and advocating the need for greater parental control over children. At the state and local level, parents and politicians responded, mobilizing against marijuana. State laws regulating the drug and drug paraphernalia began to proliferate.

Bourne's successor was his deputy Lee I. Dogoloff, a social worker with limited experience in dealing with drug addicts; he seems to have been selected because the disarray in the White House precluded searching for someone with more appropriate qualifications for the position. Looking for ways to address the drug issue, he was quickly influenced by parent groups who provided reams of information about the harms of marijuana and who presented emotional appeals about the dangers young children were facing as a result of the hold medical professionals had over national drug policy. Dogoloff became convinced that marijuana, not heroin, was the embodiment of the drug threat. Carter, too, in a fight for re-election, understood that public opinion on drugs was changing. Within a year, the White House unveiled its "Adolescent Drug Abuse Prevention Campaign" to discourage use of illicit drugs, particularly marijuana. And, in the administration's final drug policy report, Dogoloff concluded that

> A permissive societal attitude has posed particular difficulties for law enforcement officials and teachers in the performance of their duties, as well as for parents who are striving to impart the values and attitudes of responsible citizenship to their children.[29]

As the war clouds were gathering, treatment advocates got one last gasp of hope as the threat of a new epidemic began to reveal itself. Rising reports of addicts seeking treatment and being put on waiting lists pushed the White House into action. An emergency injection of $10 million was secured for treatment efforts; but with the inflation of the period even that input meant that treatment funds had fallen in real terms since Nixon's administration.[30]

Carter's presidential term, like the search for a way to live with the reality of the drug phenomenon, came to a close in shambles. Supporters of an Iranian revolution, identifying the United States as evil, seized the U.S. embassy in Tehran and took hostages; the Soviets invaded Afghanistan; the oil producers' cartel, OPEC, continued its grip on production and international distribution; and the U.S. economy faltered in the face of a shaky dollar. All of this confused, frightened, and angered the voting public. Carter's call for the United States to recognize the limits of its power and live within its means fell on deaf ears.

Ronald Reagan campaigned in 1980 on a platform that promised to renew the greatness of the United States. He and his advisors articulated the message that the country could achieve many things, including a cheap and reliable oil supply and a restructured and dynamic economy, if government would get out of the way and let people take care of their own lives. He did advocate a few legitimate roles for the federal government: win the cold war, make the United States powerful and respected once again, and limit crime. It was a program that resonated with the U.S. electorate and gave Reagan a landslide victory.

Methadone programs were immediately suspect in Reagan's new national drug strategy. Methadone was a drug itself, and Reagan's belief was that heroin addicts simply became dependent on methadone at the taxpayers' expense. Instead of treatment, deterrence became the means to solve the drug problem. In Reagan's first year, the law enforcement portion of the national drug budget rose 20 percent, while that for treatment fell 25 percent. When combined with Carter's stable drug budget, the result was that in 1981 the treatment budget was less than one-fourth the level of the budget in 1974.[31]

A changing focus of federal policy did not mean that marijuana stopped attracting the attention of parents. The National Academy of Sciences released the results of a multiyear study on marijuana in 1982, disputing claims of permanent brain or nervous system damage or decreases in fertility and calling for decriminalization. The report was denounced, then ignored. The Reagan administration was quite comfortable with the argument that there were no soft or hard drugs; all illegal drugs were inherently bad.

Instead, it moved forward with its prohibition agenda. First Lady Nancy Reagan brought the prestige of her office to the newly invigorated fight against drugs. She worked closely with parents to promote the message that the government could not solve the drug problem, but that families and communities could if they became involved. These early efforts exposed her to a broad spectrum of youthful ex-users and evolved into her "Just Say No" campaign as the war on drugs heated up in the mid-1980s.

Cocaine was becoming a topic of concern in the early 1980s, even before Peter Bourne's fear of the impact of a fall in its price came to pass. The profits from cocaine were sufficiently large that drug dealers began to fight in the streets over territory. Miami, Florida, was the city primarily affected by these territorial struggles because of its position on the transit route between Colombia and the United States, but many cities felt the heat from this new outbreak of crime. The press and Hollywood found the topic to be quite profitable, too, as they hawked stories more violent and lurid with each telling.[32]

In January 1982, the Reagan administration created the South Florida Task Force under the direction of Vice President George H. W. Bush. More than three hundred agents from different federal law enforcement agencies, supported by the U.S. Navy, were tasked to interdict marijuana. Instead, they discovered large quantities of cocaine being smuggled into the country. Despite this early warning, the DEA would not shift its focus from marijuana to cocaine until the mid-1980s, at the height of the cocaine epidemic.[33]

In June 1982, Reagan named Carlton Turner as director of the new Drug Abuse Policy Office. Invoking the bloody WWI battle at Verdun in France, Reagan said

> We can put drug abuse on the run through stronger law enforcement, through cooperation with other nations to stop the trafficking, and by calling on the tremendous volunteer resources of parents, teachers, civic and religious leaders, and State and local officials.... We're taking down the surrender flag that has flown over so many drug efforts. We're running up a battle flag.[34]

Drug policy now took a decidedly punitive turn. Funds for rehabilitation, even in prisons, were cut. Turner later explained the shift in policy:

> If people can afford to go out and buy cocaine, why should the government pay for their treatment?... This country has a problem accepting the fact that there are really bad people in society. We've got the belief that nobody's bad—that we can rehabilitate everybody.... I made a conscious decision that we were going to get rid of all the damned psychiatrists.[35]

Money went instead to pursue everyone involved in the illicit drug trade: consumers, traffickers, producers, and money launderers. Congress could read the writing on the wall of public opinion; it agreed with the president and changed the law. It did so over the Pentagon's reluctance to permit the armed forces to participate in domestic law enforcement activities. The Pentagon's budget for participation in the drug war went from $1 million to $196 million in five years.[36] State governments followed suit with their own punitive policies, supported by a massive infusion of funds. The Supreme Court began to ease restrictions on law enforcement and weaken protections for the accused.

The national data on drug use that accompanied these policy shifts showed a continuation of the downward trend for the appeal of marijuana that had begun in 1979. Past month use of any illicit drug also continued to fall for twelve- to twenty-five-year-olds. Although twenty-six- to thirty-four-year-olds experienced an increase in past month illicit drug use until the mid-1980s, this number fell as well after 1985.[37] All of these past month use rates dropped precipitously in the late 1980s until 1992, when they generally leveled off at rates lower than those found in the early 1970s. Ecstasy, Oxycontin, and methamphetamines were the exceptions; use of these drugs rose sufficiently fast to provoke stories and pronouncements of epidemics.

Accompanying this decline in marijuana use was a dramatic increase in the prison population at both the state and federal levels. Drug arrests increased by 72.4 percent from 1984 to 1989;[38] at the state level, the number of drug-related prisoners rose more than 1,000 percent from 1980 to 1992.[39] In California alone, the number of people in prison for violating drug laws increased from 5,116 in 1985 to 23,853 in 1990, and would double again in the 1990s.[40]

STUDY QUESTIONS

1. Begin by getting a sense of the entire case. Specifically, how did the focus of national drug policy change over time?
2. When did illicit drug use first attract national attention?
   - Was there any debate about how illegal drug use should be conceived, as socially deviant, alternative norms, individual choice, or threats to national security?

- Which important political actors held which views? What types of evidence did they present to support their position?
3. Once the drug issue got on the national agenda, what individuals or groups were given the task to design national drug policy?
   - What was the professional background of these individuals or the members of these groups?
   - Were there any disagreements among individuals, especially within specific groups? If so, were compromises reached or was common ground found?
   - What proposal was finally put forth? If there was more than one, why was this the case?
4. What individuals or groups needed to accept the proposed policy design in order for it to become national drug policy?
   - Were there any debates among these actors about the proposed policy? If so, what were they? If not, why not?
   - How did the policy that was accepted differ from the one that was proposed by the policy design group? Why did it differ?
5. Which groups benefited from the policy ultimately adopted and which groups paid the costs? What were the costs and benefits of the policy for society as a whole?

Answer the following questions for each change in national drug policy over time.

6. Why did the policy change? Consider:
   - Who objected to it?
   - Why did they object to it?
   - How they were able to influence officials so that a revision of national policy was made?
   - If the resulting change in policy provided the critics of the old policy with what they wanted. If not, why not?
7. Which groups benefited from the new policy and which groups paid the costs? What were the costs and benefits of the new policy to society as a whole?

Chapter 9 The Netherlands
From Drug War to Dynamic Harm Reduction, 1960–2002

Summary

Like other countries, Holland signed on to the major international treaties that, by the 1920s, outlawed opium, heroin, and cocaine.[1] Marijuana, however, had not been made a part of those treaties, and the Dutch ignored the drug, having little to no experience with it. In contrast to a number of other developed nations, the Dutch never outlawed alcohol.

However, the use of psychoactive substances other than alcohol and nicotine became a concern in the Netherlands in 1960 as consumption of these nontraditional substances increased. The Dutch national government initially adopted an active prohibitionist policy that included prison terms for marijuana consumers. Local governments subsequently began adopting harm reduction strategies, and national drug policy was reformed in 1976 along similar lines. Policies underwent further refinement in the 1990s in response to French and German protests about Dutch policy and the increasing demand for Ecstasy. Policy, nevertheless, remained firmly rooted in a harm reduction paradigm that subsequently recognized the need for vigilance because new drugs and new circumstances meant new harms.

The Context for Modern Dutch Drug Policy

Social and Economic Characteristics. Holland is geographically small, about the size of South Carolina, with a medium-sized population. Consequently, the nation has the greatest population density in the European Union (EU). In the 1950s, it was ethnically a very homogeneous society, although it had a former colony in Southeast Asia (Indonesia) and colonies in the Americas (Aruba and Suriname).

It was a middle-class society, an original signatory to the European Common Market (now the European Union), and in the 1950s, it was experiencing positive economic growth. Flush with success, the Netherlands developed an extensive social welfare system that provided its citizens health care, education, and housing. It also developed a legal system that emphasized rehabilitation over punishment and the importance of prevention (an individual does not consider violating the law) rather than deterrence (an individual wishes to violate the law but is deterred by a fear of punishment). Crime was

135

not an important public policy issue in the country. The press was in the hands of the private sector and expressed a broad range of opinion.

Political Characteristics. Today, the Netherlands is a decentralized parliamentary democracy with a queen. The country has a history of political and religious conflict, including a succession of foreign rulers (German, Spanish, and French); the subsequent breaking away of the regions of present-day Belgium and Luxembourg; Catholics versus Protestants; and the rise of militant trade unionism.

Since most individuals had little in common, the danger of further fragmentation was addressed by creating a consociational system of government.[2] Such a proportional representation electoral system in a society with deep divisions meant no party could win a majority and rule alone. The commitment of elites to consensus meant pragmatic ruling coalitions that reflected what has been called "the ordering principles of Dutch political life—religious or ideological devotion, political deference, consensual decision-making, and collective responsibility."[3]

Distribution of Political Power. Political power is dispersed widely among five main parties as well as between the national and local governments. The Labor Party (PvdA) is a social democratic party, without formal ties to the trade unions. The Liberal Party (VVD) is a classical liberal party, advocating the importance of free enterprise and individualism; in the United States it would be seen as a conservative party. Three other parties are based on religion: the Catholic People's Party (KVP), the Anti-Revolutionary Party (ARP), and the Christian-Historical Union (CHU). These mainstream religious parties identify themselves as lying between the focus on individualism of the Liberals and the statist project of the Labor Party. Every government coalition from 1924 to 1994 included a religious party.[4] Within this national context, drug policy at the local level was made by negotiations among the town council, the public prosecutor, and law enforcement.

Drug Use. Despite signing the early international prohibition treaties, Dutch authorities have long viewed addiction as a medical rather than a penal problem. Physicians had the authority to prescribe opiates or cocaine based on their medical judgment of the case at hand. Law enforcement tolerated those who used drugs recreationally without harming others. They were especially lenient toward residents of Chinese origin, who smoked opium, and prostitutes, who sniffed cocaine. Trafficking in these substances was pursued without targeting the user. Heroin use was virtually unknown in Holland in the 1950s.[5]

The use of illegal drugs in the Netherlands at the end of the 1950s was low. Marijuana and amphetamine use, however, were beginning to rise, the former more significantly than the latter. While mainstream Dutch society was still largely immune to, and ignorant of, these drugs, U.S. troops in Europe were among the main users of marijuana in Holland. With no history of marijuana legislation and no constituency speaking for the new and growing number of drug users, the KVP/VVD government coalition responded by enforcing prohibition through the arrest and imprisonment of users.[6]

Summary of Potential Players. In this context, the potential players in Dutch drug policy included the ministries of an activist national government, interest groups representing private health services, local governments, parents, youth, consumers, political parties, and a broad-ranging press.

Drug War: 1960–1965

As arrest and imprisonment of users increased, the Dutch press began running stories in 1961 that questioned this punitive response, particularly toward those using marijuana. In fact, the punitive response was a default devised when the Ministry of Social Affairs and Public Health failed to devise a policy response to the growing use of marijuana. Deviance paradigms were dominant in Dutch health and criminology circles, especially a variant of the "labeling" theory. According to this theory, subgroups with acceptable differences from mainstream society can be pushed into deviance if they are rejected, that is, identified as deviant or sick, by the mainstream. Health services were expected to provide treatment and counseling services to bring those who had strayed from the acceptable limits back into the mainstream.

The problem was that the ministry didn't believe that marijuana could be used medicinally, as doctors were doing with opiates and cocaine, and although it believed marijuana use was harmful, it knew little about the drug and thus could not devise appropriate treatment regimens. Psychiatric detoxification had been imposed on some users, but this was not a viable national strategy because of the expense and the increase in government power it implied. At the same time, the Dutch Foreign Ministry was participating in the UN meetings that produced the 1961 UN Single Convention on Narcotic Drugs, which prohibited the legalization of cannabis. In this context, the Ministry of Social Affairs and Public Health punted the ball to the Ministry of Justice.[7]

The confusion over whether and how marijuana represented a threat to Dutch society presented itself just as that society and its political system were beginning to undergo great changes. As a result of modernization and economic growth, the traditional social and political divisions were weakening. The religious parties began to lose support; reformers attacked the emphasis on consensus for the sake of stability. A new party, the Liberal Democrats 66 (D66) was founded with a platform that called for reforming the Dutch political system. In this context, government stability deteriorated badly, with four governments coming to power in five years (1963–1967), all led by religious parties.

With traditional divisions deteriorating but no indication of what the new basis for politics would be, party elites continued to seek accommodation of policy positions to create new and stable governing majorities.[8] Indicative of the growing importance of the youth movement, the government created a Ministry of Culture, Recreation and Welfare to coordinate its youth policy, which included subsidizing youth employment and overseeing youth centers.[9] On this initiative, this new ministry had to work closely with local governments, which often funded and regulated the centers.

These local governments were made of members of a Dutch public that was becoming increasingly aware of marijuana use through the press. The media did not link drugs to crime, however, but rather to alternative lifestyles.[10] Yet, the Ministry of Justice was growing concerned by the failure of increasing convictions to stem the rising use of marijuana among middle-class Dutch youth. It faced both criticism from the press and parents for punishing users without a credible rationale, as the press and professional journals were skeptical about the alleged harms of the drug, and because the Ministry of Social Affairs and Public Health could offer no treatment programs to end use.

De Facto Harm Reduction: 1967–1976

Dutch society and government had other problems in the late 1960s through the mid-1970s. Inflation was an issue, and the government imposed wage and price controls that were followed by tax increases in 1971. Also in 1971, the KVP lost its leadership in the elections and became a minority partner in the new ARP-led government. That government fell the next year, and in 1973 the PvdA headed a five-party coalition that sought to stimulate the economy via minimum wage increases, rent control, and housing subsidies. When the government negotiated full independence for Suriname in 1975, tens of thousands of new immigrants from that South American country exercised their right of Dutch citizenship and immigrated to Holland. The result was an increase in unemployment at the same time that the ethnic make-up of the country began to shift.

Into this mixture of political and policy instability stepped local governments and the private sector. Cities, in particular Amsterdam, adopted an informal policy of tolerance toward marijuana sales and use. Town councils, public prosecutors, and law enforcement believed that it was necessary to keep middle-class Dutch users away from drug traffickers who peddled not just marijuana but also hard drugs, such as opium. Guidelines were developed for sales at youth centers that permitted only the sale of marijuana and hashish.[11]

The National Federation of Mental Health Organizations, representing both public and private health groups, decided to fund research on Dutch drug users and to create a drug policy commission. The task of the commission was "to clarify factors that are associated with the use of drugs, to give insight into the phenomenon as a whole, and to suggest proposals for a rational policy. . . ." Membership included treatment experts with experience on alcohol, psychiatrists, a sociologist, law enforcement officials, and a medical sociologist already studying the phenomenon. The commission was chaired by a criminal law professor, Louk Hulsman, known for his skepticism about the effectiveness of criminal law for dealing with social issues.[12]

The undersecretary of health, a doctor critical of marijuana use, wanted a different voice on the issue and set up a competing Narcotics Working Party in 1968. Its charge was "to investigate causes of increasing drug use, how to confront irresponsible use of drugs, and to propose a treatment system for those who developed dependence of these drugs." The group was dominated by medical and legal personnel from the Ministries of Social Affairs and Public Health and Justice.

Perhaps because this membership just reproduced the stalled debate between the ministries, the group floundered for a year. The Ministry of Culture, Recreation and Sport lobbied to be part of the group and for the inclusion of behavioral scientists. In 1970, the Narcotics Working Party was reconfigured with broader membership, including some of those serving simultaneously on the Hulsman Commission. Pieter Baan, a chief inspector of mental health, was appointed its chair.[13]

At the time that the Hulsman and Baan commissions were beginning their work, the first large Dutch survey of drug users was becoming public. Herman Cohen, a member of both commissions, had surveyed a thousand users and published his results in 1968. His work concluded that users had a relatively high level of education, rarely became addicted, and the most harm to them came from the threat of imprisonment.

The press reported the study extensively. A national conservative newsweekly, *Elsevier*, decided to do its own direct reporting on drug users in 1970. The six-page article contained interviews with attendees of an open-air rock concert in Rotterdam, medical personnel at the event, and policymakers, including parliamentarians on public health and justice subcommissions. The newsweekly concluded that drug use was not a problem in Holland and that marijuana consumers were nice people who were neither out of control nor addicts.[14]

In 1970, an advisory group to the Ministry of Culture, Recreation and Sport advocated reforming the marijuana laws to make them similar to those regulating alcohol.[15] Also in that year, the public prosecutor's office characterized criminal law as inadequate for dealing with drug users. The report opined that drug information and prevention policies would have a greater impact than prosecution.[16]

The Hulsman Commission report was completed in 1971 and advocated the eventual legalization of all drugs. It concluded that illicit drug use could be controlled and limited by the individual and that marginalizing subcultures of drug users was inadvisable. It also rejected the gateway theory in regard to marijuana and recommended the separation of marijuana use from other drug using subcultures. The report likened drug use to parents who refused to vaccinate their children on religious grounds, arguing that the government could not disapprove of the behavior of those with different "concepts of life." It went on to warn that a law enforcement strategy would require a constantly increasing police force that would result in polarization and increased violence in Dutch society.

Other recommendations included legalizing the use and possession of small quantities of cannabis, although its production and distribution should remain misdemeanors in the short term. Use and possession of other psychoactive substances should also be misdemeanors in the short term and adequate treatment facilities should be provided for users who required them, in addition to drug treatment evaluation, a system for providing information about drugs, and more research.[17]

The Baan Commission issued its report in 1972. This official commission not only rejected the gateway theory of marijuana, it quoted a study that concluded that drug use was not a result of social misery or pathology, or necessarily more than an experimental phase in the lives of most individuals. That report went on to say that users "not only read more about drugs but also read more about other things than drugs: art, politics, science and philosophy than youths from the two control groups."

The commission proposed a distinction between soft drugs (marijuana and hashish), which produced "acceptable risks," and hard drugs (every other illegal drug), which generated "unacceptable risks." It suggested working for a change in the status of cannabis, and an amendment to policy in regard to it, in the 1961 UN Convention. Until this change in status occurred, it advised that marijuana and hashish trade of twenty-five grams or less be considered simply a misdemeanor. For hard drugs, the Baan report advocated using the law to direct users into treatment.[18]

The Baan Commission's distinction between soft and hard drugs provided a rationale for a police crackdown on opium trafficking beginning in 1972, which resulted in virtually drying up the supply. Before law enforcement could react, opiate users turned to heroin, resulting in a heroin epidemic. Despite the increased presence of heroin and the rising crime associated with it,[19] Dutch voters in the 1970s still did not rate crime as an important priority.[20]

The Ministry of Social Affairs and Public Health continued to oppose efforts to decriminalize marijuana despite the reports of the Hulsman and Baan Commissions and the concurrence of the Ministry of Justice and the Ministry of Culture, Recreation and Sport. But in 1972, the ARP/KVP coalition lost the elections after just one year in office and a PvdA/KVP government took office in 1973.[21] The new government was more favorably disposed toward the de facto decriminalization strategies of local government and the two national commission reports. A new Minister of Health was appointed, who also happened to be the mother of a radio talk host who provided information about the price and quality of different sources of marijuana on the air.[22]

For the next two years, policymakers in the Ministry of Social Affairs and Public Health; the Ministry of Justice; the Ministry of Culture, Recreation and Sport; and the Ministry of Foreign Affairs searched for a way to legalize marijuana and decriminalize other drugs. But the 1961 UN Convention and concerns from France and Germany, both of which were pursuing drug war strategies at the time, about the direction of Dutch policy proved insurmountable obstacles to that goal.[23]

Official Harm Reduction: 1976–1995

In 1976, the Dutch government decided to proceed with what seemed possible.

> The Dutch Opium Act punishes possession, commercial distribution, production, import, and export of all illicit drugs. Drug use, however, is not an offense. The act distinguishes between "hard" drugs that have "unacceptable" risks (e.g., heroin, cocaine, Ecstasy), and "soft" drugs (cannabis products). One of the main aims of this policy is to separate the markets for soft and hard drugs so that soft drug users are less likely to come into contact with hard drugs.[24]

The goals of the act also include not marginalizing drug users by turning them into criminals because such ostracization creates harm in and of itself.[25] Hallucinogenic mushrooms were not listed as either soft or hard and remain completely legal in their fresh form; however, in the reforms of 1996, processed magic mushrooms were placed into the List 1 category of banned substances.[26]

There were dissenting voices to these changes in Holland,[27] but they were in the minority. Even when the PvdA lost the elections in 1977, ushering in another seventeen years of Christian Democratic Alliance-led coalition governments,[28] the basic harm reduction emphasis of Dutch drug policy remained.

At first the act merely tolerated the sale of cannabis, but parliament quickly realized the need for some regulation.[29] The Ministry of Justice developed guidelines for commercial sale of cannabis and hashish. Such sales would be permitted only if sellers abided by five rules: they could not advertise, sell hard drugs or alcohol, sell to minors, sell more than thirty grams to any one customer, or create a nuisance.

In 1980, the Ministry of Justice devolved enforcement to local authorities. Some towns enforced the rules so strictly as to discourage the opening of coffeehouses, whereas cities, especially Amsterdam, were quite lax. In Amsterdam there were nine coffeehouses in 1980, all on back streets. The number grew to 71 in 1985 and 102 in 1988, with many of these now on prominent streets.[30] Continued rapid expansion in the early 1990s outstripped the cities' ability to monitor and enforce regulations. As coffeehouses began violating the rules, complaints against them grew.

Contrary to what one may think hearing the increasing numbers of coffeehouses, decriminalization of cannabis did not initially produce an increase in its use. The most systematic survey of drug use in the Netherlands is carried out by the Ministry of Social Affairs and Public Health and involves the city of Amsterdam only.[31] However, because this is where most of the coffeehouses are to be found, it can safely be assumed that the results of this survey represent the extreme end of the real picture for the country as a whole.

Decriminalizing consumption of cannabis and permitting its sale on a small scale, as well as tolerating the consumption of other drugs, produced great tension in Dutch drug policy. Small-scale production and distribution of anything other than marijuana, as well as the supplying of cannabis to coffeehouses, remained an illegal activity. With no legal sources of supply, cannabis businesspeople and consumers of all drugs turned to those who had it: illegal traffickers. Because Holland is an open economy and has the world's largest port, Rotterdam, it is difficult to determine how much Dutch drug policy contributed to the development of the illegal drug trade in Holland. Despite Dutch government protests that countries with drug prohibition also experienced the illegal drug trade, the correlation between Dutch decriminalization and the growth of Dutch trafficking was an enticing point for many critics.

In 1988, the Dutch police created the Central Investigation Information bureau (CRI) to help them understand the growing presence of criminal groups in the country. One of their first efforts was to inventory the number of criminal groups, but they were not sure what criteria to use to determine whether a criminal group existed.[32] Using their original set of criteria, the CRI determined that three such groups existed in 1988. CRI and Ministry of Justice analysts, however, believed that number to be too low, so they changed the criteria and came up with a figure of 599 for the next report, which now seemed far too high. Another methodology netted a figure of ninety to one hundred organized crime groups in 1993.[33] Whatever the real figure, the sense among the Dutch public and government was that crime was real and increasing, although it never reached the stage of dominating public opinion.[34]

Despite the heightened awareness of drug-related crime, Holland has the lowest level of heroin addiction in the European Union. In addition, the number of heroin addicts is not rising, as evidenced by an average age for users of thirty or older; an average age that increases year by year. Studies continue to demonstrate that an increase in marijuana use does not promote heroin use.[35] The Dutch public accepts this conclusion, although many Dutch people and tourists do consider the presence of heroin addicts and petty crime a nuisance.[36]

Even with such relatively unexceptional use of heroin, however, Holland does rank third highest in level of amphetamine addiction in Europe.[37] In addition, the rise in use of cocaine and Ecstasy (3–4 methylenedioxymethamphet-

Table 9.1　Cannabis Consumption, Amsterdam (percentage who have ever used)

Age group	Year (percentage of total in age group)		
	1987	1990	1994
12–15	4.7	2.9	5.8
16–19	25.5	21.7	28.7

SOURCE: Reinarman, "Drug Policy Debate in Europe," citing Ministry of Health figures.

amine [MDMA], known as XTC in Holland) that affected the world in the 1980s did not skip the Netherlands, although it did not produce the level of street crime in the Netherlands that it did in the United States, Colombia, and Mexico. Evidence of this was the fact that law and order concerns in the 1980s clustered with public health and social welfare concerns far behind the voters' leading concerns of unemployment, the economy, and war and peace.[38]

The correlation of cocaine use with marijuana use was weaker in the Netherlands than in the United States. In the early 1990s, 22 percent of Dutch age twelve or older who had used cannabis at least once had tried cocaine. In the United States the comparable figure for cocaine use was 33 percent—50 percent higher.[39]

Ecstasy use caught the Dutch by surprise. Its use was popularized in the press as something focused on youth in the newly expanding entertainment culture and in affiliation with the innovative music known as "house." Little was known about the drug, and the press provided plenty of reports about young people dancing for hours in old, overheated warehouses with little water and few bathrooms. But use was spreading among other youth groups, soccer fans, old hippies, and New Agers as well.

Initially, the Dutch government was reluctant to add more substances to the banned substances list, especially when little was known about how it was being used and which harms were inherent to the actual drug. Other countries quickly added Ecstasy to their lists, but the Dutch held out until 1988, when international pressure proved too strong to resist. Analogs—other pharmacological versions of Ecstasy—sprang up, requiring that they also be added to the list in later years. In the meantime, parliament, local authorities, social workers, and parents were concerned about the lack of policy and guidance.[40]

Dynamic Harm Reduction: 1995–2002

By 1995 the unforeseen elements omitted from the 1976 drug policy reform required serious attention. What to do about them fell to a new governing coalition formed after the 1974 elections. Although the CDA was the plurality winner, it could not find a governing partner. Consequently, the social democratic PvdA created a broad coalition with the conservative VVD, the classical liberal D66, and a new party representing pensioners, the AOV. The coalition was stable enough to govern for two terms, until 2002, and to craft a new phase in Dutch drug policy.[41]

Cannabis

Because the Dutch rationale in decriminalizing marijuana was a harm reduction strategy, a dramatic rise in marijuana consumption was not favored. By the mid 1990s Amsterdam had an estimated 500 coffeehouses; another 1500 were spread about the country. The increased number coincided with an increase in the number of marijuana users, so that by some studies the Dutch were now smoking as much as users in the United States. Dutch border towns were complaining that French, German, and Belgian "drug tourists" were overrunning their locales, and the home governments of the tourists complained that they returned with the drugs.[42] Some sympathetic analysts were even concerned that the Dutch decriminalization model was becoming one of commercialization.[43]

In response, the government reformed the regulations governing coffeehouses and gave cities more authority to close and limit their number. The amount permitted for sale was decreased dramatically, from thirty grams to five. The stated goal of the Ministry of Social Affairs and Public Health was to reduce the number of cannabis outlets to the point that the minimum supply compatible with not stimulating a black market was reached. In 1996, the ministry also decided to invest in demand reduction programs, mainly educational information through school programs and the mass media.[44] In 2002, cannabis herb became available on prescription for medicinal purposes, relieving patients from having to violate the five-gram-a-day limit on purchases from a single supplier.[45]

Ecstasy

The Ministry of Social Affairs and Public Health stood by the traditional Dutch position that the use of illegal drugs, including Ecstasy, would never be fully eliminated. Therefore, it undertook efforts to learn more about Ecstasy and the house parties (known as raves in the United States) where it was distributed. It also investigated how the harms associated with Ecstacy's use could be minimized. National and local health officials, law enforcement, people involved in the promotion of house culture, nongovernmental groups that set up pill testing facilities at the clubs and parties, and users themselves were consulted and surveyed by research teams.

As a result of these studies, the ministry issued practical guidelines in 1995 to help local authorities make large-scale music events safer for all attendees, including for those who used illegal drugs. These recommendations covered such things as security and restroom facilities, but also chill-out rooms, in which overheated and exhausted dancers could relax. The Ministry of Social Affairs and Public Health then embarked on a campaign to discourage Ecstasy use in 1997 and continued to call for more research into the drug, its use, and its potential harms.[46]

Heroin

The ministry also looked for new ways to deal with the heroin users among the Dutch population. In 1998, the Dutch initiated a small program to supply addicts with heroin. Heroin maintenance programs had been tried before in Great Britain and were once again under discussion in a number of countries. The Dutch experience went well enough that it was expanded the following year.[47] Dutch heroin addicts profit by the Dutch policies as HIV rates are kept low by free access to clean needles. Government-sponsored methadone clinics reach three-quarters of the nation's heroin addicts, helping them deal with their addiction and live better lives.[48]

Crime and International Cooperation

Although Dutch drug policy reforms did not give law enforcement a prominent role, the intent was never to tolerate major crime, including international trafficking, associated with drugs. Beginning in the mid-1990s, the Dutch government began putting more effort to this end. To house the expected increase in convicted criminals, the government constructed fourteen new prisons between 1994 and 1996, a number that represents 38 percent of the total number of prisons in Holland as of 2001.[49]

In 1995, Portugal, Spain, France, Germany, Luxembourg, Belgium, and the Netherlands agreed to abolish internal borders. But France, Germany, and Belgium insisted that Holland take a more active role in controlling its drug trade or they would not implement the agreement. In response, the Dutch government increased interdiction and vigilance efforts at the Amsterdam airport and the Rotterdam port. Special attention was given to the production and trafficking of synthetic drugs. Police exchanges and cooperation among the four countries also grew.[50] The U.S. government has noted the progress made by Dutch law enforcement, but points out that Holland continues to be a center for production, distribution, and consumption of most illicit drugs.[51]

STUDY QUESTIONS

1. Begin by getting a sense of the entire case. Specifically, how did the focus of national drug policy change over time?
2. When did illicit drug use first attract national attention?
   - Was there any debate about how illegal drug use should be conceived, as socially deviant, alternative norms, individual choice, or threats to national security?
   - Which important political actors held which views? What types of evidence did they present to support their position?
3. Once the drug issue got on the national agenda, what individuals or groups were given the task to design national drug policy?
   - What was the professional background of these individuals or the members of these groups?
   - Were there any disagreements among individuals, especially within specific groups? If so, were compromises reached or common ground found?

- What proposal was finally put forth? If there was more than one, why was this the case?
4. What individuals or groups needed to accept the proposed policy design in order for it to become national drug policy?
   - Were there any debates among these actors about the proposed policy? If so, what were they? If not, why not?
   - How did the policy that was accepted differ from the one that was proposed by the policy design group? Why did it differ?
5. Which groups benefited from the policy ultimately adopted and which groups paid the costs? What were the costs and benefits of the policy for society as a whole?

Answer the following questions for each change in national drug policy over time.

6. Why did the policy change? Consider:
   - Who objected to it?
   - Why did they object to it?
   - How they were able to influence officials so that a revision of national policy was made?
   - If the resulting change in policy provided the critics of the old policy with what they wanted. If not, why not?
7. Which groups benefited from the new policy and which groups paid the costs? What were the costs and benefits of the new policy to society as a whole?

Chapter 10

**Sweden
From Harm Reduction to
Drug War, 1965-1993**

Summary

Swedish drug policy evolved from an unregulated harm reduction strategy in 1965 to a major offensive against both supply and demand, which is the hallmark of a drug war strategy, in the 1990s. The process was not a simple one, as during the intervening years, the government attempted to combine de facto harm reduction with prohibition and then became increasingly coercive in the 1980s as the nation sought to build on the early successes of harm reduction to achieve a drug-free society.

Background

Nineteenth-century Swedish society, like many of that time, was concerned about the effects of psychoactive substances on human behavior and health. A small group of doctors, psychiatrists, teachers, and politicians promoted the view that excessive use of caffeine and tobacco created dangerous social problems.[1] But well into the 1920s most of Swedish society was focused on the debate concerning alcohol, morphine, and cocaine. The temperance movement narrowly missed winning a national referendum to support alcohol prohibition in 1922.

The vote against prohibition did not favor unlimited alcohol consumption, however. Sweden controlled alcohol via the Bratt system, named after its innovator, Dr. Ivan Bratt: the government discouraged drinking by imposing a government monopoly on production, imports, and sales; limiting the days and times alcohol could be sold; and taxing it at sufficiently high rates to discourage consumption without attracting a black market. The drinking age was set at twenty-five, and individuals were provided with a ration book stipulating the quantities that an individual could purchase based on gender, income, and personal behavior. Treatment was also available for alcoholics.[2] In short, Sweden had rejected both the prohibition and full legalization strategies for alcohol, opting for a complex harm reduction approach.

Eventually, the temperance movement began losing its influence in Sweden because of the social changes brought on by industrialization and urbanization. Labor had allied with the temperance movement because union leaders and workers believed that sobriety was necessary to build a social welfare state. But once the welfare state became a reality, the allies parted ways. Rather than finding common cause with the temperance movement, unions now opposed the Bratt system for discriminating against workers, since rations were influenced by income.

The Context for Modern Swedish Drug Policy

Social and Economic Characteristics. Sweden is a geographically large country with a small population; Stockholm is its capital and the largest city. The country is very homogeneous ethnically, although migration began to rise in the 1950s, and identifies far more as a part of Scandinavia—along with Norway, Finland, and Denmark—than as a part of continental Europe. Beginning in the 1930s, the country developed an extensive social welfare system that provided a safety net as industrialization and urbanization spread after World War II. Perhaps because of a strong sense of community and Swedish culture, the penal system emphasized rehabilitation over punishment.

Political Characteristics. Sweden was a de facto parliamentary democracy with a monarch from 1917 to 1974; a new constitution in 1975 turned the country into a formal parliamentary and democratic government, yet still with a monarch. Because its large territory was sparsely populated, Sweden developed systems of government that were decentralized even before it became a modern democracy. Its parliament consisted of two houses, until a constitutional reform in 1970 made it unicameral. Members are elected in a proportional representation system that was heavily weighted toward the plurality party before constitutional changes in 1974; changes in that year have made it more likely that a coalition government will emerge from the elections.

Distribution of Political Power. Sweden has four major political parties: the Social Democrats (SD), Center (formerly Agrarian Party), Liberals, and Conservatives. Other parties that have played important roles as members of coalition governments since 1990 include the former Communist Party, now the Left Party; the Green Party; and the Christian Democrats. The SD have dominated electoral politics, governing continuously from 1932 to 1976, returning to office from 1982 until 1991 and again from 1994 through 2005. Consistent with Sweden's history of decentralization, city and town governments have a great deal of autonomy.

Pyschoactive Substance Use. In 1955, the Bratt system was repealed and alcohol consumption rose, along with the number of problem drinkers. The medical profession was expected to provide treatment for these individuals, who could be involuntarily committed to a facility if their behavior was determined to be a threat to society. The repeal of the Bratt system made doctors and social workers more relevant to the discussion of alcohol and gave impetus to the search for a scientific explanation of what "harm" is and how to treat it.

Illicit drug use in the 1950s was overwhelmingly concentrated on amphetamines, much of that use intravenous; there was some opiate use, and even some marijuana use for medicinal purposes. By the 1960s, marijuana use was increasing. Sweden's experience with amphetamine addiction contrasted with that of the rest of Europe, in which heroin was the main drug of concern.[3]

The number of people tried and convicted for use of illicit drugs rose dramatically after 1957. In the period from 1954 to 1957, a total of fourteen people were convicted of illicit drug use. Then 18 were convicted in 1958 alone; by 1965, convictions reached 318 just for that year. Stockholm accounted for 70 percent of the arrestees in this period, but even rural areas and small cities experienced rising drug arrests (11 percent of the total). The drugs associated with these arrests were cannabis (11 percent), opiates (5 percent), and central stimulants, particularly amphetamines, (84 percent).[4]

Summary of Potential Players. In the early 1960s, Sweden was a highly organized society with temperance and Christian groups engaged in treatment and social work. Organized labor was very loyal to the SD party, and the press was an oligopoly of public and private firms, subsidized by the government through the political parties as part of a modern social welfare society. Medical professionals, law enforcement, parents, youth, and drug consumers were not yet organized as interest groups in the early 1960s.[5]

Harm Reduction: 1965

From April 1965 until May 1967 the city government of Stockholm, frustrated with the national government and anxious to alleviate the social disruptions caused by a rising addict population, tolerated an experimental drug maintenance program designed to reduce harm to the individual addict and society. The program echoed the heroin maintenance program that was already decades old in Britain, but in Sweden the target audience was mainly amphetamine addicts, although others were included in a haphazard fashion.

The experiment was not a scientific one, as it began with ten addicts selected nonrandomly and did not have a control group against which to test the results of the pilot treatment: the prescription of amphetamines, methadone, and morphine to drug addicts. But the project included ten medical doctors; was supported by the ex-drug users' organization, the Swedish Association for Assistance to Drug Users (RFHL); and would later be adopted by the Health Inspectorate. Over the two years of the project, a total of 120 addicts participated in the program for at least three months.[6] Hence, the project was considered a legitimate effort at the time.

The experiment was very much the project of one man, Dr. Sven-Erik Ahström. Although he was a police doctor, he had already established a reputation for having liberal ideas about drug addiction and treatment. Among those ideas was that addicts needed to be treated with respect and trusted if they were to function well in society; hence, he allowed some patients to distribute drugs to other patients and even take drugs home. If patients ran out of drugs before the allotted time for renewal of the prescription, he increased the prescription.[7]

The other doctors became aware of the lax controls on the patients very quickly, and abandoned the project within the first ten months. By the next year, the RFHL withdrew its support. Ahström seemed oblivious to the dangers created by addicts selling their unlimited prescriptions on the street, the deaths that occurred among the patients, and the fact that crime associated with drug addicts in Stockholm was not going down. The experiment was finally shut down following a public uproar when a patient administered morphine and amphetamines to a teenage girl who was not a patient and she died from an overdose.

At the same time as Ahström's experiment was being carried out in the streets of Stockholm, another police doctor was undertaking another nonscientific study of addicts. Dr. Nils Bejerot hypothesized that addiction derived from the biochemical properties of the drugs, rather than from the social and psychological characteristics of the users. That meant that everyone would fall into addiction if they consumed beyond a point that no one could predict. He also believed that addiction had epidemic characteristics and would spread rapidly if the carriers were not isolated from others.

Bejerot was the supervisory medical officer at the detention center where all people in Stockholm arrested for crimes were held while awaiting trial. He believed that this was an ideal setting for testing his hypothesis about the epidemic patterns of drug addiction, as well as the link between drugs and crime. His procedure was simple: trained nurses would examine the arms of all arrestees for needle marks and the percentage of users in the total group would be noted. Some interesting numbers developed: from 1965 to 1967, a "permissive" time in Stockholm with respect to drugs, the percentage of inmates who were intravenous drug users rose from 20 percent to 25 percent to 33 percent. Bejerot was quick to publicize these findings as proof of the link between drugs and crime, despite a host of issues that questioned their scientific validity.[8]

In 1965 the Swedish police organized into a national federation and, indicative of their concern over the drug issue, created a national drug commission to articulate police viewpoints.[9] Also in 1965, the national government, in a typical Swedish approach that brought together experts, government agencies, and interest groups to deal with important issues,[10] created the Committee on the Treatment of Drug Abuse. The committee provided reports on treatment, prohibition, and control. In addition, the government began a large campaign in the media and in the schools against drugs.[11] The press presented no dissenting views about the way in which drugs were being portrayed, not only because it received government subsidies, but also because editors believed in the policy and the duty of the press to articulate it unambiguously.[12]

Most of the public supported the government's approach as well. In regards to alcohol, many Swedes accepted the government's regulation and treatment approach toward the substance only because of its roots in Sweden's past and culture. Since these new drugs had no cultural history in Sweden, some pro-hibitionists believed that it was possible to nip the problem in the bud by mak-ing it impossible for these drugs to gain a foothold. With the prohibitionists leading the way, the public saw tough laws as necessary and promising.[13]

Prohibition with Harm Reduction: 1968

The Swedish parliament moved quickly in the direction of prohibition, heav-ily influenced by Ahström's failure, Bejerot's theories, and the second of two reports that the Committee on the Treatment of Drug Abuse published in 1967. Bejerot had warned that anyone could become an addict if they took drugs; recreational use was impossible to control by the individual because the biochemical properties of the substances overwhelmed personal characteris-tics and social experiences. The committee's report on reducing addiction noted that both demand and supply factors needed to be addressed. Its first report had dealt with treatment, the results of which had a decidedly secondary impact on lawmakers designing the new national drug legislation.[14]

The Narcotic Drugs Act of 1968 was based on a punitive approach toward supply and a treatment approach for users. In line with Bejerot's theories, it rejected the notion of a distinction between soft and hard drugs. Drug offenses were categorized into three types by severity. Minor drug offenses were punishable by a fine, and by Swedish law they were therefore eligible to be dismissed by a judge. Normal drug offenses could be eligible for a fine or a prison term of up to two years. Major drug offenses could receive penalties ranging up to four years' imprisonment. The prosecutor general wanted users to go into treatment, not prison, and so he provided guidelines that autho-rized waivers of the charges for possession of up to three grams of cannabis and one hundred amphetamine tablets—a normal-level offense.[15] The guide-lines, however, were implemented in a manner that effectively decriminalized personal consumption, as police paid the most attention to drug traffickers.

Ahström's disastrous experiment confirmed the worst fears of many Swedes and they were unhappy with the 1968 legislation for not going far enough. Parents were already concerned by the many research studies coming out in the 1960s that indicated that Swedish children were developing in ways that would make them self-centered and insensitive adults.[16] Dr. Bejerot's study carried a great deal of weight with the national police board and with those already convinced that drugs were an unacceptable threat.[17] Many organized into Parents Against Drugs to lobby for prohibition.

The next year, Hassela, a small but devoted group that used innovative and controversial residential treatments for detoxification, created its own interest group, Hassela Solidarity, to promote prohibition.[18] Also in 1969, Bejerot organized the Association for a Drug Free Society (RNS), which began a door-to-door membership drive. All three organizations were articulate and had good contacts with the press; their editorials and reports found ready outlets.

Responding to this public outcry, in 1970 parliament increased penalties for major drug offenses to six years. The deterrent impact of these measures seemed to be working, as the number of drug addicts stabilized after passage of the law. Believing that the law had stopped the expected epidemic from materializing (Bejerot's theory), parliament again increased penalties for major drug offenses in 1972. Penalties were raised to a maximum of ten years imprisonment. The conditions under which treatment could be made compulsory were broadened, and a majority of tranquillizers and sedatives were added to the list of narcotic drugs.[19]

Consumers of illegal drugs whose behavior did not push them into the category in which they would be subject to compulsory treatment continued to be largely ignored at this time. The changes to the drug laws in 1972 still made it possible for someone with a week's supply of cannabis to get a waiver of prosecution, and the police preferred to pursue major traffickers, virtually ignoring consumers and small-scale street dealers.[20] Consequently, Sweden had a de facto decriminalization of personal drug use and small-scale sale at this time.

Pursuing the Drug-Free Society: 1976

In 1976, under new electoral rules, the Social Democrats lost an election for the first time since 1932, which ushered in a new era of electoral competition. The coalition that defeated the Social Democrats was led by the Center Party and included the other two major parties, the Liberals and Conservatives. The threat posed by drugs was one of the important campaign themes stressed by the Conservatives.[21] Unfortunately, the coalition was a highly unstable one, and the government would fall in 1978 over disagreements about nuclear energy policy.

Although there was no evidence of escalating drug use at the time, the new government appointed a committee and charged it with recommending "further measures to curb the acceleration of drug abuse." The committee brought in a report that convinced the parliament to unanimously approve the goal of Swedish national drug strategy as the creation of a drug-free society.[22]

The move to a drug-free agenda was incompatible with the de facto decriminalization of consumption. Accordingly, the government took a series of steps to force law enforcement and the judicial system to prosecute personal use. In 1980, dismissal of charges for minor offenses was limited to cases in which the drugs not only were for personal use but the quantity was also too small to be further divided. Heroin, cocaine, and morphine were excluded from the waiver policy because they were considered too dangerous. The prosecutor general also moved cannabis into the same category as amphetamines, citing new studies that claimed that cannabis was harmful. Minimum terms for minor drug offenses were doubled, from one to two years, and the maximum sentence for normal drug offenses went from two to three years. Under the new drug control guidelines, the number of recorded drug offenses rose dramatically, from 22,500 in 1979 to 68,000 in 1982.[23]

The new efforts to deal with consumers were not limited to punitive measures. When parliament passed a new social welfare bill in 1981, it added legislation that made it easier to subject young adults "over 15 if behavior constitutes a serious danger of health or development" to compulsory care (Law on Treatment of Young People [LUV]) and alcohol and drug users (Law on Treatment of Abusers [LVM]).[24] The right-center government was dismantling the social welfare state in many areas, but increasing the power of the state on other matters, such as drugs.[25]

In 1982, a new player emerged on the drug issue. The Swedish Carnegie Institute created a research center to study and disseminate information on drugs, criminality, and related matters. Dr. Bejerot took the position of scientific director until his death in 1988. The center's director frequently published in law enforcement publications. The police and the institute coordinated their efforts to promote what they considered to be appropriate policies for achieving the drug-free society.[26]

When the Social Democrats returned to power in 1982, a new direction on drug policy was a given. In fact, the Social Democrats had included the drug issue in their campaign. Utilizing the symbolic expression of Swedish social democracy, *Folkhemmet* (the people's home), the party declared that the country must be clean of drugs. The new government thus appointed its own drugs commission to generate new proposals to further control drugs and drug use. Penalties were once again increased for drug infractions, and more activities, such as facilitating a drug deal, became subject to criminal law. But the government's commission still rejected criminalizing drug use, believing that it would negatively affect treatment policies.[27]

The refusal by the Social Democrats to criminalize consumption of illicit substances encountered serious opposition in Swedish society. One national survey claimed that 95 percent of the population favored the change. The FMN and RNS circulated a petition for criminalization that garnered close to half a million signatures; the groups then organized a large march from the countryside to Stockholm to emphasize their position.[28]

But the drug issue was not sufficiently important to deny the Social Democrats victory in the 1985 and 1988 elections. Although the social forces favoring criminalization continued their protests, the government maintained its position, arguing that not even the public prosecutor's study on drugs had recommended criminalization of use. Nonetheless, the Social Democrats continued to move further along the punitive spectrum by making minor offenses subject to imprisonment for the first time and removing the possibility of a fine for normal drug offenses, essentially mandating a conviction. By the end of the 1980s, the Social Democrats reluctantly acceded to criminalizing drug use, but to reinforce their conviction that treatment rather than prison was the proper policy, limited the penalty to a fine. The fine was expected to be a signal that Sweden and the Social Democrats found drug use unacceptable.[29]

Reinforcing the hard-liners' beliefs, the decade of the 1980s, with tougher law enforcement progressively implemented, experienced a decline in drug use, particularly of marijuana.

Pursuing the Drug War: the 1990s

Severe economic problems in the 1990s produced high youth unemployment and a fiscal crisis for government at the national and local levels. Budget cuts abounded at the national level as the welfare state continued to be dismantled;[30] all treatment for drugs and alcohol was paid by municipal social services at the time.[31] In 1996, the National Board of Health and Welfare criticized the fact that fewer drug abusers were being reached and that the shift to outpatient care provided less coverage than did the old model of residential care.[32] Treatment, however, was and still is expensive and the focus on crime resulted in a shift of the scarce funds for the drug issue from treatment to law enforcement.[33]

The Social Democrats lost the 1991 elections and were replaced by a four-party coalition of Conservatives, Liberals, Centrists, and Christian Democrats. The Liberals were given the Ministry of Health and Social Welfare as one of their portfolios. The new minister, who was also the leader of the Liberal Party, quickly declared it necessary for the police to be able to do urine tests on suspected drug users so that they might be identified and given treatment. (Under Swedish law one cannot be forced to undergo a police examination unless one is arrested for an offense that could result in a prison sentence.) The minister's cause was helped by a 1992 survey that showed that the number of heavy drug users was about 40 percent higher in 1992 than in 1979.[34] In 1993, the penalty for drug use was raised to include imprisonment, completing the process of criminalizing consumption that the Social Democrats had resisted.[35]

All of this was not the only reason 1993 was an important year for the drug debate. Accession to the European Union (EU) was being negotiated at this time. Opinion polls indicated that the more harm reduction-oriented tenor of the EU was a great concern to Swedish voters. Authorities of a number of large cities in the EU countries met in Frankfurt, Germany, and created an organization to promote harm reduction policies, the European Cities on Drug Policy (ECDP).

In response, the Conservative city council in Stockholm hosted a counter-conference and a competing organization; the European Cities Against Drugs (ECAD) was created to promote prohibition within the EU. Stockholm's city council also took the lead within Sweden in persuading cities to shut down government supported treatment facilities and cut public monies for treatment by one-third. The goal of the Conservatives was for local and outpatient facilities to take care of the drug users who would not be deterred by the new get-tough policies.[36]

Across the political spectrum, drugs and youth crime were increasingly linked in the 1990s political discourse throughout Sweden. The disagreement among the political parties was over where to lay the blame. Conservative newspaper editorials always focused on individual responsibility, with the Liberals coming to that position only in the 1990s as a result of their growing disenchantment with taxes for the welfare state. The editorials of the Social Democrats, in contrast, looked to the cutbacks in social services for their inspiration.[37]

The Social Democrats returned to office in 1994 and have been there for four terms (2006 will be another election year). They appointed a new drugs commission in 1998 to evaluate prevailing policy. The commission found that the Swedish emphasis on reaching a drug-free society is correct, as is the emphasis on prohibition, control, and treatment. It recommended renewed efforts to implement the national drug strategy. A drug czar's office was created to coordinate drug policy, and a national campaign, Mobilization Against Drugs, was launched.[38]

A few dissenting voices were heard. Becoming a member of the EU made the harm reduction strategies that began to proliferate among the ECDP cities seem more relevant, and therefore these received more comment in the press. In preparation for a 1998 UN drug summit, twelve Swedish academics and intellectuals penned their signatures to an international appeal to the UN secretary general that called for a dialogue about drug policy options.[39] The new commissioner of the Swedish National Police also expressed frustration in a 1996 interview with the RNS magazine *Narkotikafrågan* asking, "Why are you always so terribly repressive?" and "Why do you always want a lot of things done to people who have not committed any crimes?"[40]

The 1990s ended with both recreational and problematic drug use back on the rise, reaching levels close to those that existed in the 1970s before the big punitive push on drug policy.[41] Attitudes of young people were changing as well, becoming slightly more accepting of drug use.[42] The punitive thrust of policy that had been adopted to drive use down even lower than had been achieved in the 1980s now became an effort to reverse the growing tide of drug use.

Arrests for minor offenses increased dramatically—70 percent from 1991 to 1997—but use climbed as well. By 2000, the number of overdose deaths in Sweden was among the highest in the EU and its 90 percent hepatitis C infection rate among intravenous drug users was the highest.[43]

The economic costs of the punitive strategy were diminished by new means of depriving convicted individuals of their freedom, including civil commitment (1988), community service (1990), and electronic monitoring (1994). Probation subject to attendance of drug rehabilitation was also a lower-cost option that a judge could impose. Still, about one-third of inmates in 1998 were serving time for a drug crime, and 47 percent of all inmates had been drug addicts.[44]

By the start of the millennium, Sweden had moved from a society with modest drug usage, treatment of users, and vigorous pursuit of traffickers—a traditional harm reduction strategy—to a period of increased use paired with reduced treatment, criminalization of use, and increasingly stringent criminal procedures—a typical drug war strategy. It was a strategy Sweden wished to take to the world. In the words of the Social Democrats' Minister of Health and Social Welfare, Margot Wallström

> We must also fight a strategy of liberalization, and ultimately of legalization, as it would make it impossible to solve the narcotics problem. The young people in our countries must get a clear, uniform message which is negative to drugs.
>
> Classifying different narcotic substances by degree of harm they are supposed to inflict does not offer any solution either. We know today that there are no harmless drugs. And last, but not least, we must give higher priority to narcotics questions in national and international agendas such as the United Nations, the Council of Europe, and within the European Union.[45]

STUDY QUESTIONS

1. Begin by getting a sense of the entire case. Specifically, how did the focus of national drug policy change over time?
2. When did illicit drug use first attract national attention?
   - Was there any debate about how illegal drug use should be conceived, as socially deviant, alternative norms, individual choice, or threats to national security?
   - Which important political actors held which views? What types of evidence did they present to support their position?
3. Once the drug issue got on the national agenda, what individuals or groups were given the task to design national drug policy?
   - What was the professional background of these individuals or the members of these groups?
   - Were there any disagreements among individuals, especially within specific groups? If so, were compromises reached or was common ground found?
   - What proposal was finally put forth? If there was more than one, why was this the case?
4. What individuals or groups needed to accept the proposed policy design in order for it to become national drug policy?
   - Were there any debates among these actors about the proposed policy? If so, what were they? If not, why not?
   - How did the policy that was accepted differ from the one that was proposed by the policy design group? Why did it differ?

5. Which groups benefited from the policy ultimately adopted and which groups paid the costs? What were the costs and benefits of the policy for society as a whole?

Answer the following questions for each change in national drug policy over time.

6. Why did the policy change? Consider:
   - Who objected to it?
   - Why did they object to it?
   - How they were able to influence officials so that a revision of national policy was made?
   - If the resulting change in policy provided the critics of the old policy with what they wanted. If not, why not?

7. Which groups benefited from the new policy and which groups paid the costs? What were the costs and benefits of the new policy to society as a whole?

8. Compare the development of national drug policy among the three case studies.
   - Why do countries adopt a drug war policy?
   - Why do countries adopt a harm reduction policy?

Notes

Chapter 1

1. "Afghanistan: Interview with a Female Poppy Farmer," *Bitter-Sweet Harvest: Afghanistan's New War.* August 2004. IRIN Web Special on the threat of opium to Afghanistan and the region. www.irinnews.org/webspecials/opium/intfem. asp. Accessed December 27, 2004.
2. For the Paris cannabis market and U.S.–Paris marijuana seed trade, see "The World Geopolitics of Drugs 1998/1999," *Observatoire Geopolitique des Drogues,* April 2000, 99–102.
3. J. E. Brooks, *The Mighty Leaf: Tobacco Thru the Centuries* (Boston: Little, Brown, 1952), 56, 71, as cited in "National Commission on Marihuana and Drug Abuse, History of Tobacco Regulation," based in part on a paper prepared for the commission by Jane Lang McGrew, an attorney from Washington, D.C. http://druglibrary.org/schaffer/LIBRARY/studies/nc/nc2b.htm.
4. H. Richard Friman, *NarcoDiplomacy* (Ithaca: Cornell University Press, 1996), 4–34; Ethan A. Nadelmann, "Global Prohibition Regimes: The Evolution of Norms in International Society," *International Organization* 44:4 (Autumn 1990): 504–511.
5. Dipak K. Gupta, *Analyzing Public Policy: Concepts, Tools and Techniques* (Washington, D.C.: CQ Press, 2001), 46–66.
6. To compare, see Samuel Popkin, *The Reasoning Voter* (Chicago: University of Chicago Press, 1991).
7. President Richard M. Nixon appointed the National Commission on Marijuana and Drug Abuse in 1971, the National Academy of Sciences issued a report in 1982, and the Institute of Medicine of the National Institutes of Health (NIH), responding to calls from President William Clinton's drug czar, General Barry McCaffrey, issued its report in 1999.
8. Theodore Hamm, "Our Prison Complex," *The Nation,* October 11, 1999. www.thenation.com/doc.mhtml%3Fi=19991011&s=hamm.
9. "Hallucinogens Addiction Information at Support Systems Provided by the National Institute on Drug Abuse," National Institute on Drug Abuse. www.drug-rehabilitation.com/hallucinogens.htm. Accessed April 4, 2004.
10. "Research Report Series—Hallucinogens and Dissociative Drugs," National Institute on Drug Abuse. www.nida.nih.gov/ResearchReports/hallucinogens/halluc2.html; Alan I. Leshner and George F. Koob, "Drugs of Abuse and the Brain," Proceedings of the Association of American Physicians 111: 2, 99–108.
11. Bonnie B. Wilford, ed., ASAM Publications, e-mail communication, August 8, 2001. BBWilford@aol.com.
12. Craig Lambert, "Deep Cravings," *Harvard Magazine,* March–April 2000.
13. Jerald W. Cloyd, *Drugs and Information Control: The Role of Men and Manipulation in the Control of Drug Trafficking* (Westport, Conn.: Greenwood Press, 1982), 17–58.
14. Bill Moyers, *Close to Home* PBS television series, 1998.
15. Klaus von Lampe, "Definitions of Organized Crime." www.organized-crime.de.
16. Paul Tough, "The OxyContin Underground," *New York Times Magazine,* July 29, 2001, 33–37, 52.

17. Quotes on the system are taken from Ray A. Goldberg and Leonard M. Wilson, *Agribusiness Management for Developing Countries—Latin America* (Cambridge: Harvard University Press, 1974), 3–5.
18. Ibid, 4.
19. Ibid, 6.

Chapter 2

1. Christopher A. Szechenyi, "Ecstasy Bust Leads to Israel Organized Crime, Officials Say," *Boston Globe*, April 26, 2000. www.boston.com/news/daily/26/ecstasy.htm. Accessed May 10, 2000.
2. Howard B. Kaplan and Robert J. Johnson, *Social Deviance* (New York: Kluwer Academic, 2001), 3–10.
3. For example, the official Web site of D.A.R.E. (Drug Abuse Resistance Education) notes "The DARE program gives kids the life skills they need to avoid involvement with drugs, gangs, and violence." The implication is that these youth never picked up the life skills appropriate to nondeviant behavior.
4. Howard Parker, Judith Aldridge, and Fiona Measham, *Illegal Leisure: The Normalization of Adolescent Recreational Drug Use* (London: Routledge, 1998), 25; National Institute on Drug Abuse, *Drug Abuse Prevention for the General Population* (Washington, D.C.: National Institutes of Health, 1997); and National Institute on Drug Abuse, *Drug Abuse Prevention for At-Risk Individuals* (Washington, D.C.: National Institutes of Health, 1997).
5. Philip C. Baridon, *Addiction, Crime, and Social Policy* (Lexington, Mass.: Lexington Books, 1976), 86–88.
6. To compare, see Mark Bowden's *Killing Pablo* (New York: Penguin Books, 1992) and Terrence E. Poppa's, *Drug Lord, the Life and Death of a Mexican Kingpin* (Seattle: Demand Publications, 1998).
7. There are multiple versions of the study of how politics and economics relate; however, the use of insights from economics to study political phenomena ("rational choice") is the leading one.
8. To compare, see David W. Rasmussen, Bruce L. Benson, and H. Naci Mocan's "The Economics of Substance Abuse in Context: Can Economics Be Part of an Integrated Theory of Drug Use?" *Journal of Drug Issues*, 28: 3 (1998): 575–592.
9. For addiction rates, recall the discussion around Table 1.1 in Chapter One; for variations in drug use by narcotics addicts, see Ted Goldberg's, *Demystifying Drugs* (New York: St. Martin's, 1999), 51–59.
10. John Gerard Ruggie, "What Makes the World Hang Together? Neo-utilitarianism and the Social Constructivist Challenge," *International Organization*, 52: 4 (Autumn 1998): 857.
11. Martha Finnemore and Kathryn Sikkink, "International Norm Dynamics and Political Change" *International Organization* 52: 4 (Autumn 1998): 892.
12. To compare, see the exhaustive analysis in Denise B. Kandel, ed., *Stages and Pathways of Drug Involvement: Examining the Gateway Hypothesis* (New York: Cambridge University Press, 2002).
13. Hans Morgenthau, *Politics among Nations*, 6th edition (New York: McGraw-Hill, 1985); Kenneth Waltz, *Theory of International Relations* (Weston: Mass.:

Addison-Wesley, 1979); John J. Mearsheimer, "The False Promise of Institutionalism," *International Security* 19: 3 (Winter 1994–1995).

14. For example, the fungal herbicide Fusarium oxysporum is used in Colombia as a means to eradicate marijuana but was rejected by Florida's Departments of Agriculture and Environment to destroy marijuana grown in the state. Northeast Ohio Sierra Club, "The Herbicide Threat." http://ohio.sierraclub.org/northeast/Herbicide.html. Accessed August 10, 2005.

15. Waltz, *Theory of International Relations.*

16. To compare, see the Drug Policy Alliance, "Facts on the Drug Czar's Accounting Fraud," February 2003. www.drugpolicy.org/library/factsheets/ondcp-fuzzy/index.cfm.

Chapter 3

1. National Archives, "When Nixon Met Elvis." www.archives.gov/exhibits/when_nixon_met_elvis/part_3_1.html; John Cassidy, "Presley's Death on Prescription Finally Revealed," *Sunday Times* (London), December 23, 1990. Lexis/Nexis. Accessed November 7, 2002; Dan Baum, *Smoke and Mirrors: The War on Drugs and the Politics of Failure* (Boston: Little, Brown, 1996), 45–47.

2. For an analysis of the surveys, see Denise B. Kandel, "The Social Demography of Drug Use" in Ronald Bayer and Gerald M. Oppenheimer, eds., *Confronting Drug Policy: Illicit Drugs in a Free Society* (New York: Cambridge University Press, 1993), 24–77.

3. European School Survey Project on Alcohol and Other Drugs (ESPAD), "Summary of the 2003 Findings." www.espad.org/diagrambilder/summary.pdf. Accessed March 18, 2005.

4. Organization of American States, Inter-American Drug Abuse Control Commission (CICAD), "Comparative Report on Nationwide School Surveys in Seven Countries: El Salvador, Guatemala, Nicaragua, Panama, Paraguay, Dominican Republic and Uruguay 2003," Washington, D.C., November 2004, pdf file.

5. To compare, see, Office of Applied Statistics, Substance Abuse and Mental Health Services Administration, "Detailed Emergency Dependency Tables from the Drug Abuse Warning Network, 2001," Department of Health and Human Services, Washington, D.C. www.samhsa.gov/oas/oas.html. Accessed November 17, 2002.

6. Office of National Drug Control Policy (ONDCP), "Drug Policy Information Clearinghouse Fact Sheet: Ecstasy 2004." www.whitehousedrugpolicy.gov/publications/factsht/mdma/index.html. Accessed August 11, 2005.

7. Substance Abuse and Mental Health Services Administration (SAMHSA), "National Household Survey 2001, Chapter 2," Department of Health and Human Services. www.samhsa.gov/oas/nhsda/2k1nhsda/vol1/chapter2.htm#2.driv. Accessed October 15, 2002.

8. ESPAD, "Summary of the 2003 findings," 25, Table 3.

9. CICAD, comparisons of Table N4, Chart N11, and Chart N13.

10. Substance Abuse and Mental Health Services Administration (SAMHSA), "Results from the 2003 National Survey on Drug Use and Health: Detailed Tables," p. i, Department of Health and Human Services. http://oas.samhsa.gov/phsda/2k3tabs/PDF/2k3TabsIntro.pdf. Accessed March 18, 2005.

11. Office of Applied Statistics, "Appendix D: Key Definitions, 2002," Substance Abuse and Mental Health Services Administration (SAMHSA). www.oas.samhsa.gov/nhsda/2k2nsduh/Results/appD.htm.
12. www.oas.samhsa.gov/NHSDA/2kSNSDUH/Results/2k2results.htm. Accessed March 29, 2004.
13. The National Survey can be found at CONACE's Web site, split into a general report and a report on specific substances, www.conacedrogas.cl/inicio/obs _naci_encu_tema1.php. Accessed March 25, 2005. Data reported here are from pages 88 and 64, respectively.
14. Substance Abuse and Mental Health Services Administration (SAMHSA), "Results from the 2001 National Household Survey on Drug Abuse: Summary of National Findings," vol. 1 (Rockville, Md.: Office of Applied Studies, 2002), 109, Table H.1; 110, Table H.2; 102, Table G.4; and 22, Table H.14. as cited in www.drugwarfacts.org/druguse.htm. Accessed November 6, 2002.
15. National Institute on Drug Abuse (NIDA), *Monitoring the Future, Secondary School Students*, vol. I (Bethesda, Md.: NIH Publication), 89–90.
16. Office of Applied Studies, Substance Abuse and Mental Health Services Administration, "Results for the National Survey on Drug Use and Health: Detailed Tables," U.S. Department of Health and Human Services. www.oas.samhsa.gov/nhsda/2k3tabs/PDF/Sect1peTabs43to47.pdf. Accessed March 23, 2005.
17. Bureau of Justice Statistics, "Substance Abuse and Treatment, State and Federal Prisoners, 1997," *Special Report, January 1999* (Washington, D.C.: U.S. Department of Justice, Office of Justice Programs), 7.
18. Seventy-one percent of prisons tested inmates. Bureau of Justice Statistics, according to Mary Barr, "Drugs in Prison," *The Drug Policy Letter*, May–June 2000, 8.
19. www.oas.samhsa.gov/NHSDA/2kSNSDUH/Results/2k2results.htm. Accessed March 29, 2004.
20. www.oas.samhsa.gov/NHSDA/2kSNSDUH/Results/2k2results.htm. Accessed March 29, 2004.
21. Peter Bourne, "An Epidemiological Model of Heroin Addiction" in Peter Bourne, ed., *Addiction* (New York: Academic Press, 1974).
22. Robert J. MacCoun and Peter Reuter, *Drug War Heresies* (New York: Cambridge University Press, 2001), 30–32; National Institute on Drug Abuse (NIDA), *Monitoring the Future, Secondary School Students*, vol. II (Bethesda, Md.: NIH Publication), 30–32.
23. NIDA, *Monitoring the Future*, vol. II, 30.
24. Paul Tough, "The OxyContin Underground: How a Prescription Painkiller Is Turning into a Pernicious Street Drug," *New York Times Magazine*, July 29, 2001, 32–37, 52; Barry Meier, "Maker Chose Not to Use a Drug Abuse Safeguard," *New York Times*, August 13, 2001 via Lexis/Nexis. Accessed August 13, 2001; CNN, "FDA Warns OxyContin Maker on Ads," January 23, 2003. http://opioids.com/oxycodone/oxycontin.html. Accessed March 25, 2005.
25. General Barry McCaffrey, op-ed, "Don't Legalize Those Drugs," *Washington Post*, June 29, 1999.
26. Substance Abuse and Mental Health Services Administration, *National Household Survey on Drug Abuse: Population Estimates 1998* (Rockville, Md.: U.S. Department of Health and Human Services, 1999), 19, 25.

27. Article in *Journal of Drug Policy;* Denise Kandel and Kazuo Yamaguchi, "From Beer to Crack: Developmental Patterns of Drug Involvement," *American Journal of Public Health* (June 1993), 83: 6: 851–855.

28. Substance Abuse and Mental Health Services Administration, *Summary of Findings from the 1999 National Household Survey on Drug Abuse* (Rockville, Md: U.S. Department of Health and Human Services, 2000), G-49, G-60, and G-61.

29. Mark Thorton, "Alcohol Prohibition Was a Failure," Policy Analysis 157, CATO Institute. www.cato.org/pubs/pas/pa-157.html. Accessed March 27, 2005.

30. Recipes from Web sites will not be referenced here; www.dancesafe.org; www.experienceamsterdam.com/DRUGINFO-Ecstasy.html#dt; an example of an organization that provides harm reduction information but does not test pills is RaveSafe in South Africa: www.ravesafe.org/safehouse/welcome.htm

31. Quote is from G. Dimijian, "Contemporary Drug Abuse" in A. Goth, ed., *Medical Pharmacology: Principles and Concepts* (New Hartford, N.Y.: American College of Clinical Pharmacology, 1961), 299; also D. Musto and M. Ramos, "Follow-Up Study of the New England Morphine Maintenance Clinic of 1920," *New England Journal of Medicine* 30: 1075–1076; J. Ball and J. Urbaitis, "Absence of Major Medical Complications among Chronic Opiate Addicts" in J. Ball and C. Chambers, eds., *The Epidemiology of Opiate Addiction in the United States* (Springfield, Ill.: Charles C. Thomas, 1970), 301–306. All as cited in excerpt from Jara A. Krivanek, *Heroin: Myths and Reality* (Boston: Allen & Unwin, 1988), accessed via www.heroin-information.org/heroin/pages/how_bad_withdrawal.html. Accessed August 19, 2001.

32. M. L. Martin, M. J. Khoury, J. F. Cordero, and G. D. Waters, "Trends in Rates of Multiple Vascular Disruption Defects, Atlanta, 1968–1989: Is There Evidence of a Cocaine Teratogenic Epidemic?" *Teratology* 45 (1992): 647–653. All as cited in www.drugwarfacts.org/crack.htm. Accessed November 6, 2002.

33. Hallam Hurt, MD, Elsa Malmud, PhD, Laura Betancourt, Leonard E. Braitman, PhD, Nancy L. Brodsky, PhD, Joan Giannetta, "Children with In Utero Cocaine Exposure Do Not Differ from Control Subjects on Intelligence Testing," *Archives of Pediatrics & Adolescent Medicine,* 151 (1997): 1237–1241. All as cited in www.drugwarfacts.org/crack.htm. Accessed November 6, 2002.

34. L. Klein and R. L. Goldenberg, "Prenatal Care and Its Effect on Pre-term Birth and Low Birth Weight," in I. R. Merkatz and J. E. Thompson, eds., *New Perspectives on Prenatal Care,* (New York: Elsevier, 1990), 511–513; S. N. MacGregor, L. G. Keith, J. A. Bachicha, and I. J. Chasnoff, "Cocaine Abuse during Pregnancy: Correlation between Prenatal Care and Perinatal Outcome," *Obstetrics and Gynecology* 74 (1989): 882–885; C. Chazotte, J. Youchah, and M. C. Freda, "Cocaine Use during Pregnancy and Low Birth Weight: The Impact of Prenatal Care and Drug Treatment," *Seminars in Perinatology* 19 (1995): 293–300. All as cited in www.drugwarfacts.org/pregnant.htm. Accessed November 6, 2002.

35. Xiaobin Wang, MD, MPH, ScD, Barry Zuckerman, MD, et al., "Maternal Cigarette Smoking, Metabolic Gene Polymorphism, and Infant Birth Weight," *Journal of the American Medical Association* 287: 2 (January 9, 2002): 200; and Scott M. Montgomery and Anders Ekborn, "Smoking During Pregnancy and Diabetes Mellitus in a British Longitudinal Birth Cohort," *British Medical Journal* 321 (January 5, 2002): 27. As cited in www.drugwarfacts.org/pregnant.htm. Accessed November 6, 2002.

36. H. A. Flynn, S. M. Marcus, K. L. Barry, et al. 2003. "Rates and Correlates of Alcohol Use Among Pregnant Women in Obstetrics Clinics," *Alcoholism: Clinical and Experimental Research* 27: 1 (2003): 81–87, as cited in SAMHSA, *Fetal Alcohol Spectrum Disorders.* http://fascenter.samhsa.gov/pdf/WYNKFASDCenter3newad1.pdf. Accessed March 23, 2005.

37. Data on mortality is from www.drugwarfacts.org. Accessed November 2005. Also from *The Drug Policy Letter,* May–June 1999, 13.

38. Office of Applied Statistics, "Detailed Emergency Department Tables from the Drug Abuse Warning Network, 2001," Table 1.7, Substance Abuse & Mental Health Services Administration, Department of Health and Human Services. www.samhsa.gov/oas/DAWN/DetEDAnnual/2001/Text/DetEDtext.pdf. Accessed November 7, 2002.

39. www.drugwarfacts.org and sources cited therein. Accessed November 6, 2002.

40. MacCoun and Reuter, *Drug War Heresies,* 274–276.

41. Bureau of Justice Statistics, "Substance Abuse and Treatment, State and Federal Prisoners, 1997," *Special Report,* January 1999, U.S. Department of Justice, Office of Justice Programs.

42. Jesse Katz, "Past Drug Use, Future Cops" *Los Angeles Times,* June 18, 2000, Part A; Part 1; Page 1. Accessed via Lexis/Nexis September 23, 2002.

Chapter 4

1. Elaine Monaghan, "Whiff of Doom over U.S. Tobacco Fields," *The Times* (London), June 28, 2003. Accessed via Lexis/Nexis March 30, 2004.

2. Andean peasant, quoted in Catherine J. Allen, *The Hold Life Has: Coca and Cultural Identity in an Andean Community,* 2d ed. (Washington, D.C.: Smithsonian Institution Press, 2002), 193.

3. Jorge Dominguez, Linda Head, and William Rosenau, *Arciniega's War in the Upper Huallaga Valley,* Case Studies in Public Policy and Management, 1044.0 John F. Kennedy School of Government, Harvard University, 1990.

4. Isaías Rojas, "Peru: Drug Control Policy, Human Rights and Democracy" in Coletta A. Youngers and Eileen Rosin, eds., *Drugs and Democracy in Latin America: The Impact of U.S. Policy* (Boulder: Lynne Rienner, 2004), 185–230.

5. Canadian drug bust ephedrine.

6. Paul Tough, "The Alchemy of OxyContin," *New York Times Sunday Magazine,* July 29, 2001.

7. David Gates, "Odyssey of a Psychonaut," *Newsweek,* June 10, 1996, 92.

8. John M. Broder, "F.T.C. Charges Joe Camel Ad Illegally Takes Aim at Minors," *New York Times,* May 29, 1997, A1.

9. Robert J. MacCoun, Peter Reuter Jr., and Charles Wolf, *Drug War Heresies: Learning from Other Vices, Times, and Places* (New York: Cambridge University Press, 2001), 286–296.

10. In 2002, Sydney, Australia, five German cities, and twenty Dutch cities, as well as "some in Switzerland and Spain" officially sanctioned SIRs. Nat M. J. Wright and Charlotte E. J. Thompson, "Supervised Injecting Centres," *British Medical Journal* 238 (2004): 100–102. http://bmj.com. Accessed April 28, 2005, via DrugScope. www.drugscope.org.uk/news_item.asp?a=1&intID=1071; Andrew Byrne "Injecting Room Up and Running in Sydney," *Drug Policy Alliance*

(July 2001). Accessed via www.drugpolicy.org/library/sydney_injection.cfm on August 13, 2005.

11. Drug Enforcement Agency (DEA) Intelligence Brief, "The Changing Face of European Drug Policy," Office of International Intelligence, Europe, Asia, Africa Strategic Unit, April 2002. www.usdoj.gov/dea/pubs/intel/02023/02023p .html. Accessed August 29, 2003.

12. National Organization for the Reform of Marijuana Laws (NORML), "European Drug Policy: 2002 Legislative Update." www.norml.org/index.cfm?Group _ID=5446. Accessed August 29, 2003.

13. Elizabeth Joyce, "New Drugs, New Responses: Lessons from Europe," *Current History* (April 1998).

14. A perusal of the Internet turned up multiple sites that offer formulas and directions, complete with disclaimers that warn that the drug is illegal and that it would be a crime to produce it.

15. Geopolitical Drug Watch, "A Drug Trade Primer for the Late 1990s," *Current History* (April 1998). www.mapinc.org/drugnews/v98.n386.a06.html.

16. Single Convention on Narcotic Drugs, 1961, as amended by the 1972 Protocol Amending the Single Convention on Narcotic Drugs, 1961. www.unodc.org/ pdf/convention_1961_en.pdf.

17. Observatere Global de Drugs (OGD), *The World Geopolitics of Drugs 1998/99*, 30–32.

18. Barbara Crossette, "Taliban's Ban on Poppy a Success, U.S. Aides Say," *New York Times,* May 20, 2001 p. A5.

19. Steven R. Weisman, "On Visit to U.S., Afghan Leader Defends Opium Fight," *New York Times,* May 23, 2005, A1.

20. In the 1970s, at the height of Mexico's heroin boom, the author met a Mexican heroin farmer in exactly these conditions when the heroin producer was bringing his infant child, suffering from a gastrointestinal infection, from which the child was on the verge of dying because of the resulting dehydration, to the city. (Their hamlet had neither potable water nor electricity for refrigeration; consequently, these types of illnesses were quite common.) The trip by mule and four-wheel truck took more than twenty-four hours.

21. OGD, *The World Geopolitics of Drugs,* 99–102.

22. Patrick L. Clawson and Rensselaer W. Lee III, *The Andean Cocaine Industry* (New York: St. Martin's, 1996), 133–134.

23. Scott Wilson. "In Columbia, coca declines but the war does not; fighting spikes in province despite anti-drug program," *Washington Post,* December 21, 2003, A Section, A24.

Chapter 5

1. Mark Thornton, "Alcohol Prohibition Was a Failure" Cato Institute Policy Analysis No. 157, July 17, 1991. www.cato.org/pubs/pas/pa-157.html. Accessed May 9. 2005.

2. Libertarian Party leaflet.

3. Thomas C. Schelling, "What Is the Business of Organized Crime?" reprinted in *Choice and Consequence* (Cambridge: Harvard University Press, 1984); Margaret E. Beare and R. T. Naylor, "Major Issues Relating to Organized Crime: Within

the Context of Economic Relationships," Nathanson Centre for the study of organized crime and corruption, Law Commission of Canada, April 14, 1999.
www.ncjrs.org/nathanson/organized.html. For testimony supplied by Proctor &
Gamble that applied the organized crime concept to Amway Corporation, see G.
Robert Blakely "Report of G. Robert Blakely," Notre Dame Law School, 1998.
www.amquix.info/pdfs/Blakely_expert_report.pdf.

4. National Drug Intelligence Center (NDIC), "California Central District Drug
    Threat Assessment," May 2001. www.usdoj.gov/ndic/pubs0/668/meth.htm.

5. See the critique in Joseph Albini, "The Distribution of Drugs: Models of Crimi-
    nal Organization and Their Integration," in Thomas Mieczkowski, ed., *Drugs,
    Crime and Social Policy: Research, Issues, and Concerns* (Boston: Allyn and Bacon,
    1991), 101.

6. Ada Becchi, "Italy: 'Mafia-dominated Drug Market'?" in Nicholas Dorn, Jorgen
    Jepsen, and Ernesto Ugo Savona, eds., *European Drug Policies and Enforcement*
    (New York: MacMillan, 1996), 119–130.

7. For cocaine and heroin prices in the U.S. market, see Washington Office on Latin
    America, "Are We There Yet? Measuring Progress (Or Not) in the U.S. War on
    Drugs in Latin America," *Drug War Monitor* (November 2004). www.wola
    .org/ddhr/ddhr_data_measures2.htm. Accessed May 30, 2005.

8. Christopher A. Szechenyi, "Ecstasy Bust Leads to Israel Organized Crime, Officials
    Say," *Boston Globe*, April 26, 2000. www.boston.com. Accessed May 10, 2000.

9. Peter Reuter and John Haaga, *The Organization of High-Level Drug Markets: An
    Exploratory Study* (Santa Monica, Calif.: RAND, 1989), xii, 35–40. See also the
    discussion of the London drug markets in Vincenzo Ruggiero and Nigel South,
    Eurodrugs: Drug Use, Markets and Trafficking in Europe (London: University
    College London Press, 1995), 109–144.

10. Mark Harrison Moore, *Buy and Bust: The Effective Regulation of an Illicit Mar-
    ket in Heroin* (Lexington, Mass.: Lexington Books, 1977), 52–53.

11. Dan Waldorf and Sheigla Murphy, "Perceived Risks and Criminal Justice Pressures
    on Middle Class Cocaine Sellers," *Journal of Drug Issues* 25: 1 (1995): 11–32.

12. Mangai Natarajan and Mathieu Belanger, "Varieties of Drug Trafficking Organiza-
    tions: A Typology of Cases Prosecuted in New York City," *Journal of Drug Issues*
    28:4 (1998): 1113. Although the study suffers from sampling problems (p. 1121),
    its findings at the micro-level of the neighborhood are consistent with those done by
    other scholars. Cf. Bruce D. Johnson, Ansley Hamid, and Harry Sanabria, "Emerg-
    ing Models of Crack Distribution" in Thomas Mieczkowski, ed., *Drugs, Crime and
    Social Policy: Research, Issues, and Concerns* (Boston: Allyn and Bacon, 1991), 71.

13. In addition to the sources cited elsewhere in this chapter, see Albini, "Distribu-
    tion of Drugs," 101.

14. Natarajan and Belanger, "Varieties of Drug Trafficking Organizations," 1009–1010.

15. Reuter and Haaga, "Organization of High-Level Drug Markets," xii.

16. But we do not actually know. Christopher S. Wren, "Phantom Numbers Haunt
    the War on Drugs," *New York Times*, April 20, 1997, E4.

17. Phil Williams, "The Nature of Drug-Trafficking Networks," *Current History*
    (April 1998): 154–159.

18. Reuter and Haaga, *Organization of High-Level Drug Markets*, xii, 8.

19. Peter Andreas, "The Political Economy of Narco-Corruption in Mexico," *Cur-
    rent History* (April 1988): 160–163; Phil Williams, "Nature of Drug-Trafficking
    Networks," 159.

20. Coletta A. Youngers and Eileen Rosin, "The U.S. 'War on Drugs': Its Impact in Latin America and the Caribbean" in Coletta A. Youngers and Eileen Rosin, eds., *Drugs and Democracy in Latin America: The Impact of U.S. Policy* (Boulder: Lynne Rienner, 2004), 5–7.

21. Barbara Denton and Pat O'Malley, "Gender, Trust and Business: Women Drug Dealers in the Illicit Economy," *British Journal of Criminology* 39: 4 (Autumn 1999): 523, 527–528.

22. Thomas Mieczkowski, as cited in Barbara Denton and Pat O'Malley, "Gender, Trust and Business," 523.

23. Reuter and Haaga, *Organization of High-Level Drug Markets*, 24–25.

24. cf. Ruggiero and South, *Eurodrugs*, 114.

25. Johnson, Hamid, and Sanabria, "Emerging Models of Crack Distribution," 67.

26. Bruce A. Jacobs, "Crack to Heroin? Drug Markets and Transition," *British Journal of Criminology* 39: 4 (Autumn 1999): 557.

27. Johnson, Hamid, Sanabria, "Emerging Models of Crack Distribution," 58.

28. Douglas D. Koski, "A Critical Perspective on Drug Selling in the United States: Can Transposition of the Dutch Model Succeed?" *Contemporary Drug Problems* 26: 2 (Summer 1999).

29. Roger Alford, "Doctors Arrested for Prescribing OxyContin to Addicts: Crackdown in Appalachia Began after Cancer Painkiller Showed up on Black Market," *The Gazette* (Montreal, Quebec) May 12, 2003, A17. "Seven People Tried to Smuggle 240 Pounds of High Potency Marijuana into United States on Canadian Military Vehicles," August 15, 2000, *USA Today;* Karen DeYoung, "U.S. Colonel to Plead Guilty in Colombia Drug Probe; Officer Said to Help Wife Hide Money Laundering," *Washington Post,* April 4, 2000, A01.

30. K. Bruum, L. Pan, I. and Rexed, *The Gentlemen's Club: International Control of Drugs and Alcohol* (Chicago: University of Chicago Press, 1975).

31. Peter Reuter, Robert MacCoun, Patrick Murphy, et al., *Money from Crime: A Study of the Economics of Drug Dealing in Washington, D.C.* n.p.: RAND, 1990, vi–x.

32. Steven Levitt and Sudhir Venkatesh, "An Economic Analysis of a Drug-Selling Gang's Finances," *Quarterly Journal of Economics* 115 (August 2000): 755–789. These researchers found a similar situation among the gang members they studied.

33. Levitt and Venkatesh "Economic Analysis of a Drug-Selling Gang's Finances"; Johnson, Hamid, and Sanabria, "Emerging Models of Crack Distribution," 64 citing Kolata, 1989; Ruggiero and South, *Eurodrugs*, 129–133.

34. Reuter, MacCoun, and Murphy, *Money from Crime*, viii; Waldorf and Murphy, *Perceived Risks*, 14–15.

35. Ruggiero and South, *Eurodrugs*, pp. 84–85.

36. Ibid, 145–151.

37. Johnson, Hamid, and Sanabria, "Emerging Models of Crack Distribution," 70–71.

38. Reuter, MacCoun, and Murphy, *Money from Crime*, x, xi.

39. Johnson, Hamid, Sanabria, "Emerging Models of Crack Distribution," 63.

40. National Criminal Justice Reference Service, "Survey Results: Youth Gangs and Crime," 2. www.ncjrs.org/html/ojjdp/jjsum_11_00/survey10.html#drug . Accessed May 9, 2005.

41. Cheryl L. Maxson, *Street Gangs and Drug Sales in Two Suburban Cities.* Research in Brief series (Washington, D.C.: National Institute of Justice, 1995).

42. Peter H. Reuter and Robert J. MacCoun, "Street Drug Markets in Inner-City Neighborhoods: Matching Policy to Reality" in James B. Steinberg, David W.

Lyon, and Mary E. Viana, eds. *Urban America: Policy Choices for Los Angeles and the Nation* (Santa Monica, Calif.: RAND, 1992), 227–230, citing Malcolm W. Klein, Cheryl L. Maxson, and Lea C. Cunningham, " 'Crack,' Street Gangs, and Violence," *Criminology* 29: 4 (1991): 623–650.

43. Denton and O'Malley, "Gender, Trust and Business," 519.
44. Reuter and Haagas, *Organization of High-Level Drug Markets,* 39, 45.

Chapter 6

1. Tim Golden, "U.S. Report Says Salinas' Banker Ignored Safeguards," *New York Times,* December 4, 1998, A8; Nick Anderson, "Citibank Admits Lapses in Oversight Helped Foreigners Launder Millions," *Los Angeles Times,* November 10, 1999, C3.
2. Financial Action Task Force on Money Laundering, "Basic Facts about Money Laundering." www1.oecd.org/fatf/MLaundering_en.htm. Accessed April 15, 2003.
3. Timothy Egan, "Montana Has Mountains Like Switzerland and Wants Numbered Accounts," *New York Times,* January 18, 1998, 16; Tom Lutey, "State's Offshore Banking Coffers Remain Empty," Associated Press, July 31, 2002. Both pieces accessed via Lexis/Nexis.
4. Department of the Treasury, *The National Money Laundering Strategy for 1999,* 35. www.treas.gov/press/releases/ps113.htm. Accessed May 10, 2000.
5. John Marzulli, "Guilty? Now He Sez No," *Daily News* (New York), March 1, 2004, 30.
6. Noguchi, Motoo, "Help Needed for the 'Unbanked,' " *Washington Post,* March 26, 2004, A23.
7. Federal Reserve Board, Fedwire and National Settlement Services Annual Data. www.federalreserve.gov/paymentsystems/fedwire/wireannual.htm.
8. The Clearing House Interbank Payments System (CHIPS). www.chips.org.
9. The G-10 is a group of countries, originally ten, now eleven, whose central banks work together to provide funds to and to oversee international financial institutions, such as the International Monetary Fund (IMF). These nations are: Belgium, Canada, France, Germany, Italy, Japan, the Netherlands, Sweden, Switzerland, the United Kingdom, and the United States.
10. The SWIFT 2003 annual report can be found at www.swift.com/index.cfm?item _id=42722.
11. Federal Money Laundering Statutes, Section 1957, Appendix 1, 68. www.treas .gov/press/releases/docs/money.pdf.
12. Solveig Singleton " 'Know Your Customer' as Incoherent Privacy Policy." Testimony before the U.S. House of Representatives Committee on the Judiciary Subcommittee on Commercial and Administrative Law, March 4, 1999. www.cato .org/testimony/ct-ss030499.html.
13. Mark Motivans, PhD, "Money Laundering Offenders, 1994–2001," Bureau of Justice Statistics, U.S. Department of Justice. www.ojp.usdoj.gov/bjs/abstract/ mlo01.htm. Accessed August 14, 2005.
14. Golden, "U.S. Report Says Salinas' Banker Ignored Safeguards."

15. Gene L. Dodaro, United States General Accounting Office, "Testimony: Asset Forfeiture: An Update." Testimony before the U.S. House of Representatives Committee on the Judiciary Subcommittee on Crime, April 24, 1989.

Chapter 7

1. Commission of the European Communities, *Communication from the Commission to the Council and the European Parliament on the Implementation of the EU Action Plan on Drugs (2000–2004)*, Brussels, 08.06.2001 COM(2001) 301 final EU Action Plan Drugs.
2. Robert O. Keohane, *After Hegemony: Cooperation and Discord in the World Political Economy* (Princeton: Princeton University Press, 1984); Art Stein, *Why Nations Cooperate* (Ithaca: Cornell University Press, 1993).
3. Keohane, *After Hegemony.*
4. David G. Savage, "Supreme Court's Abduction Case Could Affect War on Terrorism," *Seattle Times*, December 2, 2003. http://seattletimes.nwsource.com/html/nationworld/2001805275_scotus02.html; "The Long Arm of U.S. Law Enforcement: Cross-Border Abductions and 'Americanisation,' " bi-monthly supplement of *Latin American Weekly Report;* "Diplomacy," WR-94-10, March 17, 1994, ii. Accessed via Lexis/Nexis on August 14, 2005.
5. Wayne Crawford, "Toeing the U.S. Line on Heroin," *Hobart Mercury* (Australia), March 6, 1999. Accessed via Lexis/Nexis on August 14, 2005.
6. Susan Taylor Martin, "U.S. Policy not Limited to Borders," *St. Petersburg Times,* July 29, 2001, 1A; "Marijuana Law Concerns U.S., Harper Says," *The Ottawa Citizen*, December 2, 2004, A6. Accessed via Lexis/Nexis.
7. Raphael Perl, "Drug Control: International Policy and Approaches," Congressional Research Service, Issue Brief for Congress, Order Code IB88093. Updated June 7, 2005. Accessed August 1, 2005.
8. Stephen E. Flynn (Commander, U.S. Coast Guard), "U.S. Support of Plan Colombia: Rethinking the Ends and Means," Strategic Studies Institute, U.S. Army War College, Special Series, *Implementing Plan Colombia,* May 2001, 3–4.
9. United Nations Office on Drugs and Crime: www.unodc.org/unodc/index.html.
10. France Diplomatie, www.diplomatie.gouv.fr/index.gb.html; Tom Lappin, "Resin d'etre," *The Scotsman* (United Kingdom), November 24, 1995.
11. To compare, see "Euro-Ibero American Seminar: Co-operation on Drugs and Drug Addiction Policies," Oporto, Portugal, October 8–9, 1998, European Monitoring Centre for Drugs and Drug Addiction. www.emcdda.eu.int/index.cfm?fuseaction=public.Content&nNodeID=432&sLanguageISO=EN.
12. Elizabeth Joyce, "Lessons from Europe: New Drugs, New Responses," *Current History* (April 1998).
13. United Nations Office on Drugs and Crime, www.unodc.org/unodc/index.html.
14. Robert Graham, "Drug Summit Agrees on Moves to Curb Demand." *Financial Times,* April 12, 1990, 6; Robert Graham, "U.S. Hard Line May Affect Success of Drug Summit," *Financial Times,* April 11, 1990, 4.
15. *Plan Colombia: Plan for Peace, Prosperity, and the Strengthening of the State,* United States Institute of Peace Library. www.usip.org/library/pa/colombia/adddoc/plan_colombia_101999.html.

16. David Spencer and Heather Noss, "Colombia: Strategic End State, Goals, and Means ... A Workshop Report" Center for Strategic Studies, CNA Corporation, Alexandria, Va. MISC D0002740.A1/November 2000, 12; "The U.S.-Colombia Initiative," International Office of National Drug Control Policy Fact Sheet. www.whitehousedrugpolicy.gov/publications/international/factsht/us-columbia .html.
17. Joaquin Roy, *European Perceptions of Plan Colombia: A Virtual Contribution to a Virtual War and Peace Plan?* Strategic Studies Institute, U.S. Army War College, Special Series, *Implementing Plan Colombia* May 2001, 1.
18. To compare, see Decision 552, *Andean Plan to Prevent, Combat and Eradicate Illicit Trade in Small Arms and Light Weapons in all its Aspects,* Eleventh Meeting of the Andean Community Council of Foreign Ministers, June 24–25, 2003, Quirama, Antioquia, Colombia. www.saferafrica.org/DocumentsCentre/ Monographs/Decision552/DECISION552.asp.
19. To compare, see Bureau of Western Hemisphere Affairs, *Support for Plan Colombia,* U.S. Department of State. www.state.gov/p/wha/rt/plncol. Accessed August 14, 2005.
20. To compare, see Coletta A. Youngers and Eileen Rosin, eds., *Drugs and Democracy in Latin America: The Impact of U.S. Policy* (Boulder: Lynne Rienner, 2004), 113–137.

Chapter 8

1. Dan Baum, *Smoke and Mirrors: The War on Drugs and the Politics of Failure* (Boston: Little, Brown, 1996), 9.
2. Harry G. Levine and Craig Reinarman, "From Prohibition to Regulation: Lessons from Alcohol Policy for Drug Policy" in Ronald Bayer and Gerald M. Oppenheimer, eds., *Confronting Drug Policy: Illicit Drugs in a Free Society* (New York: Cambridge University Press for The Milbank Memorial Fund, 1993), 161–163. See also The Women's Crusade in Xenia, Ohio (affiliated with Ohio State University Department of History). http://prohibition.osu.edu/xenia.htm.
3. Mark Thornton, "Alcohol Prohibition Was a Failure" Cato Institute Policy Analysis No. 157, July 17, 1991. www.cato.org/pubs/pas/pa-157.html. Accessed June 20, 2005.
4. Gerald M. Oppenheimer, "To Build a Bridge: The Use of Foreign Models by Domestic Critics of U.S. Drug Policy" in Ronald Bayer and Gerald M. Oppenheimer, eds., *Confronting Drug Policy: Illicit Drugs in a Free Society* (New York: Cambridge University Press for The Milbank Memorial Fund, 1993), 196–197.
5. David F. Musto, *The American Disease: Origins of Narcotic Control,* 3d ed. (New York: Oxford University Press, 1999), 238; Mike Gray, *Drug Crazy* (New York: Random House, 1998), 72–86.
6. Edward M. Brecher et al., *The Consumers Union Report on Licit and Illicit Drugs,* 1972, Chapter 56. Accessed via Schaffer Library of Drug Policy. www.druglibrary .org/schaffer/Library/studies/cu/cu56.html. Accessed August 21, 2005.
7. Peter Bourne, ed., *Addiction* (New York: Academic Press, 1974).
8. Baum, *Smoke and Mirrors,* 19–31.
9. Michael Massing, *The Fix* (New York: Simon & Schuster, 1998), 113.

10. John Ehrlichman, quoting President Nixon, as cited in Massing, *The Fix*, 109.
11. Massing, *The Fix*, 106–117; I want to thank Ariana Valle for pointing this out to me.
12. Ibid., 124, 129.
13. Ibid., 119–120.
14. Ibid., 121.
15. Committee on Data and Research for Policy on Illegal Drugs, et al., *Informing America's Policy On Illegal Drugs: What We Don't Know Keeps Hurting Us* (Washington, D.C.: National Academies Press, 2001), 192–193. See also Common Sense for Drug Policy, "Drug War Distortions." www.drugwardistortions .org/distortion1.htm.
16. Massing, *The Fix*, 136–137.
17. Ibid., 119–120.
18. Ibid., 126–128; Baum, *Smoke and Mirrors*, 80–81.
19. Baum, *Smoke and Mirrors*, 86.
20. Gerald R. Ford's Special Message to the Congress on Drug Abuse, April 27, 1976. www.ford.utexas.edu/library/speeches/760368.htm. Accessed August 20, 2005.
21. Massing, *The Fix*, 166–167.
22. The reference to alcohol may have been influenced by First Lady Betty Ford's alcohol problems, although neither Baum nor Massing mention its potential influence.
23. Baum, *Smoke and Mirrors*, 86–87.
24. Massing, *The Fix*, 135.
25. Betty Ford wrote two books about her struggles with drugs and established the Betty Ford Center at the Eisenhower Medical Center to help others overcome their drug dependencies.
26. *The Opium Convoys* from The Heroin Wars Series (Oley, Penn.: Bullfrog Films, 1996).
27. Massing, *The Fix*, 145–146; Baum, *Smoke and Mirrors*, 101–102.
28. Massing, *The Fix*, 150–151.
29. Baum, *Smoke and Mirrors*, 134–136.
30. Massing, *The Fix*, 154.
31. Ibid., 160–161.
32. Ibid., 164–165.
33. Ibid., 165.
34. Baum, *Smoke and Mirrors*, 166.
35. Massing, *The Fix*, 169.
36. Baum, *Smoke and Mirrors*, 168.
37. Office of Applied Statistics, "Summary of Findings from the 1998 National Household Survey on Drug Abuse," Substance Abuse and Mental Health Services Administration (SAMHSA), U.S. Department of Health and Human Services, 12. http://oas.samhsa.gov/nhsda/98SummHtml/TOC.htm.
38. Bruce L. Benson, et al., *Part 1. Independent Policy Report: Illicit Drugs and Crime* (Oakland, Calif.: The Independent Institute 1996). www.drugpolicy.org/library/ drugs_crimep1.cfm. Accessed August 21, 2005.
39. Drug Policy Alliance, *Drug Prohibition & the U.S. Prison System*. www.drugpolicy .org/library/research/prison.cfm. Accessed August 21, 2005.
40. Justice Policy Institute, *Poor Prescription: The Costs of Imprisoning Drug Offenders in the United States*, July 2000. www.drugpolicy.org/docUploads/PoorPrescription .pdf. Accessed August 21, 2005.

Chapter 9

1. Dirk J. Korf, "Windmills in Their Minds? Drug Policy and Drug Research in the Netherlands," *Journal of Drug Issues* (Summer 1999) and Ed Leuw, "Drugs and Drug Policy in the Netherlands," *Crime and Justice* 14 (1991): 241–242.

2. Arendt Lijphart, *The Politics of Accommodation. Pluralism and Democracy in the Netherlands* (Berkeley: University of California Press, 1968).

3. Erik Jones "Politics Beyond Accommodation? The May 2002 Dutch Parliamentary Elections," *Dutch Crossing* 26: 1 (Summer 2002): 68.

4. Ibid.

5. Peter Cohen, "The Case of the Two Dutch Drug Policy Commissions. An Exercise in Harm Reduction, 1968–1976," paper presented at the 5th International Conference on the Reduction of Drug-related Harm, March 7, 1994. Accessed via CEDRO (centrum voor drugonderzoek). www.cedro-uva.org/lib/cohen.case.html on July 20, 2005.

6. Marcel de Kort, "The Dutch Cannabis Debate, 1968–1976," *Journal of Drug Issues* 24: 3 (1994): 418.

7. Ibid., 421.

8. Paul Pennings, "Parties, Voters and Policy Priorities in the Netherlands, 1971–2002," *Party Politics* 11: 1 (2005): 70–71.

9. de Kort, "Dutch Cannabis Debate," 419, 421.

10. None of the sources consulted indicated either that the Dutch public was concerned about crime in general during the 1960s or that they linked crime and drugs. Citations to the harm question, however, are presented repeatedly. On the characterization of the press coverage concerning alleged harms caused by marijuana, de Kort, "Dutch Cannabis Debate," 419, 422, 423.

11. Ibid., 419, 423.

12. Cohen, "The Case of the Two Dutch Drug Policy Commissions," 2.

13. de Kort, "Dutch Cannabis Debate," 421 and Cohen, "The Case of the Two Dutch Drug Policy Commissions," 2.

14. Cohen, "The Case of the Two Dutch Drug Policy Commissions," 6.

15. de Kort, "Dutch Cannabis Debate," 424.

16. Cohen, "The Case of the Two Dutch Drug Policy Commissions," 5.

17. Ibid., 2–4.

18. Ibid., 4–6.

19. Jay Branegan, "Dutch Dilemma: Drugs 'R' Us?" *TIME International* 147: 18 (April 29, 1996). www.time.com/time/international/1996/960429/drugs.html.

20. Pennings, "Parties, Voters and Policy Priorities," 35.

21. Leuw, "Drugs and Drug Policy," 247.

22. Hassela News Network, "The Failure of Dutch Drug Policy." Found in Drug Prevention Network of the Americas. www.dpna.org/drugissues/failure_of_dutch_drug_policy.htm. Accessed July 23, 2005.

23. de Kort, "Dutch Cannabis Debate," 424–425.

24. U.S. Department of State, Bureau of European and Eurasian Affairs, "Background Notes: The Netherlands," May 2005. www.state.gov/r/pa/ei/bgn/3204.htm. Accessed July 20, 2005.

25. Craig Reinarman and Peter Cohen, *Is Dutch Drug Policy the Devil?* (Amsterdam: Centre for Drug Research, Universiteit van Amsterdam, 1999). www.cedro-uva.org/lib/reinarman.devil.html. Accessed July 15, 2005.

26. Manja D. Abraham, "Places of Drug Purchase in the Netherlands," paper presented at the 10th Annual Conference on Drug Use and Drug Policy, Vienna, September, 1999. Accessed via CEDRO. www.frw.uva.nl/cedro/library/places.pdf. See also Dana Larsen, "Holland Allows Only Fresh Shrooms," *Cannibis Culture* (August 28, 2003). www.cannabisculture.com/articles/3056.html. Accessed July 29, 2005.

27. Hassela News Network, "The Failure of Dutch Drug Policy."

28. *Microsoft Encarta Online Encyclopedia 2005* "Netherlands, The," http://encarta.msn.com. Accessed July 17, 2005. In 1980 the religious parties KVP, ARP, and CHU merged into the Christian Democratic Appeal, CDA.

29. Reinarman and Cohen, *Is Dutch Drug Policy the Devil?*

30. Robert MacCoun and Peter Reuter, "Interpreting Dutch Cannabis Policy: Reasoning by Analogy in the Legalization Debate," *Science* 278 (October 3, 1997): 49.

31. Craig Reinarman, "The Drug Policy Debate in Europe: The Case of *Califano vs. The Netherlands*," *International Journal of Drug Policy* 8: 3 (1997). Accessed via CEDRO at www.cedro-uva.org/lib/reinarman.califano.html. Accessed July 24, 2005.

32. See my discussion in Chapter Five regarding the ambiguity of the concept "organized crime."

33. Reinarman, "The Drug Policy Debate in Europe." Footnote 20 contains an extended discussion of the variations in the methodologies used by the CRI.

34. Pennings, "Parties, Voters and Policy Priorities," 35.

35. Peter Cohen, "Shifting the Main Purpose of Drug Control: From Suppression to Regulation of Use," *International Journal of Drug Policy* (1999): 10. Accessed via CEDRO www.cedro-uva.org/lib/cohen.shifting.pdf on July 15, 2005.

36. Branegan, "Dutch Dilemma."

37. Australian Institute of Criminology, Australian Government, "Illicit Drugs and Alcohol: International and Overseas Responses, The Netherlands" www.aic.gov.au/research/drugs/international/netherlands.html.

38. Pennings, "Parties, Voters and Policy Priorities," 35. The cold war heated up in the first half of the 1980s.

39. Studies cited in MacCoun and Reuter, "Interpreting Dutch Cannabis Policy," 50.

40. Van de Wijngaart, "Ecstasy Use at Large-Scale Dance Events in the Netherlands," *Journal of Drug Issues* (Summer 1999).

41. Jones, "Politics Beyond Accommodation?" 63.

42. Branegan, "Dutch Dilemma."

43. See the description in Robert J. MacCoun and Peter Reuter's "Does Europe Do it Better? Lessons from Holland, Britain and Switzerland," *The Nation* (September 20, 1999).

44. Ministry of Health, Welfare and Sport, "Drugs Policy in the Netherlands," April 1997. As cited on UK Cannabis Internet Activists (UKCIA) Web site. www.ukcia.org/research/dutch.htm.

45. Australian Institute of Criminology, "Illicit drugs and alcohol."

46. Ministry of Health, Welfare and Sport, "Drugs Policy in the Netherlands;" de Wijngaart, "Ecstasy Use at Large-Scale Dance Events."

47. Australian Institute of Criminology, "Illicit Drugs and Alcohol."

48. Branegan, "Dutch Dilemma."

49. Barbara Nazareth Andrade de Oliveira, "Prison Service—Netherlands," LegislationOnLine. www.legislationline.org/index.php?country=44&org=0&eu =0&topic=12.
50. Ministry of Health, Welfare and Sport "Drugs Policy in the Netherlands."
51. U.S. Department of State, "The Netherlands."

Chapter 10

1. Sven Ake Lindgren, "A Criticism of Swedish Drug Policy." www.drugtext.org/ library/articles/923207.htm.
2. Ted Goldberg, "The Evolution of Swedish Drug Policy." *Journal of Drug Issues* (Summer 2004). Accessed via www.findarticles.com on June 15, 2005.
3. Jan Blomqvist, "Sweden's 'War on Drugs' in the Light of Addicts' Experience" in P. Rosenqvist, J. Blomqvist, A. Koski-Jannes, and L. Ojesjo, eds., *Addiction and Life Course* (Helsinki: NCA, 2004), 139–171; Tim Boekhout van Solinge, *The Swedish Drug Control System* (Amsterdam: CEDRO, 1997), 35. Accessed via www.cedro-uva.org/lib/boekhout.swedish.html on June 15, 2005.
4. Leonard Goldberg, "Drug Abuse in Sweden (II)," *United Nations Office on Drugs and Crime Bulletin,* (January 1, 1968): 9–36. www.unodc.org/unodc/en/ bulletin/bulletin_1968-01-01_2_page004.html#s240. Accessed June 25, 2005. Data cited from an unnamed 1967 Narcotics Drug Committee report on which Goldberg served.
5. Hugh Heclo and Hendrik Madsen, *Policy and Politics in Sweden* (Philadelphia: Temple University Press, 1987), 27–28.
6. van Solinge, *Swedish Drug Control System,* 42–43.
7. Ted Goldberg, *Demystifying Drugs* (London: MacMillan, 1999), 176–177.
8. van Solinge, *Swedish Drug Control System,* 42–44.
9. Ibid., 80–81.
10. Heclo and Madsen, *Policy and Politics in Sweden,* 5–46; Torbjörn Bergman, "Sweden: Democratic Reforms and Partisan Decline in an Emerging Separation-of-Powers System," *Scandinavian Political Studies* 27: 2 (2004): 214.
11. Gerald Lafreniere, "National Drug Policy: Sweden," report prepared for the Senate Special Committee on Illegal Drugs, Parliament of Canada, April 18, 2002. www.parl.gc.ca/37/1parlbus/commbus/senate/com-e/ille-elibrary-e/geralde .htm. Accessed July 9, 2005.
12. Ted Goldberg, "Evolution of Swedish Drug Policy;" Arthur Gould, "Drug Issues and the Swedish Press," *The International Journal of Drug Policy* (1996), 7: 2. Accessed via www.drugtext.org/library/articles/96724.htm on June 10, 2005.
13. Ted Goldberg, "Evolution of Swedish Drug Policy."
14. van Solinge, *Swedish Drug Control System,* 42.
15. Ibid., 50.
16. Heclo and Madsen, *Policy and Politics in Sweden,* 28.
17. van Solinge, *Swedish Drug Control System,* 36–38.
18. The group has been accused by former clients of engaging in physical and psychological abuse, as well as of violating laws regulating compulsory commitment of individuals to treatment centers. Ted Goldberg, *Demystifying Drugs,* 205–219; van Solinge, *Swedish Drug Control System,* 51.
20. van Solinge, *Swedish Drug Control System,* 47–48.

21. Ibid., 63.
22. Ibid, 56–57; Wallström, "Guiding Principles."
23. van Solinge, *Swedish Drug Control System*, 58–61; Wallström, "Guiding Principles."
24. Lindgren, "Criticism of Swedish Drug Policy"; Goldberg, *Demystifying Drugs*, 182–183.
25. Bergman, "Sweden," 217.
26. van Solinge, *Swedish Drug Control System*, 81.
27. Leif Lenke and Boerje Olsson, "Swedish Drug Policy in the Twenty-First Century: A Policy Model Going Astray," *The Annals of the Academy of American Political and Social Science*, 582 (July 2002): 70; van Solinge, *Swedish Drug Control System*, 79.
28. Per Johansson, address at a meeting of the RNS—The National Association for a Drug-free Society in Stockholm, July 12, 1998. Johansson is the secretary general of the RNS. Speech available at www.rns.se/english. Accessed June 10, 2005; van Solinge, *Swedish Drug Control System*, 79.
29. van Solinge, *Swedish Drug Control System*, 65–66.
30. Lenke and Olsson, "Swedish Drug Policy," 71; Bergman, "Sweden," 207.
31. Bergman, "Sweden," 217; Alec Carlberg, "Time for a New and Humane Swedish Drug Policy," The Swedish Association for Help and Aid to Drug Abusers. www.rfhl.se/rfhl_special_001/pressmed/4.htm. Accessed July 20, 2005; van Solinge, *Swedish Drug Control System*, 121–122, 163, 178; Wallström "Guiding Principles."
32. Ted Goldberg, *Demystifying Drugs*, 200–201.
33. Jeremy Bransten "Europe: Drugs—Sweden's Strict Policies (Part 4)," Radio Free Europe/Radio Liberty Inc. www.rferl.org/features/2000/11/30112000154646.asp. Accessed August 20, 2005.
34. Wallström, "Guiding Principles."
35. van Solinge, *Swedish Drug Control System*, 114.
36. Bransten, "Europe."
37. Felipe Estrada "The Transformation of the Politics of Crime in High Crime Societies," *European Journal of Criminology* 1: 4 (2004): 434–435.
38. Blomqvist, "Sweden's 'War on Drugs,' " 142.
39. Ted Goldberg, "Evolution of Swedish Drug Policy."
40. *Narkotikafrågan* 5–6 (1996) as cited in van Solinge, *Swedish Drug Control System*, 83.
41. Blomqvist, "Sweden's 'War on Drugs,' " 142; Morgan Johansson, Swedish Social Services Minister, "International Dimension for European Drug Policy." Speech delivered in Brussels, Belgium, March 1, 2005. Speech available at www.regeringen.se/sb/d/1182/a/42927. Accessed June 10, 2005.
42. Wallström, "Guiding Principles."
43. Blomqvist, "Sweden's 'War on Drugs';" Bransten, "Europe."
44. Hanns von Hofer, "Notes on Crime and Punishment in Sweden and Scandinavia," Resource Material Series No. 57 (Stockholm: Department of Criminology, 1997). See also Om NOS, Kriminalstatistikk (1995), 303. www.unafei.or.jp/english/pdf/PDF_rms/no57/57-21.pdf. Accessed July 26, 2005.
45. Wallström, "Guiding Principles."

For Further Research

Resources on Analytic Perspectives:

SOCIAL DEVIANCE

Downes, David, and Paul Rock. *Understanding Deviance: A Guide to the Sociology of Crime and Rule Breaking.* New York: Oxford University Press, 1998.

CONSTRUCTIVISM

Wendt, Alexander. *Social Theory of International Politics.* New York: Cambridge University Press, 1999.

Risse, Thomas, Stephen C. Ropp, and Kathyrn Sikkink. *The Power of Human Rights: International Norms and Domestic Change.* Cambridge, United Kingdom: Cambridge University Press, 1999.

RATIONAL CHOICE

Shepsle, Kenneth A., and Mark S. Bonchek. *Analyzing Politics: Rationality, Behavior and Institutions.* New York: W. W. Norton, 1997.

Bueno de Mesquita, Bruce. *Principles of International Politics,* 3d edition. Washington, D.C.: CQ Press, 2006.

REALISM

Krasner, Stephen D. "Global Communications and National Power: Life on the Pareto Frontier." *World Politics* 43 (April 1991), 336–356.

Mearsheimer, John J. *The Tragedy of Great Power Politics.* New York: W. W. Norton, 2003.

Journals:

British Journal of Criminology
Journal of Drug Issues
Crime, Law and Social Change

Web Sites for Tracking Consumption:

Drug Abuse Warning Network (DAWN): www.dawninfo.net
European School Survey Project on Alcohol and Other Drugs: www.espad.org
National Institute for Drug Abuse (NIDA): www.samhsa.gov
National Organization for the Reform of Marijuana Laws (NORML):
    www.norml.org/index.cfm
Substance Abuse and Mental Health Services Administration: www.samhsa.gov
Trimbos-institute, Netherlands Institute of Mental Health and Addiction (for access
    to European data): www.trimbos.nl/indexuk.html
United Nations Office for Drug Control and Crime Prevention:
    www.odccp.org/odccp

Index